An Introduction to the Bond Markets

For other titles in the Wiley Finance Series
please see www.wiley.com/finance

An Introduction to the Bond Markets

Patrick J. Brown

John Wiley & Sons, Ltd

Copyright © 2006   John Wiley & Sons Ltd, The Atrium, Southern Gate, Chichester,
West Sussex PO19 8SQ, England

Telephone   (+44) 1243 779777

Email (for orders and customer service enquiries): cs-books@wiley.co.uk
Visit our Home Page on www.wiley.com

All Rights Reserved. No part of this publication may be reproduced, stored in a retrieval system or transmitted in any form or by any means, electronic, mechanical, photocopying, recording, scanning or otherwise, except under the terms of the Copyright, Designs and Patents Act 1988 or under the terms of a licence issued by the Copyright Licensing Agency Ltd, 90 Tottenham Court Road, London W1T 4LP, UK, without the permission in writing of the Publisher. Requests to the Publisher should be addressed to the Permissions Department, John Wiley & Sons Ltd, The Atrium, Southern Gate, Chichester, West Sussex PO19 8SQ, England, or emailed to permreq@wiley.co.uk, or faxed to (+44) 1243 770620.

Designations used by companies to distinguish their products are often claimed as trademarks. All brand names and product names used in this book are trade names, service marks, trademarks or registered trademarks of their respective owners. The Publisher is not associated with any product or vendor mentioned in this book.

This publication is designed to provide accurate and authoritative information in regard to the subject matter covered. It is sold on the understanding that the Publisher is not engaged in rendering professional services. If professional advice or other expert assistance is required, the services of a competent professional should be sought.

Other Wiley Editorial Offices

John Wiley & Sons Inc., 111 River Street, Hoboken, NJ 07030, USA

Jossey-Bass, 989 Market Street, San Francisco, CA 94103-1741, USA

Wiley-VCH Verlag GmbH, Boschstr. 12, D-69469 Weinheim, Germany

John Wiley & Sons Australia Ltd, 42 McDougall Street, Milton, Queensland 4064, Australia

John Wiley & Sons (Asia) Pte Ltd, 2 Clementi Loop #02-01, Jin Xing Distripark, Singapore 129809

John Wiley & Sons Canada Ltd, 22 Worcester Road, Etobicoke, Ontario, Canada M9W 1L1

Wiley also publishes its books in a variety of electronic formats. Some content that appears in print may not be available in electronic books.

Library of Congress Cataloging-in-Publication Data

Brown, Patrick J.
  An introduction to the bond markets / Patrick J. Brown.
    p. cm.
  Includes bibliographical references and index.
  ISBN-13: 978-0-470-01583-4 (cloth : alk. paper)
  ISBN-10: 0-470-01583-7 (cloth : alk. paper)
 1. Bonds.   2. Bond market.   I. Title.
  HG4651.B685 2006
  332.63′23—dc22
                                            2006004502

British Library Cataloguing in Publication Data

A catalogue record for this book is available from the British Library

ISBN 13 978-0-470-01583-4 (HB)
ISBN 10 0-470-01583-7 (HB)

Typeset in 10/12pt Times by TechBooks, New Delhi, India
Printed and bound in Great Britain by Antony Rowe Ltd, Chippenham, Wiltshire
This book is printed on acid-free paper responsibly manufactured from sustainable forestry
in which at least two trees are planted for each one used for paper production.

To my wife, Katy

...so I decided to go East and learn the bond business. Everybody I knew was in the bond business, so I supposed it could support one more single man.
The Great Gatsby – F. Scott Fitzgerald

Contents

Preface   xi

Disclaimer   xv

Introduction   xvii

1 What is a Bond and Who Issues Them?   1
  1.1 Description of a bond   2
    1.1.1 The issuer   2
    1.1.2 Size and currency   2
    1.1.3 Type   2
    1.1.4 Coupon payments and frequency   2
    1.1.5 Redemption amount and maturity dates   3
    1.1.6 Embedded options   4
    1.1.7 Guarantee   5
    1.1.8 Where quoted and traded   6
  1.2 The difference between corporate bonds and equities   7

2 Types of Bonds and Other Instruments   9
  2.1 Fixed-rate bonds   9
    2.1.1 Straight coupon bonds   9
    2.1.2 Zero-coupon bonds   10
    2.1.3 Undated or irredeemable bonds   11
    2.1.4 Strippable bonds and strips   11
    2.1.5 Bonds with sinking funds   13
    2.1.6 Step-up or graduated-rate bonds   14
    2.1.7 Annuities   15
  2.2 Floating-rate notes   16
    2.2.1 Undated or perpetual floating-rate notes   19
  2.3 Index-linked bonds   19
  2.4 Hybrid bonds   22

	2.5	Other instrument types		22
		2.5.1 Treasury bills		22
		2.5.2 Certificates of deposit		22
		2.5.3 Commercial paper		23
		2.5.4 Medium-term notes		24
		2.5.5 Preference shares		25
		2.5.6 Permanent interest bearing shares		26
3	**How Do You Price and Value a Bond?**			**27**
	3.1	Compound interest		27
	3.2	Discounting and yield considerations		29
	3.3	Accrued interest		32
	3.4	How Bonds are quoted		34
	3.5	Bond pricing		36
	3.6	Yields and related measures		38
		3.6.1 Current yield		39
		3.6.2 Simple yield to maturity		40
		3.6.3 Redemption yield		41
		3.6.4 Life and duration		47
		3.6.5 Modified duration		52
		3.6.6 Convexity		56
		3.6.7 Dispersion		57
	3.7	Floating-rate notes		59
		3.7.1 Simple margin (FRN)		59
		3.7.2 Discounted margin (FRN)		60
	3.8	Real redemption yield		62
	3.9	Money market yields and discounts		63
4	**Bond Options and Variants**			**65**
	4.1	Callable bonds		65
	4.2	Putable bonds		67
	4.3	Convertible bonds		69
	4.4	Dual Currency bonds		73
	4.5	Mortgage-backed securities		73
	4.6	Collateralized debt obligations		74
	4.7	Bonds with conditional coupon changes		75
	4.8	Reverse floaters		75
	4.9	Bonds with warrants attached		77
5	**Yield Curves**			**79**
	5.1	Yield curve shapes		79
	5.2	Zero-coupon or spot yield curves		82
	5.3	Forward or forward–forward yield curves		84
	5.4	Par yield curves		85
	5.5	Investment strategies for possible yield curve changes		88

			Contents	ix

6 Repos — 95
- 6.1 Classic repos — 100
- 6.2 Sell/buy-backs — 103
- 6.3 Stock borrowing/lending — 104

7 Option Calculations — 107
- 7.1 Buying a call option — 107
- 7.2 Writing a call option — 108
- 7.3 Buying a put option — 108
- 7.4 Writing a put option — 110
- 7.5 Theoretical value of an option — 110
- 7.6 Combining options — 111

8 Credit and Other Risks and Ratings — 115
- 8.1 Credit risk — 115
  - 8.1.1 Covenants — 116
  - 8.1.2 Ratings — 117
- 8.2 Liquidity — 119

9 Swaps, Futures and Derivatives — 123
- 9.1 Swaps — 123
  - 9.1.1 Interest rate swap — 123
  - 9.1.2 Asset swap — 130
  - 9.1.3 Cross-currency swap — 130
  - 9.1.4 Basis swap — 132
  - 9.1.5 Forward rate agreement — 132
- 9.2 Credit risk in swaps — 133
- 9.3 Swaptions — 133
- 9.4 Futures — 133
- 9.5 Credit default swaps — 137

10 Portfolio and Other Considerations — 141
- 10.1 Holding period returns — 141
- 10.2 Immunization — 143
- 10.3 Portfolio measures — 144
- 10.4 Allowing for tax — 145

11 Indices — 147
- 11.1 Bond Index classifications — 147
- 11.2 Choosing indices — 148
- 11.3 Index data calculations — 149
- 11.4 Index continuity — 150
  - 11.4.1 Large changes in the constituents of the index — 150
  - 11.4.2 Gaps in subindex calculations — 151
  - 11.4.3 Bonds dropped due to lack of prices — 151
  - 11.4.4 Ratings downgrade — 152

x   Contents

Appendix A. Using the Companion Website   **153**

Appendix B. Mathematical Formulae   **155**
- B.1 Accrued interest   155
- B.2 Current yield   158
- B.3 Simple yield to maturity   158
- B.4 Redemption yield   159
- B.5 Duration   162
- B.6 Modified duration   163
- B.7 Convexity   164
- B.8 Dispersion   165
- B.9 Annuities   166
- B.10 Simple margin   167
- B.11 Discounted margin   167
- B.12 Real redemption yield   168
- B.13 Convertible calculations   169
- B.14 Discount   170
- B.15 Money market yield   171
- B.16 Certificate of deposit yield   171
- B.17 Warrant calculations   171
- B.18 Compounding frequency adjustments   172
- B.19 Portfolio yield   174
- B.20 Portfolio Macaulay duration   175
- B.21 Portfolio modified duration   175

Appendix C. Bond Market Glossary   **177**

References   **215**

Index   **217**

Preface

In contrast to the equity markets, why is it that to the average private investor or non-bond market professional that bonds and the bond markets around the world are a closed book? This is surprising when you consider that:

- Bonds are intrinsically safer investments than equities.
- Bonds are usually easier to value than equities. After all, they often have predefined returns.
- The size of the bond markets and the trading of derivatives based on bonds between financial institutions is many, many times larger than that of the equity markets. Worldwide the size of the bond markets is measured in trillions of US dollars ($1 trillion = $1 000 000 000 000). For example, the repo markets (essentially a form of short-term secured borrowing using bonds as collateral) in Europe have a daily turnover in excess $1 trillion; the interest rate and currency swap markets have outstanding transactions with a nominal value in excess of $180 trillion, etc.

However, possibly the question has been put the wrong way round. We should possibly be asking, why are the equity markets so attractive? Many people like to have a gamble, and they regard the equity markets as an attractive place to do this. People like to think that they are able to assess the prospects of a company, presumably better than the market, and in the process make a fortune. Holding bonds, on the other hand, with their predefined returns, does not offer this possibility. After all, how many people are prepared to put £1 into a sweepstake, which has a 1 in 1000 possibility of producing a payout of £1000, compared with the number who are prepared to accept £1 if there is a 1 in 1000 chance that they are prepared to pay out £1000. The odds for both strategies are identical.

This lack of sex appeal of bonds is only part of the problem, and even this can be removed with the use of futures, swaps and other derivatives, although these are often not directly available to the private investor. However, this approach, with its highly mathematical basis, makes the bond markets even more remote and unattractive to many people.

Another significant reason for the lack of interest in the bond markets, in spite of their size, is their lack of transparency. With the equity markets many, if not most, national newspapers publish daily closing prices of leading equity shares. It is true that they also publish closing prices for domestic government bonds, but the great majority of outstanding bonds are not issued by governments. Even the *Financial Times* produces daily prices for well under 100 bonds, out of the many thousands of outstanding public bonds in Europe. The bond price discovery process is much more complicated than for equities, for although many eurobonds are quoted on the Luxembourg or London stock exchanges, nearly all the trading is done off-exchange.

Lack of transparency in the bond market does not stop with price discovery. With equity shares, companies have to produce annual accounts and periodic updates which are made available to all shareholders and which can be easily obtained by other interested parties. These help in evaluating the worth of the shares. On the other hand, with bonds, at least in Europe, the annual accounts do not normally identify the breakdown of the outstanding debt. Similarly, it is often quite difficult, at least for an individual, to find the individual terms and guarantees associated with the debt instruments.

The purpose of the book is to give an introduction to the bond markets to readers who have an interest in understanding what they are, how they work and how they can be used, but who do not want to be intimidated by mathematical formulae. As a result it is hoped that readers will be able to evaluate the appropriateness of investing in the bond markets. This is achieved by frequently illustrating the points graphically, relegating most of the mathematical formulae to Appendix A and supplementing the book with a companion website.

The book stands up in its own right without using the website. However, in order to take full advantage of it, users will need a PC with Excel. The website enables readers to:

- enter bond details and calculate expected returns;
- calculate annuity payments;
- produce a variety of yield curves and from them project expected interest rates in the future;
- calculate returns for the reader's own bond market portfolio of investments, based on a variety of scenarios about future interest rates and the user's investment time horizon; etc.

Another objective of this book is to try to demystify at least some of the bond market terminology, so that it is possible for non-bond market professionals to understand how the instruments work and to appreciate the expected gains. To illustrate this let us consider two examples.

If you are offered two, otherwise identical investments, one that pays 4 % every six months (that is 8 % per year) and the other that pays 8.16 % once a year, which one should you choose, or does it not matter? This is the sort of problem that has occurred in the past in the UK, and no doubt other countries, with savings rates offered by building societies and other financial institutions. This problem has, at least partly, been solved by a requirement to publish the Annual Equivalent Interest Rate.

Another example comes from a recent advert for a UK high income ISA,[1] which proudly promotes tax-free income and:

6.57	% p.a.
Current gross running yield.	
5.79	% p.a.
Current gross redemption yield.	
Yields are as at 31.05.05 and will vary.	

---

[1] ISA stands for 'Individual Savings Account'. Such accounts, which are subject to a number of restrictions, allow UK citizens to receive interest from and realize capital gains on these accounts tax-free.

In the small print it also says: 'In order to generate a high level of income, the Trust invests in companies that offer bonds with a significant level of risk to capital.'

How many people not trading in the market actually understand what these two figures mean, and would allow for the possibility of some of the investments either defaulting or having to be sold at a loss prior to any default? I know that many of the people that I know do not.

To give the providers of the ISA their due, it does say further on in the small print that: 'It [the redemption yield] will be lower than the current running yield if the capital value of the trust is expected to decrease. Both yields will vary.' So unsurprisingly, they are expecting the capital value of the ISA to decrease!

It is very difficult, if not impossible, to predict the future return on ordinary shares. However, with fixed interest investments, subject of course to the issuer not getting into serious trouble, the future cash flows arising from the investment are usually specified, although the issuer may sometimes be able to exercise an option that changes the cash flows. Similarly, with floating rate instruments, the future returns are usually specified relative to some external measure, such as LIBOR (London Interbank Offer Rate) or EURIBOR (Euro Interbank Offer Rate).

You would think that the defined terms would be an advantage and would encourage investment in bonds. However, this means that you cannot buy a bond investment that will give you almost unlimited gains as one always hopes one can with an equity share. On the other hand, although not for the novice, it is possible to obtain similar gains, or losses, to those on equities, using bond derivatives.

Bonds are essentially intrinsically safer investments than equities. There is no reason why people should not understand how bonds work and be happy to invest in them. After all, anyone buying a house on a mortgage is in effect just issuing a bond to the company from whom they are borrowing the money.

Disclaimer

Neither the author nor John Wiley & Sons, Ltd accept any responsibility or liability for loss or damage occasioned to any person or property through using the material, instructions, methods or ideas contained herein, or acting or refraining from acting as a result of such use. The author and Publisher expressly disclaim all implied warranties, including merchantability of fitness for any particular purpose.

Introduction

Trading in bonds or loans is not a recent invention. Although stock exchanges date from the early 15th century,[1] by the beginning of the 17th century trading and speculation in government stocks and shares in the Dutch East India Company on the Amsterdam stock market was carried out in a modern way. Although Amsterdam is often referred to as the 'first stock market', state loan stocks had been negotiable much earlier in Venice, in Genoa and before 1328 in Florence. There are references to French *'Rentes sur l'Hôtel de Ville'* (municipal stocks) in 1522 and stock markets in the Hanseatic towns from the 15th century.

It appears that the *Rentes sur l'Hôtel de Ville* did not play the same role as annuities did in England, but remained a safe gilt-edged investment, which was often immobilized in an inheritance, difficult to negotiate and subject to tax on sale. Based on a French text[2] written in 1706, it compares the French situation to that pertaining in Italy, Holland or England where 'State bonds (are bought and transferred) like all buildings, with no cost or formality.' Moreover, the English annuities could also be regarded as an alternative currency, sufficiently guaranteed, carrying interest and immediately convertible into liquid cash at the Exchange. However, what was new to Amsterdam was the volume, the liquidity of the market, the publicity and the freedom to speculate.

The purpose of this book is to give a basic introduction to the workings of the securities markets and the bond market in particular. It will look at the different types of instruments, explain how they differ and are traded. It will try, at least partially, to answer questions such as:

- What is a bond?
- Who issues bonds?
- Why do people issue bonds and why do investors buy them?
- How does it differ from an equity or ordinary share?
- How safe is my investment in a bond?
- How much money will I get back?
- When will I get the money back?
- Why does a bond yield more/less than an equity?
- How do you value a bond?
- How can you make use of bonds?

---

[1] Bruges dates from 1409, Antwerp 1460, Lyons 1462, Toulouse 1469, Amsterdam 1530, London 1554: see Fernand Braudel (1982).

[2] See Fernand Braudel (1982).

This book is intended to be an introduction to the bond markets and as a result the formulae for how to calculate redemption yields, duration, convexity, discounted margins or other calculations are delegated whenever possible into Appendix B.[3] Similarly, it does not go into the details of the various traded futures and derivative contracts. Neither does it go into all the possible variations and options on the different instruments. The major security houses and hedge funds employ 'rocket scientists' to construct new variations every week, sometimes with disastrous effects. (Even today, what happened to Long Term Capital Management sends shivers around the world's capital markets.)

After the Introduction, the first chapter in the book describes what a bond is and who issues them. This is followed by a chapter that describes the main standard types of bonds, including fixed-rate, floating-rate and index-linked bonds, together with some of the tradeable money market instruments, which behave in a similar way to short-dated bonds. The description of bonds with a variety of embedded options, such as call and put options, has been relegated to Chapter 4. Chapter 3 describes how bonds are priced and valued. It introduces the concepts of accrued interest, current and redemption yields, Macaulay and modified durations, convexity and dispersion, together with why they are calculated. For floating-rate notes, it also describes the simple and discounted margin calculations, and real redemption yields for index-linked bonds. The results of the calculations are often illustrated graphically with the formulae relegated to Appendix B. The next chapter, Chapter 4, describes bonds with a variety of options, together with the effect that the options can have on the valuation of the instrument.

Chapter 5 on yield curves describes the different types of yield curves, including spot, par and forward curves, and how they can be calculated. It also discusses how yield curves can be used to develop strategies that may increase the return on a bond portfolio. A discussion of the repo market follows in the next chapter. Repos are essentially just a form of short-term secured borrowing which are used extensively and help in making the financial markets run smoothly. It also discusses the differences between classic repos, sell and buy-back agreements and stock lending.

Chapter 7 looks at the profits and losses that can be achieved by buying and writing options, together with a flavour of how they can be used. Non-structural instrument risks are discussed in the next chapter. This includes credit risk and bond ratings, together with the liquidity risk that can occur if it is necessary to realize a holding in a non-benchmark bond before its maturity.

Chapter 9 describes swaps, futures and other derivatives. It looks at the size and variety of standard interest rate swaps together with a number of variations, including asset swaps, cross-currency swaps, basis swaps and forward rate agreements. It goes on to discuss futures and credit default swaps.

Chapter 10 discusses a variety of topics including holding period returns, immunization, the calculation of portfolio durations and yields and allowing for tax on interest payments and capital profits. This is followed by a chapter on bond indices. It discusses the appropriateness of using one index against another when comparing the performance of a portfolio.

Appendix A describes the programs that have been supplied on the companion website. Some of the programs allow users to create their own bonds and simulate the effect of various changes in rates or prices. Others allow you to create and modify yield curves, and see their effect on bond values. Appendix B gives the mathematical formulae for most of the calculations described and used in the preceding chapters, while Appendix C is a bond market glossary.

---

[3] Many of these formulae can be found in Patrick Brown (1998).

1
What Is a Bond And Who Issues Them?

Over many years whenever I mentioned the bond market socially, people would often enquire 'What is a bond?', as if bonds were something from outer space. This would never happen if one were to mention the equity or share markets. On explaining that if bank loans or mortgages were tradeable they could be regarded as types of bonds and that many governments raise money by issuing bonds, many people immediately lost interest. This need not be the case; bonds can be sexy! However, unlike equities, except in the case of a few structured deals, the possibility, however remote, of a nearly infinite return is impossible.

In general terms, a bond is a loan by one party (the investor or holder) to another party (the issuer). The issuer gives the investor a guarantee that he or she will pay interest on the loan at regular intervals and repay the loan at a specified time in the future. In addition, the issuer may retain or grant embedded options that he or she or the investor can exercise in the future.

The terms 'bonds'[1] and 'loans' have been used almost interchangeably throughout the book. The description 'note' is also used extensively, but it frequently refers to a bond that was originally issued for a period of not more than five years or to a floating-rate note. In addition, bonds have sometimes been referred to as 'stocks', which is a term that has been used by the Bank of England over many years to refer to UK Government gilt-edged issues. Its use should not be confused with 'common stocks', which are equity issues. The description of a bond is often very easy to understand as in the following example.

Example 1.1 Bundesrepublik Deutschland $3\frac{3}{4}$ % Anleihe 2009

In January 1999, Germany issued €14 billion of this bond at a price of 100.34. It will pay interest every 4 January up to and including 4 January 2009, when it will be redeemed at 100. It can be traded in multiples of €0.01 and is in a fully registered form. It is listed on all the German stock exchanges, and is thus tradeable.

In the above example, the issuer, in this case the German Republic, normally guarantees the issue, but the guarantees can vary from issuer to issuer and bond to bond. 'Registered' just means that the owner of the bonds is held on a central register.

Bonds are usually referred to by a combination of the issuer name, annual coupon rate per cent and the maturity date or dates. However, the description of the bond, especially in Continental Europe, may also include the year of issue or the series number. The description does not normally specify the frequency of the coupon payments.

---

[1] Sometimes the description 'bond' refers to an investment that includes some sort of insurance guarantee and implicit premium. Such investments are not discussed here.

1.1 DESCRIPTION OF A BOND

A bond can generally be described in terms of its:

- issuer;
- size and currency;
- type;
- coupon payments and frequency;
- redemption amount and maturity dates;
- embedded options, such as whether and under what circumstances the bond can be redeemed early;
- guarantees relating to the payment of interest and return of capital; and
- where quoted and traded.

1.1.1 The issuer

From the market's point of view, there are very few restrictions as to who can issue bonds, provided they provide acceptable payment guarantees. However, financial service regulators often have different views and impose a variety of capital adequacy restrictions.

The 'issuer' of a bond may be a country, regional government, local authority, bank, company, supranational organization or even an investment vehicle that has been created specifically for the issue of this bond. The name of the bond issue is sometimes followed by either its issue number (as is the case with Japanese Government bonds) or its year of issue.

1.1.2 Size and currency

The size of a loan is often referred to as its 'principal' or 'nominal amount'. Interest and capital repayments are based on the nominal amount and not the amount of money that is raised. Bonds are frequently issued at a price that is a small discount to their nominal or 'par' value. The issuer often agrees to pay back the nominal value of the bond at redemption, although sometimes he has to pay a premium if he wants to repay it early.

The bond will also specify the currency of issue. Occasionally, usually in the past, an artificial currency unit, such as Special Drawing Rights or the European Currency Unit, has been specified. In another variant, investors have even had the right to choose the currency in which they would like the interest paid and the capital repaid.

1.1.3 Type

Nearly all bonds can be categorized into one of three different types according to how their interest and capital repayments are calculated. These are 'fixed-rate', 'floating-rate' and 'index-linked' bonds. The majority of fixed-rate and floating-rate bonds are redeemed at par, whereas with index-linked bonds the final redemption amount is also adjusted.

1.1.4 Coupon payments and frequency

The bond terms will specify the frequency and the amount of any coupon payments. The coupon rate is usually specified as an annual percentage rate, irrespective of the coupon payment frequency. The payment frequency will usually be annually, semi-annually, quarterly, monthly or only at maturity. Most fixed-rate bonds pay coupons either annually or semi-annually, whereas floating-rate notes often pay coupons quarterly or monthly.

The coupon payments may be specified as either an actual fixed amount (fixed-rate bonds), variable according to some external measure such as an interbank interest rate (floating-rate note) or index-linked to, e.g. in the case of UK index-linked issues, the UK Retail Price Index (RPI).

If a fixed-rate bond pays a coupon twice a year, except sometimes at the beginning and end of its life, the semi-annual coupon payment will be exactly half the annual rate. This is not so with floating-rate notes, where the individual payments are dependent on the exact number of days in the period and the payment dates are adjusted to make sure that they fall on a market business day.

It is quite usual for bonds to have a long or a short first coupon payment period.

Example 1.2

An issuer may find that the conditions are currently attractive for the issue of, say, a 10 year bond. However, because, for example, of when his or her income is received, or because it would be desirable to make the coupon payments coincide with those of some other bond issues, a long or a short first interest period is required.

The bond is to be issued into a market where coupons are normally paid twice a year. The issuer wishes to pay coupons in March and September each year. If the market conditions in, say, January or February are attractive for the issue, then the first coupon payment will probably be in the September, not the March immediately after the issue date. The coupon payment will then be increased to compensate the investor for the longer payment period.

Conversely, if the market conditions are not attractive for the issuance until April, the first coupon payment will frequently occur in September after issue, but the amount will now be reduced because of the shorter time period.

1.1.5 Redemption amount and maturity dates

The terms of the bond will usually specify when the issuer will repay the bond (the 'maturity date') and how much will be repaid (the 'redemption value'). The bond terms could specify several different dates and values or it could specify at any time between certain dates. These are discussed further below. Except in the case of an annuity, a zero-coupon bond being called early or a capital restructuring, the redemption amount is rarely less than the nominal value of the bond. For most fixed-rate and floating-rate bonds, unless they are called early, the redemption price is 'par', i.e. equal to the nominal value. For index-linked bonds the redemption value will rise, or in rare cases even fall, in line with the relevant index.

The terms will normally highlight the final maturity date or in the case of a serial bond (which is redeemed in a number of different tranches) a range of dates. There is, however, a number of bonds that do not specify a final maturity date. Instead, such bonds often specify that they may be redeemed by the issuer on or after a specified date, at a certain price, subject to, say, three months' notice. (This is a 'call option' – see below). Such bonds are called 'undated bonds', 'irredeemables' or 'permanent interest-bearing securities'.

1.1.6 Embedded options

As has been already indicated, bonds often give the issuer or the holder of the bond the option of a choice at some time in the future. This section highlights some of the more common options.

Sometimes the embedded option is exercised not by the issuer or the holder but as a result of some external event, e.g. if the tax status of the issue changes, making the issue unattractive, or the issuer is taken over by another company. This latter example provides extra security for investors, as it is not unknown for a company to take over another well-funded company and strip out its assets. Bond holders, unfortunately, have no say in the running of a company.

Example 1.3 Ford Motor Company $6\frac{3}{8}$ % Debentures 2029

$1.5 billion of the debentures were issued at 98.817 in February 1999. It pays interest semi-annually on 1 February and 1 August, and it will be redeemed at 100 on 1 February 2029, unless its tax status changes. If this occurs, it may be called as a whole at any time on 30 days' notice from 9 February 1999 at 100.

A 'call option' gives the issuer the right to redeem the issue early after an appropriate notice period. The terms may specify that the call option may only be exercised on or between specified dates. The terms for the call are frequently different to the terms if the bond goes to its normal maturity date. A call option is included in all undated issues, and most asset-backed issues backed by mortgages.

Example 1.4 Aetna Life and Casualty Company $7\frac{3}{4}$ % Notes 2016

The company issued $200 million in July 1986 at 101. It pays interest annually on 17 July and will be redeemed on 17 July 2016 at 100 unless it is called earlier. The bond is callable as a whole or in part at any time on 30 days' notice at the following rates: from 17 July 2001 at 106; 2002 at 105; 2003 at 104; 2004 at 103; 2005 at 102; 2006 at 101 and 2007 at 100. It is also callable if its tax status changes.

A 'put option' gives the bond holder the right to demand early redemption on one or more dates, or between specified dates. The put option may only be exercisable if a certain event occurs.

A 'convertible bond' gives the bond holder the right to convert the bonds into another instrument, e.g. the ordinary shares of the issuer. The conversion option usually occurs at a date prior to the redemption of the bond, with the result that after this date, if the option is not exercised, they revert to being non-convertible bonds.

Example 1.5 Nichiei Company Ltd $1\frac{3}{4}$ % Convertible Bonds 2014

In February 1999 the company issued JPY 50 billion of convertible bonds at 100 for redemption on 31 March 2014 unless called or converted beforehand. Interest is payable semi-annually on 31 March and 30 September.

> The bond may be called as a whole at any time on 30 days' notice from 31 March 2004. The holders have the option to convert the bond into common stock of Nichiei Company Ltd from 22 March 1999 at JPY 8610 each and from 28 September 2000 at JPY 7636.2 each. The rights expire on 25 March 2014. The holders also have the option on 14 days' notice to require early repayment (a put option) on 31 March 2004 at 100 and 31 March 2009 at 100.

A 'bond with warrants attached'. Sometimes bonds are issued with attached warrants which give the holder the option to purchase other investments at a date in the future at a predefined price. This option is frequently the right to buy an equity share, but it could be the right to buy a bond, a currency, an index or a basket of shares.

This book will concentrate on tradeable bonds, but the principles discussed apply equally to non-tradeable bonds including private mortgages. A mortgage on a property is really just a form of bond, where the borrower (the mortgagee) gives a guarantee to the lending institution that he will repay the loan over a certain period. In this particular case, the payment and capital repayment terms of the loan are frequently modified during its life and the mortgagee has a call option, possibly with a penalty.

Sometimes the bond description includes two dates: e.g. the UK Government's $7\frac{3}{4}$ % Treasury 2012/2015. This means that the security will be redeemed between 2012 and 2015 at the discretion of the issuer (the UK Government). Such a bond is said to be 'callable', i.e. subject to a call for redemption with suitable notice by the issuer between the two dates. It should be noted that the description of many callable bonds, especially corporate issues, only gives the final maturity date although they are callable over possibly many years. Other bonds may not have a redemption date specified at all in their name: e.g. $3\frac{1}{2}$ % War Loan. This bond was issued on 1 December 1932 by the UK Government with the redemption terms specified as being able to be redeemed at the discretion of the issuer, on three month's notice, at any time after 1952 at 100. Since interest rates have been considerably higher than 3.5 % for nearly all this period, the market price of the bond has been consistently below 100 and so it has not been in the interest of the government to redeem the bond.

1.1.7 Guarantee

The terms on which the issuer can issue the bond obviously depend on the guarantees that have been made about the payment of interest and repayment of the capital. Such guarantees can vary enormously from complete asset backing (where in the event of a default the investors can access assets that are worth at least the value of their loan), to a negative pledge (where the issuer has guaranteed not to issue new bonds with a higher claim on the assets, although in Europe this may even exclude bank loans), to practically no guarantee at all. Government bonds often fall into the last category, but if they are issuing domestic bonds in their own currency these are often regarded as 'risk free', since the government often has the option to print more money to satisfy any shortfall and thus service the debt. In such a situation the bond would not be truly risk free as the repayment would be in a devalued currency. It remains to be seen what emerges in the eurozone if such a situation were to occur, where the eurozone governments are restricted by the stability pact.

These days the majority of the larger publicly quoted bond issues are rated by one or more of the rating agencies. These ratings are usually provided by the ratings agency just prior to issue, and are regularly reviewed during the life of the bond. The ratings evaluate the financial strength of the issuer together with the bond's covenants. The most secure bonds are rated 'AAA' or 'Aaa', while the weakest bonds, which are usually already in default, are rated 'D'. The rating does not in any way indicate the liquidity of the issue.

1.1.8 Where quoted and traded

The fact that a bond is quoted on a stock exchange does not necessarily mean that it is normally traded on that exchange. Although this may be a reasonable assumption with some government bonds, in the Eurobond market, where the majority of public issues are quoted on either the Luxembourg or London stock exchanges, nearly all of the trading is done on the over-the-counter market directly with a market maker. The nominal stock exchange quotations are there to give investors confidence on the amount and quality of disclosure that will be provided.

A bond is not likely to have many retail investors, unless it is quoted on an exchange or the issuer has made other dealing arrangements for it. Similarly, retail investors will be eliminated if the minimum 'denomination', the minimum trading unit, of the bond is very high (e.g. $100 000).

The following are examples of typical bond profiles.

Example 1.6 Commonwealth of Australia $5\frac{3}{4}$ % Bonds 2011

In August 1998, Australia issued AUD 4 495 387 000 of the above bonds for redemption at 100 on 15 June 2011. The bonds pay interest every six months on 15 June and 15 December. They have a denomination AUD 1000 and are in registered form. The denomination statement means that they can only be traded in multiples of AUD 1000.

Example 1.7 European Investment Bank 5 % Bonds 2007

In October 1995, the European Investment Bank issued CHF 500 million of 5 % bonds at 103.375 for redemption on 18 October 2007 at 100. Interest is payable annually on 18 October and the bonds are issued in units of CHF 5000 and CHF 100 000 in bearer form. The holder of the bonds (the bearer) can go to the paying agent with the bearer certificate on the 18 October each year and get the interest payment.

Example 1.8 Bank of Scotland Subordinated Floating-Rate Notes 2010

In August 1995 £75 million were issued at 100. They will be redeemed at 100 on 2 August 2010. The notes pay interest quarterly on 2 February, May, August and November, which is set in advance at 0.45 % above the London Interbank Offer Rate for three month sterling deposits.

Example 1.9 Société Générale Subordinated Floating-Rate Notes – Perpetual

$500 million of floating-rate notes were issued in November 1996 at 100.05. Interest is payable semi-annually on 31 May and 30 November each year. The annual interest rate for each semi-annual period will be set in advance at 0.075 % above the London Interbank Offer Rate for six month US dollar deposits.

Example 1.10 Canada $4\frac{1}{4}$ % Index-linked Real Return Bonds 2026

In December 1995, Canada issued CAD 5250 million of the real return bond, which will be redeemed on 1 December 2026. It pays interest semi-annually on 1 June and 1 December. The actual interest payments and redemption amount are linked to the increase in the Canadian Consumer Price Index over the period since the issue date.

The issuer of a bond commits to pay interest on the loan and to repay the capital at some time in the future. In some jurisdictions, it is important to distinguish between these two different types of cash flows, as they may be treated differently from a tax point of view.

1.2 THE DIFFERENCE BETWEEN CORPORATE BONDS AND EQUITIES

Bonds may be issued by organizations that have equity shareholders and those that do not. The former category includes both quoted and private companies, whereas the latter includes governments, regional governments, local authorities and special-purpose investment vehicles. As discussed later, the special-purpose investment vehicles have been created so that a pool of usually mortgage loans can be securitized and taken off the balance sheet of the original company. As this entity does not have any equity, the bonds are often split into several tranches with different claims on the assets. The tranche with the lowest claim on the assets is thus acting as a pseudo-equity share, but without any upward potential.

If you look at the balance sheet of a company, you will see that it usually consists of a number of loans of various types and one or sometimes more issues of equity shares. The loans, irrespective of whether they represent short-term bank borrowing, unquoted or quoted tradeable bonds, can all be considered to be bonds, although some may have a higher priority in terms of receiving payment than the others.

The main differences between bonds and equity shares are that:

- The holders of the equity shares own the company (i.e. they own the equity of the company). Hence collectively they can determine the future direction of the company.
- The holders of the bonds, on the other hand, are only entitled to the return of the loan plus interest on it at the agreed rate. They do not have any say in the future direction of the company. Similarly, they are not entitled to any other assets of the company, unless the assets formed part of the guarantee when the bond was issued.

The differences between equities and bonds can best be illustrated by considering a simplified profit and loss account of a company:

```
    Value of sales
    Less cost of sales
    Less interest on loans, etc.
                                        = Pre-tax income
    Less tax
                                        = Earnings before dividends
    Less preference dividends
    Less ordinary dividends
                                        = Retained earnings
```

This illustrates that the retained earnings of a company are equal to the value of the sales, minus the cost of the sales, minus any financing costs (i.e. the interest on any bank or other loans) and tax payable, and minus the cost of the dividends on the preference and ordinary shares.

All the interest on the loans and the tax has to be paid before any dividend can be paid on the preference and ordinary shares. Similarly the preference dividends (which are often for a predefined fixed amount) have to be paid in full before an ordinary dividend can be paid.

Some of the loans may be entitled to interest payments before any is paid to other 'subordinated' loans. In fact, there may be several levels of entitlement. The lowest level of bonds in some recent company buyouts are called 'mezzanine bonds', whose entitlement to interest is only slightly before any equity if it exists.

The owners of the equity shares in a company, which are, by definition, more risky investments than the company's loans and bonds are compensated by:

- being able to determine the future direction of the company;
- in the event of the company going into (possibly voluntary) liquidation, being entitled to any residual assets of the company; and
- if the company is successful, being entitled to increasing dividends. If a company increases its dividend, the price of the shares is also likely to increase.[2]

---

[2] Although the stock market has often anticipated this action, the result is that the price does not instantly move in the anticipated direction.

2
Types of Bonds and Other Instruments

This chapter describes many of the different types of fixed-rate, floating-rate and index-linked bonds and short-term money market instruments that have been issued, together with some other financial instruments that work in a similar way. Some of the more common embedded bond options, such as the ability of the issuer to call (redeem early) a bond or of the holder being able to convert the bond into another issue, are described in a later chapter.

2.1 FIXED-RATE BONDS

This section looks at some of the principal types of fixed-rate bonds. In particular, it looks at straight coupon paying bonds, zero-coupon bonds, undated or irredeemable bonds, strippable bonds and strips, bonds with sinking funds, step-up or graduated-rate bonds and annuities.

2.1.1 Straight coupon bonds

These are the most common type of bonds. They are one of the easiest to understand and often the easiest to value.

A vanilla 'bullet' straight bond or 'option-free' bond gives the holder the right to receive interest periodically and have the capital returned on an agreed single date. Neither the issuer nor the investor has the right to demand early repayment of the bond.

Most fixed-rate straight bonds pay coupons once or twice a year, although a few (often older issues) pay interest four times a year. The majority of bonds in a specific market sector tend to have the same coupon payment frequency.

In the UK, US, Australian, Canadian, Italian and Japanese domestic markets, coupons are normally paid semi-annually. In the international eurodollar zone and most of the rest of Continental Europe, however, coupons on straight bonds are paid annually.

Example 2.1 $4\frac{1}{4}$ % US Treasury 15 August 2013

By 2005, the US Treasury had issued over $33 billion of this bond. It pays a coupon of 2.125 % on 15 August and another coupon of 2.125 % on 15 February each year until it is redeemed at par (100) on 15 August 2013.

Example 2.2 4 % France *Obligations Assimilables du Trésor* (OAT) 25 April 2055

In 2005, the French Treasury issued this 50 year bond. It pays a coupon of 4 % on 25 April each year up to and including its redemption at par on 25 April 2055.

Example 2.3 $2\frac{1}{2}$ % UK Consolidated Loan (Consols) – Perpetual

This security was created in 1888 as a result of consolidating three previous bonds, notably: 3 % Consolidated Annuities, originally issued in 1752; 3 % Reduced Annuities of 1752 and

> 3 % New Annuities of 1855. Since 1903 it has paid a quarterly coupon at an annual rate of $2\frac{1}{2}$ % on 5 January, April, July and October. Since 5 April 1923 it has been callable as a whole or in part on 90 days notice at 100.

It is conventional for a straight bond that pays an annual coupon to pay the same coupon each year irrespective of whether it is a leap year or not. Similarly, if they pay two coupons a year, they pay exactly half the coupon every six months. Even if you ignore weekends and bank holidays, a six month period can vary between 181 and 184 days: e.g. 1 February to 1 August is 181 days or 182 days in a leap year and 1 August to 1 February is 184 days. If the coupon falls on a Saturday, a Sunday or another non-business day, the holder has to wait until the following business day to get the payment. There is no adjustment in the amount paid for the delay. This delay also applies to any redemption amount. In the past, issuers have taken advantage of this by getting two extra days of the loan free of interest, e.g. Taylor Woodrow $8\frac{3}{4}$ % 1 December 1990, which had a redemption day on a Saturday.

In the next section you will see that payments and payment dates on floating-rate notes vary from one payment to the next, even when the underlying interest rate has not changed, due to the change in the number of days in the period and the occurrence of non-business days.

Sometimes an issuer will find that the current conditions are suitable for the issue of a new bond, but he or she would like to pay coupons at a different time of year. This can arise for a variety of reasons: it could be that the business is cyclical and the issuer would prefer to pay the interest shortly after the peak sales season, or quite frequently the issuer already has a bond in the market place and would like to make this new issue a new tranche of the same bond. This new tranche is designed to be fungible (i.e. interchangeable) with the existing bond after the first coupon date. This may help with raising capital in the future, since investors tend to prefer larger bond issues as they are often more liquid. As a result bonds are often issued with a special long or short first coupon period.

Example 2.4

Consider an 8 % semi-annual bond that was issued on 15 January with a redemption date some years later on 15 October. The issuer wants to pay the semi-annual coupons on 15 April and on 15 October, the latter date to agree with the redemption date.

The issuer has two options about when to pay the first coupon: after three months or after nine months. If the issuer elects to pay the first coupon on 15 April after the issue date, then this coupon payment will be about 2 %;[1] alternatively, if it is delayed until 15 October it will be about 6 %. After the first coupon payment all subsequent payments will be 4 %.

---

[1] The exact amount will be dependent on the accrued interest convention used by the issue.

2.1.2 Zero-coupon bonds

Some bonds are designed not to pay a coupon at all during their lifetime. In order to compensate the investor for this they are issued at a price, which is less than the redemption price. The market price of such bonds gradually moves, often erratically, from the issue price to the redemption price during its life. Such bonds are called 'zero-coupon bonds'.

> **Example 2.5   European Investment Bank 0 % 6/11/2026**
>
> The bond was issued in US dollars in November 1996 at 13.36. No coupons will be paid and it will be redeemed at par (100) on 6 November 2026.

An investor who purchased $1 million dollars nominal of the above bond at the issue date would have paid $133 600. The terms specify that 30 years later the investor will get a single payment of $1 million, which is an increase in value in dollar terms of 648 %, or a compounded annual return of 6.94 %.

2.1.3   Undated or irredeemable bonds

Historically the UK Government and more recently other issuers have issued fixed-rate bonds without a final redemption date. The issuer has given a commitment to continue paying interest at regular intervals and has retained an option to redeem the bonds on giving suitable notice. Such bonds are known as 'undated', 'perpetual' or 'irredeemable' bonds. The latter term, which is used widely in the UK gilt-edged market, is obviously not strictly correct as the issuer has the right to redeem the bonds on suitable notice.

> **Example 2.6   UK $3\frac{1}{2}$ % War Loan Stock – Perpetual**
>
> £1920 million of the stock was issued in 1929 on conversion of the 5 % War Loan 1929. It pays semi-annual interest on 1 June and 1 December each year, and is callable as a whole or in part on 90 days notice at 100 after 1 December 1952.
>
> **Example 2.7   Council of Europe Social Development Bank $5\frac{1}{2}$ % Subordinated Bonds – Perpetual**
>
> CHF 250 million of the bonds were issued in 1986 at 100. Interest is payable annually on 15 April, and the bonds may be called as a whole on 60 days notice on 15 April 2006 and every five years thereafter at 102.

Undated fixed-rate bonds behave in exactly the same way as straight fixed-rate bonds, other than not having a specified final maturity date.

2.1.4   Strippable bonds and strips

Fund managers often have future financing obligations on specific dates. As a result they would like to be able to buy investments that will give guaranteed returns which will mature just before the obligation dates. A straight fixed-rate coupon bond will only partly meet the objective, since the fund manager has no guarantee as to at what rate the coupons can be reinvested. On the other hand, this can be achieved by purchasing a suitable zero-coupon bond, but frequently appropriate bonds with the necessary security do not exist.

Although many governments do not issue zero-coupon bonds, in some cases they make it possible for fund managers to achieve their objectives by allowing market makers to 'strip' some of their existing bonds. Stripping a fixed coupon bond means splitting each future interest payment and the final capital repayment into a separate tradeable security. In effect, instead of a conventional coupon paying bond, we now have a series of zero-coupon securities with different maturity dates. This has been made possible, *inter alia*, in the US, French and UK government bond markets.

Example 2.8

In May 2005 there was £172 million nominal of the UK Government $7\frac{1}{2}$% Treasury Stock 2006 in stripped form. In other words the following zero-coupon bonds were created:

£6.45 million (= £172 million × 0.075 × $\frac{1}{2}$) being redeemed on 7 June 2005
£6.45 million being redeemed on 7 December 2005
£6.45 million being redeemed on 7 June 2006
£6.45 million being redeemed on 7 December 2006 and
£172 million of principal being redeemed on 7 December 2006

Note, in the above example, that the two tranches redeeming on 7 December 2006, one income and the other capital, have been kept separate. This is often done to allow for possible different tax treatments.

Table 2.1 lists the outstanding strippable UK gilt-edged securities on 6 May 2005. It can be seen that the amounts held in stripped form are very small compared with the total amounts

Table 2.1 Outstanding strippable UK gilt-edged securities on 6 May 2005

Security	Total amount in issue (£ million)	Amount held in strippable form at 25/04/05 (£ million)
$8\frac{1}{2}$% Treasury 2005	9 821	162
$7\frac{1}{2}$% Treasury 2006	12 133	172
$4\frac{1}{2}$% Treasury 2007	11 817	75
$7\frac{1}{4}$% Treasury 2007	11 403	130
5% Treasury 2008	14 613	30
4% Treasury 2009	13 616	7
$5\frac{3}{4}$% Treasury 2009	11 753	110
$4\frac{3}{4}$% Treasury 2010	12 505	1
5% Treasury 2012	13 714	212
5% Treasury 2014	13 410	2
$4\frac{3}{4}$% Treasury 2015	13 359	209
8% Treasury 2015	7 581	167
8% Treasury 2021	17 203	225
5% Treasury 2025	15 847	53
6% Treasury 2028	12 080	217
$4\frac{1}{4}$% Treasury 2032	14 211	585
$4\frac{1}{4}$% Treasury 2036	12 588	161
$4\frac{3}{4}$% Treasury 2038	14 643	116

Source: UK Debt Management Office.

in issue. These amounts are even smaller for the individual coupon strips. In order to partially rectify this situation, all the UK Treasury strippable bonds pay coupons on either 7 March and 7 September or 7 June and 7 December each year, and coupon strips from different bonds can be combined together. As at 25 April 2005, the total nominal value of the stripped bonds paying coupons in March and September is £743 million and that for those paying coupons in June and December is £1885 million.

Strips, which allow pension funds and insurance companies to match their expected long-term liabilities more accurately, also enable them to offer guaranteed returns over several years, since the return is not dependent on any future coupon reinvestment rate.

It is sometimes possible, as is the case with the UK market, for market makers to recombine appropriate amounts of the stripped bonds and recreate ordinary coupon paying bonds.

2.1.5 Bonds with sinking funds

Sometimes bonds are issued with sinking funds. This means that the issuer, frequently a corporate body, puts away a certain amount of money in specified years to redeem part of the issue. Depending on the bond, the sinking fund may be used to:

- Redeem a fixed proportion of each bond holding each time. Such bonds are also called serial bonds.
- Purchase bonds in the market up to a maximum price. If insufficient bonds can be purchased then the sinking fund may sometimes be used to redeem the bond shortfall by lot.
- Redeem a proportion of the bonds by drawing lots.

Sinking funds, apart from in the case of serial bonds, enable some bond holdings to be completely redeemed early whereas other holders have to wait until the final redemption date.

If the sinking fund can only be used to purchase bonds in the market place, its effect is to raise the price of the bond artificially until the allocation has been filled. However, it has no effect on the expected cash flows of a long-term investor.

Example 2.9 Wightlink Finance Ltd 8.14 % Notes 2024

In 1998 the company issued £135 million of the notes at 100. Interest on them will be paid semi-annually on 26 January and 26 July, and they will be finally redeemed on 26 July 2024.

The bonds have a semi-annual sinking fund from January 2000 which is designed to redeem 95.5 % of the bonds by serial repayment prior to the maturity date. The sinking fund amounts are 0.1 % July 2000, 0.2 % January 2001, 0.2 % July 2001, 0.3 % January 2002, ..., 3.0 % January 2019, 3.0 % July 2019, 3.2 % January 2020, 3.2 % July 2020, ..., 4.0 % July 2023 and 4.5 % January 2024.

The bonds are callable as whole or in part on a coupon date from 4 August 1999 at 100, or if higher than the price of the equivalent UK gilt-edged security (Spens clause) (see Chapter 8).

In the above example the sinking fund operates by serial repayment. This means that each bond holder has part of the capital of the bond redeemed with each sinking fund payment, with the result that the next coupon payment is calculated on the reduced capital (see Example 2.10).

Example 2.10

A bond that will be redeemed serially in four equal tranches at par on 1 May 2010, 1 May 2011, 1 May 2012 and 1 May 2013 is issued with an 8% annual coupon which is payable each year on 1 May.

Based on an original investment with a nominal value of 100, an investor would expect to get:

    1 May 2006   8% (interest)
    ....
    1 May 2009   8% (interest)
    1 May 2010   8% (interest) and 25% (return of capital)
    1 May 2011   6% (interest) and 25% (return of capital)
    1 May 2012   4% (interest) and 25% (return of capital)
    1 May 2013   2% (interest) and 25% (return of capital)

2.1.6 Step-up or graduated-rate bonds

Bonds or notes are sometimes issued with one coupon rate issued for the first few years, then a different rate for the next and then possibly further changes. In the following Canary Wharf example, the purpose was to get reasonably cheap financing for the first few years before the rental income materialized.

Example 2.11   Canary Wharf Finance Step-Up Coupon Class C First Mortgage Debentures 2027

The company issued £120 million of the bond in December 1997 at 100. The bond is due for redemption at 100 on 22 October 2027. Interest is paid quarterly on 22 January, April, July and October. There is a sinking fund by serial repayment from October 2006 every quarter, which is designed to retire 81.3% of the issue prior to maturity. The interest rate is set at 5% per annum until 22 October 1999, $6\frac{1}{4}$% until October 2001, $7\frac{3}{4}$% until October 2006 and 9.535% thereafter.

This device has also been used, *inter alia*, by the UK Government for some of its retail investments. Its purpose here is to discourage investors from selling the instrument before maturity.

Example 2.12   UK National Savings and Investments Capital Bonds – Series 23

Series 23 Capital bonds were issued to give a gross interest rate of 3.85% compounded over their five year life. Capital bonds are designed to be held for the full term to earn the guaranteed compound rate of 3.85%. The interest is calculated year by year at the following rates:

Year	Gross rates
1	3.25 %
2	3.55 %
3	3.85 %
4	4.15 %
5	4.46 %

No interest is paid on bonds repaid in the first year.

In the above example, the market in the bonds is controlled by the National Savings and Investments backed by HM Treasury at predefined rates.

2.1.7 Annuities

With an annuity the issuer agrees to pay the holder a certain amount, 'annuity payment', at regular frequencies for a specified number of years. At the end of this period the capital is deemed to have been repaid. Each payment is deemed to be part interest and part capital repayment. As time progresses the amount of interest in each payment decreases and the capital repayment increases (see Figure 2.1).

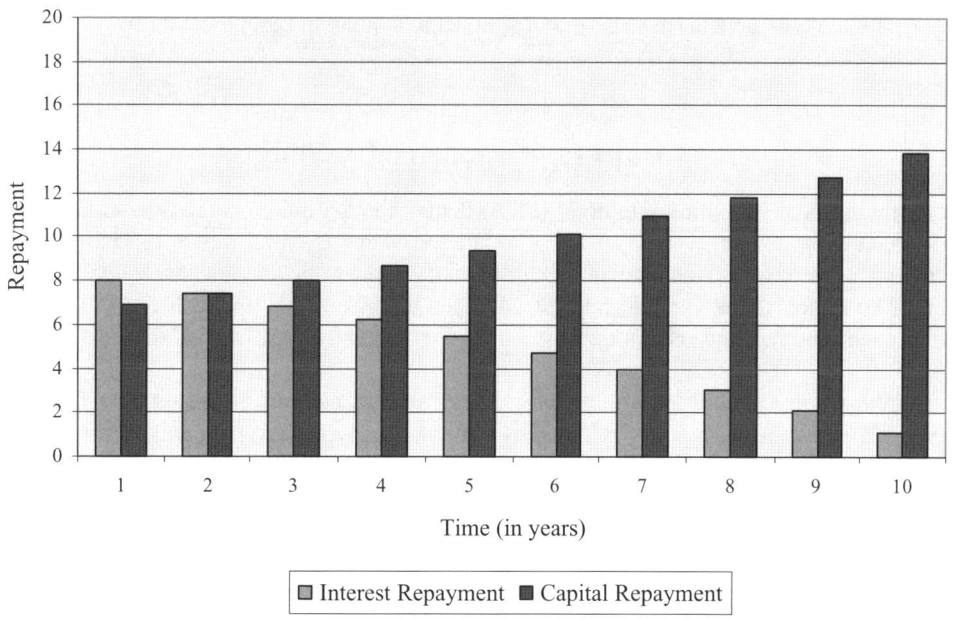

Figure 2.1 Annuity repayments.

Example 2.13

Table 2.2 shows the repayment schedule for a 10 year annuity, with interest of 8 % being paid at the end of each year.

Table 2.2 Repayment schedule for an annuity.

Time (years)	Capital outstanding. before payment	Total payment	Interest	Capital	Capital outstanding after payment
1	100.000	14.903	8.000	6.903	93.097
2	93.097	14.903	7.448	7.455	85.642
3	85.642	14.903	6.851	8.052	77.590
4	77.590	14.903	6.207	8.696	68.894
5	68.894	14.903	5.512	9.391	59.503
6	59.503	14.903	4.760	10.143	49.360
7	49.360	14.903	3.949	10.954	38.406
8	38.406	14.903	3.072	11.831	26.575
9	26.575	14.903	2.126	12.777	13.798
10	13.798	14.903	1.104	13.799	0.000

Program 2.1 Annuity

The program allows the user to enter the life, payment frequency and required interest rate for an annuity. It then calculates the annuity payments and the breakdown between interest and capital repayments. These may be displayed in tabular and graphical form.

2.2 FLOATING-RATE NOTES

A normal standard 'floating-rate note' (FRN) behaves in a similar way to a fixed-rate bond, but the coupon payments vary over time relative to some external measure. The notes are usually redeemed on a fixed date or they have a call option as they do not have a final maturity date. The effect of the variable interest payments is to keep the price of the floating-rate note much closer to the redemption price than would be the case with a similar fixed-rate bond.

On the whole, floating-rate notes have more frequent coupon payments than fixed-rate bonds. Most fixed-rate bonds pay coupons either annually or semi-annually, whereas most floating-rate notes pay coupons semi-annually, quarterly or even monthly. The coupon rate for an interest period is usually known just before the previous coupon payment. This enables the accrued interest on the note to be calculated in a relatively easy way.

The majority of floating-rate notes in Europe set their interest payments relative to the London Interbank Offer Rate (LIBOR) for the appropriate currency and period or the Euro Interbank Offer Rate (EURIBOR) for the relevant period. The LIBOR or EURIBOR interest rate period chosen usually, but not always, agrees with the payment frequency of its coupons. The following shows some typical examples.

Example 2.14 HSBC Bank plc Subordinated Floating-Rate Notes 2007

The company issued £150 million of the notes in 1997 for redemption on 27 June 2007 at 100. Interest is paid quarterly initially on 27 March, June, September and December. For each quarterly period the interest rate will be set in advance at 0.2 % above the London Interbank Offer Rate for three month sterling deposits.

Example 2.15 Barclays Bank plc Floating-Rate Primary Capital Notes – Perpetual

The company issued $600 million of the notes in 1985. Interest is payable semi-annually initially on 16 January and 16 July. For each semi-annual period it is set in advance to be $\frac{1}{4}$ % above the mean of the London Interbank Bid Rate and the London Interbank Offer Rate for six month dollar deposits.

Example 2.16 Italy Certificati di Credito del Tesoro 2008

€3 billion of the notes were issued in 2001 for redemption at 100 on 1 September 2008. Interest initially is paid semi-annually on 1 March and 1 September. The annual interest rate for each semi-annual period is set in advance at 0.3 % above the Euro Interbank Offer Rate (EURIBOR) for one year euro deposits.

Example 2.17 Oscar Funding Corporation IV Floating-Rate Notes 2004

The company issued €145 million of the note in May 1999 at 100. They will be redeemed at 100 on 11 May 2004. The notes pay interest initially on the 11th of each month. The annual rate of interest is set in advance at 0.43 % above the Euro Interbank Offer Rate for one month euro deposits.

These floating-rate note examples give a flavour of the way many of the interest rates are set. The examples show payments of different frequencies, one interest payment being set relative to the average of the bid and offer rates (the mean rate) and one that, although it pays interest every six months, calculates the interest rate relative to an annual interest rate.

Example 2.18

Bank A has issued a US dollar floating-rate note which will be redeemed at par (100) in 10 years' time. The note will pay quarterly coupons equal to the three month dollar LIBOR plus 10 basis points.[2] The LIBOR rate to be used will be the appropriate rate set two business days before the issue date or, subsequently, the previous coupon date.

Let us assume that the coupon payment dates are 17 January, 17 April, 17 July and 17 October. If the three month dollar LIBOR rates two business days before each coupon payment date are 3.0 %, 3.1 %. 3.3 % and 3.0 % respectively, then the note will pay for each period amounts at the following annual rates:

On 17 April	$3.0 + 0.1 = 3.1\%$
On 17 July	$3.1 + 0.1 = 3.2\%$
On 17 October	$3.2 + 0.1 = 3.3\%$
On the following 17 January	$3.0 + 0.1 = 3.1\%$

---

[2] A basis point is 0.01 %; thus 10 basis points is 0.1 %.

Floating-rate notes are quoted with a percentage clean price in the same way as vanilla fixed-rate bonds. As the next coupon rate is normally already known at the start of the period, there is no problem in calculating accrued interest. However, these calculations are slightly different to those of fixed-rate bonds. The main difference is that as floating-rate notes are treated as quasi-money market instruments, the coupon payment dates are modified to always occur on a day when the relevant market is open. For example, the US market is deemed to be open when the markets in New York are open, and the euro markets on Target business days.

In order to ensure that payment dates only occur on business days issuing houses frequently adopt the following convention:

> The interest payment date is the date falling n calendar months after the closing date and each date thereafter which falls n calendar months after the preceding interest payment date. If any interest payment date would otherwise fall on a day which is not a business day, it shall be postponed to the next business day unless it would thereby fall in the next calendar month. In the latter case, the interest payment date shall be the immediately preceding business day, and each subsequent payment date shall be the last business day of the nth calendar month after the month in which the preceding interest payment shall have fallen.

Example 2.19

Consider an international floating-rate note that pays a monthly coupon on Friday, 28 January 2005. If it follows the above rules then the subsequent interest payments will be on the following dates:

28 February	Monday
29 March	Tuesday (it is assumed that as Monday 28 March is Easter Monday, the market is closed)
29 April	Friday
30 May	Monday (as 29 May is a Sunday)
30 June	Thursday
29 July	Friday (as 30 July is a Saturday)
31 August	Wednesday (last business day of the month)
30 September	Friday
31 October	Monday

The effect of applying this rule is for the floating-rate note payment dates to gradually creep towards the end of the month. Hence, because the interest payment dates may change to later in the month there may be more than 365 days of interest in a non-leap year.

It can be seen that provided a floating-rate note issue is rated by the market with the same premium over its indicator rate at the beginning of a coupon period as that when it was initially issued, the price of the note should return to one that is very close to the issue price. With floating-rate notes the issue price is usually very close to par (100).

Issuers often impose restrictions on the amount of movement that is permitted on the FRN coupons. Typical restrictions include: 'caps', where irrespective of how high the indicator goes the maximum annual coupon rate is 'capped' at the specified rate; 'floors', where the coupon rate cannot fall below the specified minimum rate. In the past some issuers have issued so-called 'corridor' issues where there has been both a maximum and a minimum interest rate.

Example 2.20 Internationale Nederlanden Bank Subordinated Floating-Rate Notes 2005

The company issued $300 million of the notes in 1993 for redemption at 100 on 18 October 2005. The interest is paid semi-annually initially on 18 April and 18 October each year. The annual interest rate for each semi-annual period is set in advance at $\frac{1}{4}$ % below the London Interbank Offer Rate for six month dollar deposits, but subject to a minimum of 5 % and a maximum of 8 %.

In this example the calculated interest rate, if it was in the permitted range, was below the London Interbank Offer Rate.

2.2.1 Undated or perpetual floating-rate notes

A number of issuers, although in the main banks, have issued either hybrid fixed-rate and floating-rate or just floating-rate undated or perpetual issues. Whereas governments or government agencies are happy to issue perpetual fixed-rate issues, banks are more cautious and prefer to be able to reset the coupon rate from time to time.

Example 2.21 Abbey National 7.35 % Subordinated Capital Securities – Perpetual

The company issued $550 million of the securities in 1996 at 99.946. Interest is payable semi-annually on 15 April and 15 October. Interest will be fixed at 7.35 % per annum until October 2006; thereafter it will be reset every five years at 1.78 % above the five year US Treasury constant maturity rate.

The securities are callable as a whole every five years on 30 days' notice from October 2006 at 100, or if the tax status changes on a coupon date at 100 from October 1996.

Example 2.22 Sumitomo Bank International Finance Fixed/Floating-Rate Subordinated Notes Series B – Perpetual

The bank issued JPY 19.5 billion of the notes in 1995 at 100. The notes pay interest annually on 30 June. Until June 2005 the interest rate was fixed at 5.15 %. Thereafter the annual interest rate will be fixed in advance to be 1 % above the London Interbank Offer Rate for six month yen deposits and will be payable semi-annually on each 30 June and 31 December. The margin rate changes from 1 % to 1.5 % from June 2010.

The bond is callable as a whole or in part on coupon dates only on 25 days' notice from 30 June 2005.

2.3 INDEX-LINKED BONDS

An index-linked bond is a bond where the coupons and the redemption value are linked to some external index. This index frequently measures the inflation in the country where they are issued. Thus a holder of index-linked bonds gets a return that is inflation proof relative to the index. As a result of this inflation-proofing attribute, index-linked bonds are usually issued by governments in their domestic currency. However, there is in principle no reason why they could not be issued by a corporation with, e.g. in the case of a mining company, bonds linked to the world price of the mineral ore they are extracting.

Example 2.23

A 10 year index-linked bond is issued at 100 on 1 August 2002 with an index-linked annual coupon of 2.0% being paid semi-annually on 1 February and 1 August. The capital and coupon payments of the bond are linked to the retail price index (RPI), and the first coupon payment on 1 February 2003 has been set at 1.0%.

> The RPI for the payment on 1 February 2003 is 120.0
> The RPI for the payment on 1 August 2003 is 121.0
> The RPI for the payment on 1 February 2004 is 121.5
> The RPI for the payment on 1 August 2004 is 121.0
> The RPI for the payment on 1 February 2005 is 122.0
> The RPI for the payment on 1 August 2005 is 123.0

The payments on these dates are:

> 1 February 2003 $1 \times 120.0/120.0 = 1.0000\%$
> 1 August 2003 $1 \times 121.0/120.0 = 1.0083\%$
> 1 February 2004 $1 \times 121.5/120.0 = 1.0125\%$
> 1 August 2004 $1 \times 121.0/120.0 = 1.0083\%$
> 1 February 2005 $1 \times 122.0/120.0 = 1.0167\%$
> 1 August 2005 $1 \times 123.0/120.0 = 1.0250\%$

On the redemption date, 1 August 2012, if the relevant retail price index is RPI_{red}, then there will be a final coupon payment of:

$$1 \times RPI_{red}/120.0$$

and a return of capital of:

$$100 \times RPI_{red}/120.0$$

Figure 2.2 shows the effect on the coupon payments of a 30 year index-linked bond, with a nominal annual coupon of 2.0% if there is inflation at 3.0% per annum and at 5% per annum. It can be seen that with average inflation of 5% per annum, it is 19 years before the actual coupon rate reaches 5%, whereas if the average inflation rate is only 3%, even after 30 years the actual coupon rate is only 4.85%.

Index-linked bonds have now been issued by a variety of governments. Several countries including Canada, France, Greece, Italy, Japan, South Africa, Sweden, United States and recently the United Kingdom have standardized the methodology for calculating the accrued interest and coupon and redemption payments on a methodology originally devised by Canada in 1992.

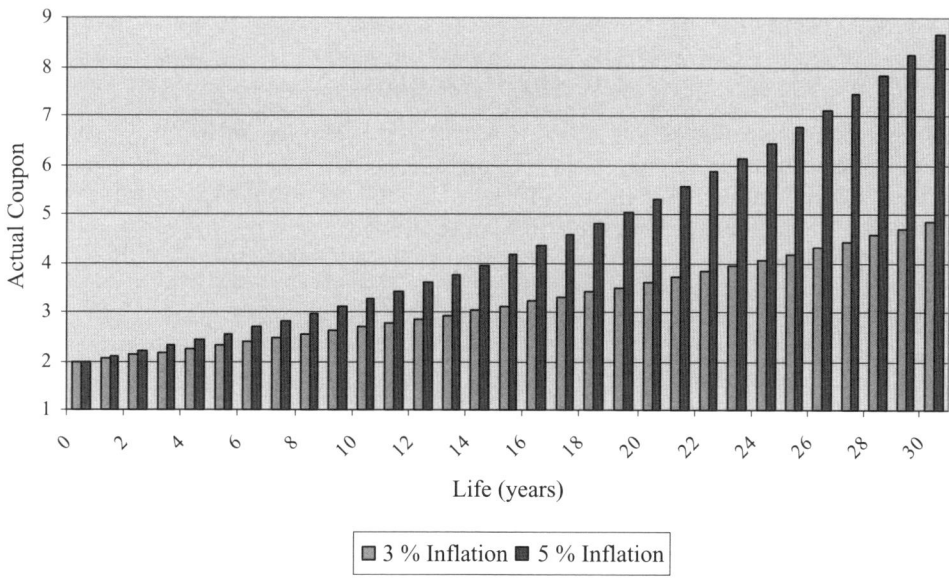

Figure 2.2 Index-linked coupon payments.

Example 2.24 United States of America $4\frac{1}{4}$ % Inflation-Linked Treasury Notes 2010 Series A

In January 2000, $11 321 million of inflation-linked notes were issued for redemption on 15 January 2010. Interest is paid semi-annually on 15 January and 15 July each year. The annual interest rate for each semi-annual period will be fixed to be CPI / 168.245 × 4.25, where CPI equals the value of the US consumer price index for the month three months prior to the beginning of the interest period. The redemption amount will be similarly adjusted.

Example 2.25 UK $2\frac{1}{2}$ % Index-Linked Treasury Stock 2024

This bond was originally issued in December 1986, but it has since had numerous additional tranches. It pays interest semi-annually on 17 January and 17 July. The interest and the capital repayments are linked to the UK Retail Price Index (RPI). The redemption value per £100 stock is set equal to £100 × RPI / 97.7, where RPI is the value for the month eight months prior to maturity. The annual interest rate for each semi-annual period is calculated as 2.5 × RPI / 97.7, where RPI is the value for the month eight months prior to the coupon payment.

It can be seen in the above examples that there is a difference in how up-to-date the relevant price index is when calculating the coupon and redemption values. The norm is now moving towards a three month lag. The three month index lag means that the bond's behaviour more closely matches the performance of the underlying index. Unfortunately, this is paid for by an increase in the complexity of the transaction calculations, as the next coupon amount is no longer known before the start of the coupon period.

2.4 HYBRID BONDS

Bonds are sometimes issued that do not conveniently fit into any of the above categories. Examples of such bonds are ones where they perform as conventional fixed-rate bonds for the first few years of their lives and then change to being a floating-rate note, or possibly the other way round. The former type are called 'fixed/floating bonds'.

Example 2.26   Skandinaviska Enskilda Banken Subordinated Step-Up Notes – Perpetual

The company issued £100 million of the notes in December 1996 at 100. Interest which will be paid annually on 11 December will be fixed at 9.04 % until December 2006 and thereafter for each semi-annual period fixed in advance at 2.5 % above the London Interbank Offer Rate for six month sterling deposits.

2.5 OTHER INSTRUMENT TYPES

2.5.1 Treasury bills

Treasury bills are short-term money market instruments, with a life to maturity of typically four weeks to 12 months. They are issued by a number of governments including the UK and US. As they do not have a specified coupon, they are in effect zero-coupon instruments and are issued at a discount to their nominal (or face) value, at which price they are redeemed.

In the UK, the Debt Management Office issues Treasury bills on a weekly basis each Monday. It offers 28 day and 91 day Treasury bills each week and 182 day ones every month. Since Treasury bills are pure discount instruments without a coupon, any new issue with the same maturity date as an existing issue is regarded as a new tranche of the existing bill. In September 2005, there were over £22 billion of UK Treasury bills outstanding.

The extract given in Table 2.3 shows the results of the Treasury bill tender offer on 2 December 2005. The length of the 28 day bill has been extended by one day as 2 January 2006 is a bank holiday.

2.5.2 Certificates of deposit

A 'certificate of deposit' (CD) is a time deposit with a bank that cannot be withdrawn until maturity. They are generally issued by commercial banks and have a fixed maturity date (usually between three months and five years) and specified coupon and payment dates. After issue, certificates of deposit are tradeable in a similar way to bonds and are often quoted on a yield basis. Short-term certificates of deposit tend to yield slightly more than a similar Treasury bill,

Table 2.3 Results of the dematerialized treasury bill tender held on 2 December 2005

29 day T Bill due 03/01/2006	ISIN Code: GB00B0HFV607
Lowest accepted yield	4.440000
Average yield	4.440000
Highest accepted yield	4.440000 (100.00 % allotted)
Average rate of discount (%)	4.424392
Average price per £100 nominal (£)	99.648473
Tail (in yield terms)	0.000000
Amount tendered for (£)	2 673 000 000.00
Amount on offer (£)	500 000 000.00
Cover	5.35
Amount allocated (£)	500 000 000.00
91 day T Bill due 06/03/2006	**ISIN Code: GB00B0HJMV49**
Lowest accepted yield	4.439000
Average yield	4.462885
Highest accepted yield	4.474000 (95.96 % allotted)
Average rate of discount (%)	4.413774
Average price per £100 nominal (£)	98.899580
Tail (in yield terms)	0.011115
Amount tendered for (£)	4 220 500 000.00
Amount on offer (£)	800 000 000.00
Cover	5.28
Amount allocated (£)	799 996 000.00
Residual amount (£)	4000.00
182 day T Bill due 05/06/2006	**ISIN Code: GB00B0HJMW55**
Lowest accepted yield	4.434000
Average yield	4.460933
Highest accepted yield	4.470000 (47.50 % allotted)
Average rate of discount (%)	4.363865
Average price per £100 nominal (£)	97.824045
Tail (in yield terms)	0.009067
Amount tendered for (£)	4 155 000 000.00
Amount on offer (£)	750 000 000.00
Cover	5.54
Amount allocated (£)	750 000 000.00

Source: UK Debt Management office.

since they are guaranteed by a bank instead of the government. However, the likelihood of a large bank failing in the short term is very slim.

2.5.3 Commercial paper

'Commercial paper' is an unsecured short-term loan issued by a corporation. It is usually issued within a program at a discount, with a maturity of between a few days and a year. Typically the maturity is only one or two months, although it can be up to one year. Some corporations find it easier to set up and manage a commercial paper program instead of always going to banks for short-term borrowing.

Example 2.27 Euro Commercial Paper Program – an extract

New South Wales Treasury Corporation (TCorp) maintain a US $5 billion Euro Commercial Paper Program to source short-dated funding from offshore markets. TCorp developed its Euro Commercial Paper Program to provide short-term investments with a broad currency choice for international investors. Issuance is conducted through an appointed panel of dealers.

Issuer	New South Wales Treasury Corporation
Guarantor	The Crown in right of NSW
Rating	• Standard & Poor's: A1+[3]
	• Moody's Investors Service: Prime-1
Issue and principal paying agent	Citibank, NA, London
Maturities	Not less than 7 days and not more than 365 days
Currencies	• Australian dollars
	• US dollars
	• Sterling
	• Yen
	• Euro
	• Hong Kong dollars
	• Other currencies subject to national regulations
Listing	The notes will not be listed on any exchange

[3] Short-term ratings are different to bond ratings.

2.5.4 Medium-term notes

'Medium-term notes' are debt securities issued by corporations under a master program agreement. Typically the notes, which are unsecured, are issued for periods of from just under one year to up to 30 years. They are issued continually by an agent over a period of time. From the issuer's point of view, the master program agreement makes it much cheaper and quicker to issue new debt.

The medium-term note (MTN) program can be very flexible. It usually specifies the maximum amount in total that can be issued under the program, the currencies of the issuance, the permissible maturity range of the bonds or notes, whether they are fixed or floating and the guarantee.

Example 2.28

The following euro medium term notes issued by United Utilities are listed on the London Stock Exchange.

Issuer	Amount (millions)	Maturity	Original term	Coupon	Ratings
UUW	EUR 120	01 Dec 2005	5 year	6 %	A2/A−
UUW	EUR 1,000	08 Nov 2007	7 year	6.625 %	A2/A−
UUW	EUR 600	18 Mar 2009	10 year	4.875 %	A2/A−

UUW	GBP 150	22 Jan 2010	7 year	5.25%	A2/A−
UUW	GBP 150	14 May 2018	15 year	5.375%	A2/A−
....	....	....	....	....	....
UU	JPY 3,000	27 Feb 2008	5 year	0.705%	A3/BBB+
UU	USD 10	29 Sep 2008	5 year	Floating	A3/BBB+
UU	EUR 10	12 Dec 2008	5 year	4.21%	A3/BBB+

UU: United Utilities plc
UUW: United Utilities Water plc (formerly known as North West Water Limited)

The medium term note programs can be extremely large and include very many different tranches.

Example 2.29   Bayerische Landesbank Girozentrale

A few years ago, the company's medium-term note program could issue notes up to the value of $7 billion. There was practically no restriction on the currency of issue. The notes could be fixed-rate, floating-rate, dual currency, index-linked or zero-coupon, with a maturity of between one month and 30 years. There were well over 500 separate deals outstanding.

In the Euromarkets, medium-term note issuance developed in the 1980s. Once issued, medium-term notes behave and are traded in a very similar way to Eurobonds. Both fixed-rate and floating-rate bonds are very common.

2.5.5   Preference shares

'Preference shares', although not strictly bonds, often behave in a very similar way. They are issued by corporations as a preferential form of equity share.

A preference share typically:

- Entitles the holder to a dividend payment that is for a fixed amount and is payable on specified dates each year.
- The preference shares may specify that they can be redeemed at a specified date.
- The preference dividend has to be paid in full before the company can pay an ordinary dividend.
- If the company does not pay a preference dividend then the holder cannot demand any payment. However, the holder in return has voting rights.

There are two main types of preference share, 'cumulative' and 'non-cumulative'. The difference between the two types is that if the issuing company fails to pay one or more preference dividends, with cumulative shares the company has to pay all the missed payments to the preference shareholders before it can restart paying an ordinary dividend. This does not apply to non-cumulative preference shares.

> **Example 2.30 Peninsular and Oriental Steam Navigation Company (P&O) 5.5 % (net) Sterling Redeemable Non-cumulative Preferred Stock**
>
> The shares, which were issued in 1987, pay a 5.5 % dividend on 1 July each year, and may be redeemed at any time after 31 December 1999 provided the directors have got an independent advisor to agree that the continuation of the shares is not in the interests of either the shareholders or the company. Each share is redeemable at par (£1) plus a premium of 20 p.

2.5.6 Permanent interest bearing shares

'Permanent interest bearing shares' (PIBS) are essentially a type of sterling preference share that arose in the UK as a result of special tax treatment for building societies. The main difference between a PIBS and a bank preference share is that the coupons on PIBS are tax deductible for building societies, whereas bank preference shares are not. Hence they can offer a higher coupon.

> **Example 2.31 Manchester Building Society 8 % Permanent Interest Bearing Shares**
>
> On 1 November 1999 the company issued £5 000 000 of PIBS in denominations of £1 000.

3
How Do You Price and Value a Bond?

This chapter starts by looking at the basic concept of compound interest. It then goes on to consider some of the factors that investors may want to take into account when they are purchasing or selling a bond. It describes the concept of accrued interest and how bonds are priced. This is followed by a description of redemption and other yield measures and related calculations. In order to try and make the chapter more comprehensible to non-mathematicians, most of the formulae have been relegated to Appendix B.

3.1 COMPOUND INTEREST

You have all heard the old adage that the value of a security is that price at which there are the same number of buyers as sellers. If the security is reasonably liquid, the price moves up and down in small steps according to the perception of the buyers and the sellers. Unfortunately, this does not help in the case of a bond which is illiquid and has not traded for six months. Here the last traded price may have very little relevance to what the bond is worth. Even if the perceived status and rating of the issue has not changed, its value may have changed considerably due to large swings in interest rates since the last transaction.

However, as bonds have predefined coupon and capital payments, albeit subject to a great variety of embedded options, there is an alternative approach. This approach defines the value of a bond as the discounted value of all expected future payments. The question now becomes: 'At what rate do you discount the future payments?'.

Before we look at some of the factors that influence the discount rate that the market puts on a bond, there is a small digression on compound interest.

A loan of £1000, which will be repaid without any interest tomorrow, is worth more to the lender than a similar loan which is repaid in one year, two years' time or even 10 years' time. If we assume the lender would like to make a return of 5 % a year on the money, the loan that is repayable tomorrow is worth almost £1000. On the other hand, a loan that is repayable in one year would be worth in today's money:

$$\frac{1000}{1 + 5/100} = £952.38$$

as investing £952.38 today at an interest rate of 5 % will give you in one year 952.38 × 1.05 = £1000.

Similarly a loan repayable in two years' time would be worth:

$$\frac{1000}{(1 + 5/100)^2} = £907.03$$

and a loan repayable in 10 years' time would be worth:

$$\frac{1000}{(1 + 5/100)^{10}} = £613.91$$

Another way of looking at this situation is to imagine the lender, who wants a return of 5 % per annum, makes a loan of £613.91 to someone who will repay the loan and the interest payments in 10 years' time. After one year the cost of the loan to the lender has increased by 5 % to:

$$613.91 \times 1.05 = £644.60$$

and after 10 years it has increased to:

$$613.91 \times 1.05^{10} = £1000.00$$

If you look at two almost identical investments which are both priced at 100, pay a 6 % coupon each year and are both redeemed at 100 in one year' time, where the only difference between them is that the first investment pays its 6 % coupon at redemption while the other one pays 3 % in six months' time and another 3 % at redemption. The second investment is obviously more valuable than the first, since the holder has the opportunity to reinvest the 3 % coupon payment that is returned before the final redemption. If it is possible to reinvest it in the same security at the same rate then by the redemption date six months later the payment would have increased from 3 % to:

$$3 \times 1.03 = 3.09\,\%$$

Another way of saying this is that a security with a 6 % coupon which is paid in equal amounts twice a year is equivalent to a similar security with a coupon of $3 + 3.09 = 6.09\,\%$, which only pays once a year. An identical relationship continues to apply if the investments are for two, three or more years.

If the above investments are now only redeemed in two years' time and you can reinvest the coupons in the same securities at the same rate, then with the security that pays 6 % annually after two years you get a total return of:

$$6 \times 1.06 + 6 = 12.36\,\%$$

However, with the semi-annual payer you get:

$$3 \times 1.03^3 + 3 \times 1.03^2 + 3 \times 1.03 + 3 = 12.55\,\%$$

The first security is still giving a return of 6.00 %, as $1.06^2 = 1.1236$, while the second is still returning 6.09 % as $1.0609^2 = 1.1255$.

This relationship between yields on investments that have been compounded with different frequencies is very important. Other things being equal, bonds that pay coupons more frequently are more valuable. Thus a quarterly coupon is more valuable than a semi-annual coupon, which in its turn is more valuable than an annual coupon.

The relationship between yields that are compounded with different frequencies is explored further in Appendix B. The principle of discounting and compound interest is fundamental to evaluating bond and money market instruments.

3.2 DISCOUNTING AND YIELD CONSIDERATIONS

Obviously bonds issued by different issuers with different guarantees and terms in different currencies will have different yields. Needless to say, when you want to estimate the discount rate or yield at which you are prepared to buy or sell a bond, there are many factors that you would like to take into account. The following lists some of the points you may wish to consider:

- *Who is the issuer?*
  Bonds are issued by many different types of issuers: governments, regional governments, local authorities, supranational organizations, companies and even special-purpose vehicles that have been set up solely to issue the bond to raise money. For example, with government bonds, the market and the ratings agencies currently regard bonds guaranteed by the US and UK governments as safer investments than those guaranteed by Argentina and Russia.
- *Do you know and understand the issuer?*
  This question is probably more relevant with corporate issuers than with government or supranational entities. If a significant proportion of the company's profits come from making a special type of widget, which you have not heard of and do not understand its potential, then you should be cautious as you might not have a feel for the risks involved. To address this concern, special-purpose vehicles normally highlight the purpose of and the risks involved in the issue.

  On the other hand, it is possible that you know and like the issuer but a further investment in the company debt will give you too great an exposure.
- *Where is the issue going to be quoted and traded?*
  Many bond issues are not quoted on an exchange in the way that equity issues are. If you look at the eurobond or international bond market, you will see that for various regulatory reasons many of them are nominally quoted on the Luxembourg Stock Exchange. However, very few of them have ever been traded on the exchange. All dealing is conducted off-exchange directly with market makers.

  Although the bond market is a global market place, there is still an investor preference for local bonds. For example, the relative ratings of World Bank and European Investment Bank bonds, where both institutions have the highest possible credit rating, are slightly different on different sides of the Atlantic.
- *What is the security offered by the issuer of the loan?*
  Companies often tend to divide their debt into different categories, which offer different levels of protection in the event of the company going through hard times. For example, a company might have divided the debt into the following categories: secured loans, senior unsecured loans and subordinated unsecured loans. In the event of a problem, the issuer will stop paying interest on all the subordinated unsecured loans before the position of the senior unsecured loans and the secured loans is considered. If the Company defaults on the interest payments or capital repayments of the secured loans, the loan holders have a right to the asset on which the loan was secured. This could be a property and could be worth more than the capital lost.

  Many eurobonds just specify in their prospectus a 'negative pledge'. As discussed later, this is just a pledge not to issue bonds in the future with a prior call on the assets of the company. However, in Europe it often does not stop the company taking out a bank loan that has a higher call on the assets.

- *What is the coupon going to be on the bond?*
  The bond could have a fixed-rate coupon, a floating-rate one, an index-linked coupon or no coupon at all. Depending on the investor's requirements, some of these options may not be appropriate. For example, a zero-coupon bond is not appropriate for an investor who wants a regular income, but it might be ideal for a pension fund or insurance company manager that has a future liability that coincides with the redemption of the bond.
- *What is the coupon payment frequency of the bond?*
  A bond that pays quarterly is worth more than one that pays semi-annually, which in turn is worth more than one that only pays interest once a year, as you get the coupons earlier.
- *What is the investor's expected direction of interest rates and over what time horizon?*
  If you expect interest rates to fall then purchasing a fixed-rate issue could be preferable to a floating-rate note, for with the latter your income will fall. Other things being equal, if your prediction is correct, the capital value of the fixed-rate issue should rise, which will not be the case with the floating-rate note.
- *What is the period of the loan?*
  Although most loans specify a final maturity date, the terms of the loan sometimes allow the issuer or the investor to demand an earlier redemption.
- *What is the duration of the loan?*
  This is different to the period of the loan. For example, compare a zero-coupon 10 year bond where you do not get any money back for 10 years with a 10 year bond that has an 8 % coupon. In the latter case the investor gets 8 % each year until the final year when he gets 108 %. The duration of the loan measures the weighted average time the investor will have to wait to get the money back. This is obviously less for the 8 % bond than the zero-coupon one.
- *What options has the issuer given himself or herself?*
  The most normal option that an issuer might have is the ability to 'call' the bond, i.e. to redeem the bond early, if circumstances make this desirable. This could mean that a strategy involving a 20 year investment could be in tatters if the bond is called next week.
- *What options has the issuer given the investor?*
  These are almost always positive in the investor's point of view. They could include a 'put' option, i.e. a right to ask for early repayment, or the option to convert the bond at predefined rates into another investment, such as the equity shares of the issuing company.
- *How great is the possibility that the issuer will not be able to repay the coupon payments and the capital in a timely way?*
  In order to answer this question at least partially, many issues have now been given a credit rating by one or more credit rating agencies. The credit rating agencies analyse the accounts of the issuer and the covenants attached to the bond, and give the bond a rating – the higher the rating, the smaller is the perceived chance of default. The highest rating that a bond can be given is AAA or Aaa (according to the rating agency). The lowest rating is D, which is awarded when the bond is already in default.
- *What is the risk-free rate of return in the currency of the loan?*
  The risk-free rate of return is conventionally defined to be the yield on domestic government securities in the currency of the loan of an equivalent life to the bond being considered. For example, the risk-free interest rate on US dollar issues is that on US Treasury notes and bonds, and that for sterling issues is the yield on UK gilt-edged securities. The logic behind this definition is that, at least theoretically, the issuer, the government, can if necessary just

print more money to service the payment of interest and the repayment of capital. Needless to say, the payments would then be in a deflated currency.

In the Eurozone the risk-free rate of interest is considered to be the cost of money to the French and German governments.

- *What is the currency of the issue?*
  Currencies that have had inflation over the recent past will need to offer investors a higher rate of return than those with low inflation.

Example 3.1

In the first half of 2005, the Japanese Government, where there has been very little inflation in the last decade, could have issued bonds with a life of less than three years with a yield to maturity of less than 0.15 % and only a yield of about 1 % for a bond with a 10 year maturity. In Switzerland, government issues of up to 10 years yield less than 2 %, whereas in the UK, gilt-edged issues, irrespective of their life to maturity, yield over 4 %.

It is unusual for bonds denominated in a currency to yield less than the equivalent domestic government bonds.

- *What is the market's expectation of the purchasing power of the currency when the payments are made?*
  This is a question that is very relevant to an international investor. For example, a US dollar domiciled investor would only make an investment in currency A, which is expected to depreciate against the US dollar by 10 % per annum if a return of considerably more than 10 % is expected in terms of currency A.
- *What is the liquidity of the security? If I want to sell, will I be able to get its proper value?*
  The stock markets and in particular the bond markets are notorious for not being able to sell your investments at a reasonable price if something unexpected occurs. Unlike the equity markets where there is always trading in the equity shares of the larger companies, the trading in a specific bond, other than major government bonds, tends to decrease as it gets older. Why is this? The majority of corporate debt is eventually purchased and put into the portfolios of pension funds and insurance companies. Such portfolios are essentially long-term holders of debt, and the bonds are used to provide for future liabilities. When a bond is first issued many other investors may purchase it on a short-term basis, giving it liquidity.

There are various other factors that effect the liquidity of a bond:

1. The size of the issue. Larger bonds tend to be more liquid.
2. Special terms. Special terms are sometimes designed to attract a specific group of investors, but they can have the effect of reducing the liquidity. They also make it harder to value the asset.
3. Number of market makers. Over several years it has been found that the most liquid bonds, other than government ones, in the eurobond market are those with the most market makers. This could be just a 'chicken and egg' situation.
4. Bonds where the market makers quote a large price spread between the buying and selling prices are almost by definition illiquid.

3.3 ACCRUED INTEREST

Unlike equity shares, bonds usually have well-defined future cash flows which are paid on specified dates, with the result that the market place makes allowance for how soon the next interest payment is going to be.

Consider a bond which pays interest of 8 % of its nominal value on 1 May each year. Other things being equal, one would expect the price you would have to pay for the bond to increase up to 30 April each year, as the time before the next interest payment of 8 % progressively decreases. Thus halfway through the year on 1 November, one would expect that the value of the bond has increased by half the annual coupon. This increase in its value allowing for the next coupon payment is called 'accrued interest'. In most cases the accrued interest associated with a bond is not included in the quoted price of the instrument, and has to be added to the price before ascertaining the purchase/sale cost.

The quoted price of a bond is called a 'clean price', if it does not include the accrued interest. If it includes the accrued interest, it is called a 'dirty' or 'gross' price.

Bonds accrue interest in a variety of ways. However, generally the accrued interest (AI) calculation is:

$$AI = g \times \frac{\text{number of days}}{\text{days in year}}$$

where:

g	annual coupon rate (%)
Number of days	number of days of accrued interest from the last coupon date or issue date to the settlement date based on the type of calendar used for the bond
Days in year	assumed number of days in the year, or the number of days in the period (i.e. between coupon dates) multiplied by the number of periods in the year

In a few markets, if you purchase a bond for settlement just before a coupon payment date, the purchaser is not entitled to the imminent coupon. It still goes to the seller. When this occurs the bond is said to be traded 'ex-coupon' or 'XD'. When a bond is traded XD, the number of days of accrued interest may be negative.

There are three main ways of calculating the number of days of accrued interest:

1. Actual calendar days.
2. Assuming that each month has 30 days (30E). This method used to be used for most eurobonds, and is still frequently used for eurodollar bonds.
3. Assuming that each month has 30 days, adjusting at the end of each month so that there are always 30 days between the end of one month and the end of the next (30U). This is used for corporate bonds in the US.

The last two methods arose in the days prior to the extensive use of computers in order to simplify the calculations. The detailed formulae for all the calculations are given in Appendix B.

Even with the actual calendar day calculation, there are variations. For example, with Japanese Government bonds, interest accrues every day except on 29 February in a leap year.

Similarly, in the denominator of the accrued interest equation, the number of days in year calculation varies from bond to bond, and even sometimes from coupon-payment period to coupon-payment period for the same bond. The number of days in a year could be 360, 362, 364, 365, 366 or 368 days.

These variations occur in a variety of ways. In practice there are five main ways of calculating accrued interest:

Actual/actual	Actual calendar days divided by actual number of days in period times number of periods in year
Actual/360	Actual calendar days divided by 360
Actual/365	Actual calendar days divided by 365
30E/360	30 day month (European method) divided by 360
30U/360	30 day month (US method) divided by 360

This list of calculation methods is not exhaustive. For example, in the swap market some instruments accrue interest at a daily rate of 1/365 of the annual coupon in a non-leap year and at a daily rate of 1/366 of the annual coupon in a leap year. Hence when a coupon period bridges both a leap and a non-leap year, the daily accrual amount is adjusted on 1 January.

In markets that accrue interest on an actual/actual basis and pay interest twice a year, such as the UK Government gilt-edged and the US Treasury markets, the number of days between one normal coupon date and the next can vary from 181 to 184 days.

The convention for fixed-rate bonds is to make all the coupon payments for full coupon periods in the year identical. Thus an 8 % bond paying coupons twice a year will make two payments of 4 %, and if it pays quarterly, it will make four payments of 2 %. Thus in order to equalize the payments over periods with different number of days, the daily accrual rate has to be suitably adjusted. In such cases another complication can arise if it is decided not to pay the first coupon until, say, nine months after the issue date. In this case the issue date will be in one 'normal' six month period with a certain number of days and the coupon payment in another with a different number of days.

Example 3.2 UK $4\frac{1}{4}$ % Treasury Stock 2032

In May 2000, Her Majesty's Treasury issued £11 580 million of the stock at 96.21. The bond will be redeemed at 100 on 7 June 2032 and pays semi-annual interest on 7 June and 7 December. The bond accrued interest from 25 May 2000 with the first interest payment being on 7 December 2000. As there are 182 days from 7 December 1999 to 7 June 2000 and 183 days from 7 June 2000 to 7 December 2000, the first interest payment thus consisted of 13 days accruing at a rate of $4.25/(182 \times 2)$ per day and 183 days accruing at a rate of $4.25/(183 \times 2)$ per day.

Example 3.3 Bundesrepublik Deutschland $3\frac{3}{4}$ % Schatzanweisungen 2003

€10 billion of the bond was issued in September 2001 at 100.18 for redemption at 100 on 12 September 2003. Interest was paid annually on 12 September and started accruing on 14 September 2001. Hence the first interest payment on 12 September 2002 consisted of only 363 days accrued interest instead of 365 days that you would get in a full year.

The convention of splitting up the year into a number of nominally identical periods for the calculation of fixed-rate coupon payments does not extend to the floating-rate market. Here, the convention is normally to accrue interest on an actual/360 basis, except in the case of sterling, where it is an actual/365 basis. As a result, over a year a non-sterling floating-rate note accrues more interest than its nominal annual coupon.

Example 3.4

Consider a US dollar floating-rate note that pays a coupon on 30 June and 31 December 2006. For both periods the nominal interest rate is 6.00 %. Assuming it accrues interest on an actual/360 basis, then as there are 181 days from 31 December 2005 to 30 June 2006 and 184 days from 30 June to 31 December 2006:

The interest amount on 30 June 2006 will be:	$6 \times 181/360 = 3.0167\%$
The interest amount on 31 December 2006 will be:	$6 \times 184/360 = 3.0667\%$
The annual amount will be:	$6 \times 365/360 = 6.0833\%$

Although the differences in the accrued interest calculations are not large, and for fixed-rate bonds average out over the year, they can be significant in the short term.

Example 3.5

Consider two otherwise identical 8.00 % bonds that accrue interest on 30E/360 and actual/365 bases. The accrued interest for each of them in a non-leap year from 28 February to 1 March is:

$$\text{(30E/360)} \quad 3\,\text{days} = 8 \times 3/360 = 0.0667\,\%$$
$$\text{(Actual/365)} \quad 1\,\text{day} = 8 \times 1/365 = 0.0219\,\%$$

However, over the year they both accrue 8.0000 % interest.

In the above extreme example, the difference in the dirty prices amounts to over four basis points,[1] which in the case of some liquid government securities is comparable to the difference between the market maker buying and selling prices.

3.4 HOW BONDS ARE QUOTED

Bonds and money market instruments are quoted in the market place in a variety of ways. This usually results in more complicated calculations than in the equity market in working out how much, excluding expenses, you have to pay for a bond purchase. With equities, if you purchase 200 shares at a price of 15 then the total cost, excluding expenses, is normally $200 \times 15 = 3000$. The calculations may be this simple for a bond transaction but usually they are more complicated.

Bond prices are normally quoted as a percentage of their 'nominal value', the nominal amount of the loan, which except in the case of index-linked bonds is normally the amount

---

[1] A basis point is 0.01 %.

you get back when the bond is redeemed. Bonds are tradeable in units, referred to as their 'denomination'. Some bonds are tradeable in very small units whereas others are not. Those bonds that are designed to be purchased by retail investors as well as institutional investors tend to have small denominations (e.g. UK gilt-edged securities have a denomination of £0.01, German Government securities €0.01 and French Government securities €1), whereas with those that are targeted solely at institutional investors, a denomination of $100 000 is not uncommon. The size of the bond's denomination only restricts the quantity you are able to buy. For example, it is not possible to purchase $50 000 worth of a bond that has a minimum denomination of $100 000.

The following lists some of the ways bonds are quoted:

- As a clean price, which is quoted as a percentage of the nominal value being purchased. The majority of bonds are quoted in this way.

    The cost of buying bonds quoted with a clean price is:

    $$\text{Cost} = (\text{clean price} + \text{accrued interest}) \times \text{nominal}/100$$

- As a dirty price, which is again quoted as a percentage of the nominal value. The dirty or gross price is the price that includes any accrued interest. The cost is now given by:

    $$\text{Cost} = \text{dirty price} \times \text{nominal}/100$$

Although this used to be a fairly common method of quoting bond prices, it is now most commonly used when the bond is in default and the accrued interest calculation is problematic.

- As an actual price. In a few cases, e.g. with French convertible issues, the bonds have a strange nominal value and often entitle the owner to purchase a single equity share. The price now reflects the cost of purchasing the share through the convertible:

    $$\text{Cost} = \text{actual price} \times \text{number of bonds}$$

- As a discount to the nominal value. This method is usually restricted to money market instruments, where the only payment is return of the principal at redemption. The cost now is given by:

    $$\text{Cost} = \left(1 - \frac{\text{discount} \times \text{fraction}}{100}\right) \times \text{nominal}$$

where:

Discount is the quoted percentage rate.
Fraction is the fraction of a year until redemption. In most markets this is calculated as actual calendar days divided by 360 (or 365 in the case of sterling).

- As a yield. When this occurs, as in the Australian Government market, the market regulator has to define exactly how a price is derived from the yield.[2]
- As an inflation adjusted price. Some index-linked bonds, such as the new UK Government three month indexation lagged bonds, quote a real clean price and a real accrued interest per

---

[2] In the UK gilt-edged market, where bonds are normally quoted on a price basis, the United Kingdom Debt Management Office has produced a booklet *'Formulae for Calculating Gilt Prices from Yields'*, (2005), which specifies how to calculate the price if it is quoted on a yield basis.

£100 of nominal. The cost of such a purchase is given by:

Cost = (real clean price + real accrued interest) × index ratio × nominal/100

where the index ratio measures the indexation factor from issue up to the settlement date of the transaction.

> **Example 3.6**
>
> The price you would pay for £100 000 nominal of a UK index-linked gilt, first issued after April 2005, with a real coupon of 2 % paid semi-annually is calculated as follows. The gilt security was issued with a reference RPI value of 200. The current reference RPI is 250. The price of the stock in the market is 90, and at the settlement date there will be 91 days of accrued interest in a period of 182 days:
>
> $$\text{Cost} = \left(90 + 1 \times \frac{91}{182}\right) \times \frac{250}{200} \times \frac{100\,000}{100} = 90.5 \times 1250 = £113\,125$$

3.5 BOND PRICING

Market makers will normally, but not always, quote a two-way price, e.g.

$$98.00 - 98.25$$

This means that they are prepared to buy the security from an investor at the lower 'bid' price of 98.00 and sell it to an investor at the higher 'offer' or 'ask' price of 98.25. The difference between the bid and the offer prices is called the 'price spread'. In some liquid markets, especially those trading government securities, market makers are obliged to quote two-way prices. However, with some less liquid securities a market maker may only quote a one-way bid price, e.g.

$$98.00 \text{ bid only}$$

This implies that the market maker is only prepared to buy the security at the specified price, as usually he or she has none of the security to sell and does not anticipate borrowing any at a reasonable cost.

Since a bond yield rises when the price falls and vice versa, if an instrument is quoted on a yield or discount basis, the bid quotation is higher than the offered one. For example:

$$3.50 - 3.45$$

This means that the market maker is prepared to buy the security on a yield of 3.50 % and sell it on a yield of 3.45 %.

Consider the following fixed-rate bond which cannot be traded ex-coupon:

Issued on 15 January 2006 at 100. Pays interest of 6.00 % each year
on the 15 January and is redeemed on 15 January 2011 at 100.

If during its five year life the expected return on this bond remains at 6.00 %, then you would expect the price you would have to pay for this bond to gradually rise throughout the year and then drop back to 100 on 15 January (see Figure 3.1). The reason for this is that the holder will

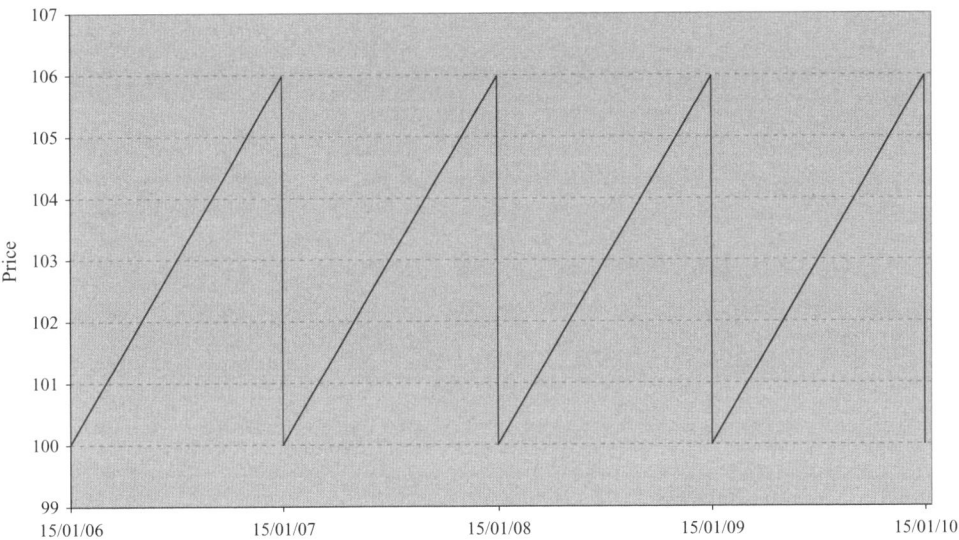

Figure 3.1 Dirty price of a bond against time.

have to wait nearly 12 months to get the next coupon payment on 16 January, but only 1 day on the 14 January.

However, the intrinsic value of the bond has not changed during its life. Hence, most stock markets now compensate for this by quoting the price of a bond without any interest that has accrued on it. This means that the purchaser of the bond has to pay the quoted price plus any accrued interest. The quoted price is called the 'clean' price and the price a purchaser would have to pay is the 'dirty' 'or 'gross' price (see Figure 3.2).

The above example assumes that the purchaser of the bond on the 14 January is entitled to the interest paid on the 15 January. However, in some markets, albeit a decreasing number, the purchaser of a bond in the days immediately before an interest payment is not entitled to the coupon. It is the seller who is entitled to the coupon. During such a period a bond is said to be trading 'ex-coupon', 'ex-dividend' or just 'XD'.

Example 3.7

In the UK gilt-edged market all fixed-rate bonds, traded for settlement in the seven business days prior to a coupon date, are traded ex-coupon. The only exception to this is $3\frac{1}{2}$ % War Stock, where the XD period is 10 business days.

Using the above 6.00 % five year bond example, if it were to go XD 7 days prior to the coupon date, the dirty price would be as shown in Figures 3.3 and 3.4.

An Introduction to the Bond Markets

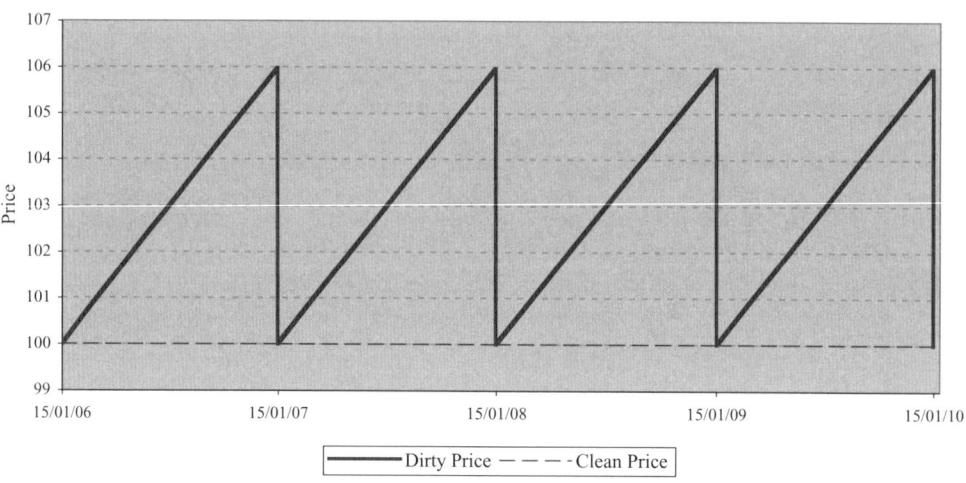

Figure 3.2 Clean and dirty prices.

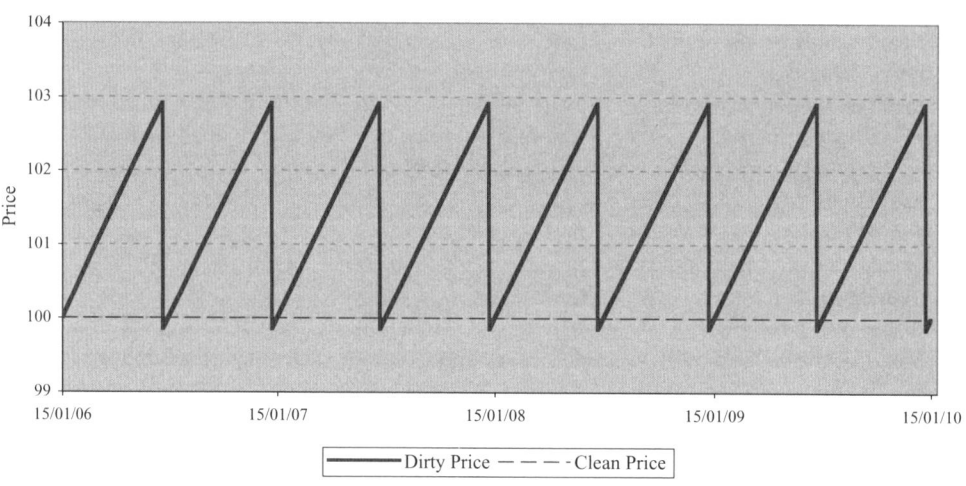

Figure 3.3 Dirty price with XD period.

3.6 YIELDS AND RELATED MEASURES

If an investor has £1000 and invests it in an instrument that gives a return of 6 % per annum, then after one year the investor would expect to see that the investment has grown to $1000 \times 1.06 =$ £1060. If at the end of the year the total proceeds are invested for a further year at 6 %, then

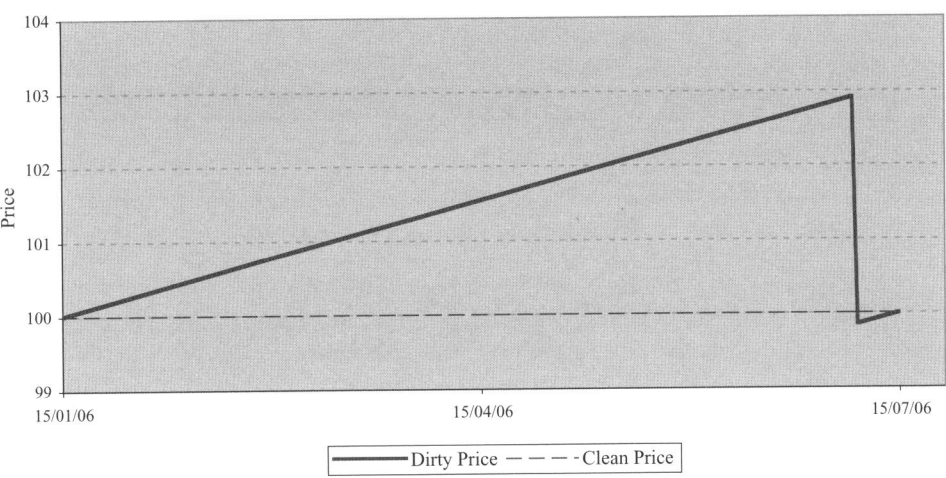

Figure 3.4 Detail of the dirty price with XD period.

the investor would expect to see the value of the investment after two years to have increased to $1060 \times 1.06 = £1123.60$.

When evaluating how much a bond is worth, the concept of a yield or expected return is both the most common and useful measure, especially when considered with its related measures such as duration and convexity. For fixed-rate bonds the market uses essentially three different types of yield. They can be categorized as: current yield, simple yield to maturity and redemption yield, although especially in the case of redemption yields there are many variations to the calculations. Although it is possible to calculate redemption yields for floating-rate notes, based on the assumption that the underlying interest or other rate will not change from its current value during the life of the note, it is much more common instead to calculate simple and discounted margins relative to the note's interest indicator rate measure.

With index-linked bonds, on the other hand, instead of calculating a standard redemption yield, which involves making assumptions about how the underlying index will perform, a 'real' redemption yield relative to the index is often calculated.

3.6.1 Current yield

The 'current yield' of a bond measures the amount of interest that an investor will get on the bond as a percentage of its current price (see Appendix B for the mathematical formula). In other words, if a bond pays an annual coupon of 4.0 % and is priced at 100, then its current yield is 4.0 % (see Figure 3.5). However, if it is priced at 80 then its current yield will be:

$$4.0 \times 100/80 = 5.0\%$$

In this calculation, by convention, the price used is the clean price without any accrued interest. This ensures that the current yield of a bond does not change if its clean price does not change. If, on the other hand, a dirty price (which includes accrued interest) was used instead, as the

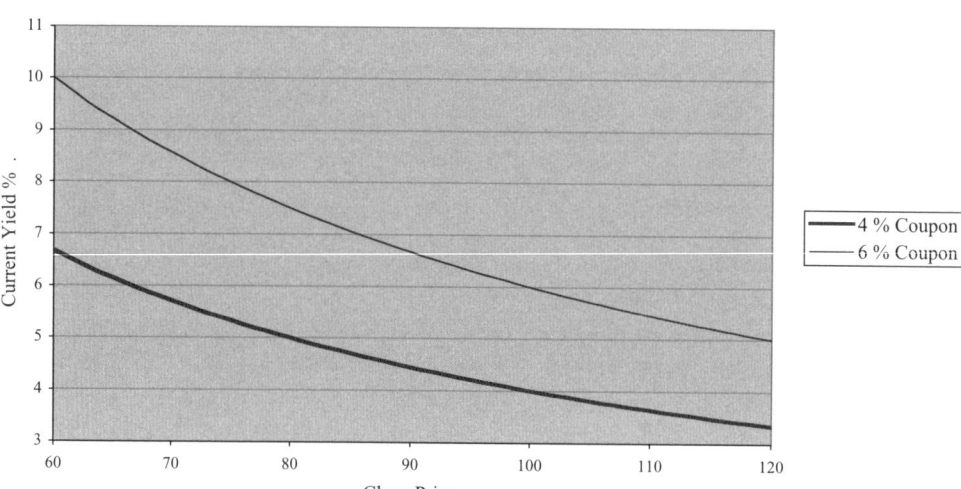

Figure 3.5 Current yield versus clean price.

accrued interest increases steadily throughout the year other than on coupon payment dates, the dirty price increases if the underlying clean price remains unchanged, and as a result there would be a reduction in the resulting yield calculation.

The current yield is also known as a 'flat yield', 'interest yield' or 'running yield'. The current yield, although a useful measurement, does have its limitations as a way of evaluating whether a bond is cheap or dear, as it does not allow for either the frequency of coupon payments or the price at which the bond may be redeemed.

3.6.2 Simple yield to maturity

The 'simple yield to maturity', which is also known as a 'Japanese yield', improves on the current yield calculation as it takes into account the effect of any capital gain or loss on redemption. However, it does this in a fairly simplistic way, which does not allow for the effect of compound interest. The capital gain or loss is assumed to be the same each year from now until the bond is redeemed.

In other words, if a bond is currently priced at 80 and it will be redeemed at 100 in 10 years' time, then it is assumed that the price will increase by $(100 - 80)/10 = 2$ per year from now until redemption, and that this increase is added to the coupon of the bond for the calculation.

Example 3.8

Consider a bond with an annual coupon of 3 % which is currently priced at 75, and which will be redeemed at 100 in 10 years' time (Figure 3.6). Then:

$$\text{Current yield} = 3 \times 100/75 = 4.0\,\%$$
$$\text{Simple yield to maturity} = [3 + (100 - 75)/10] \times 100/75 = 7.33\,\%$$

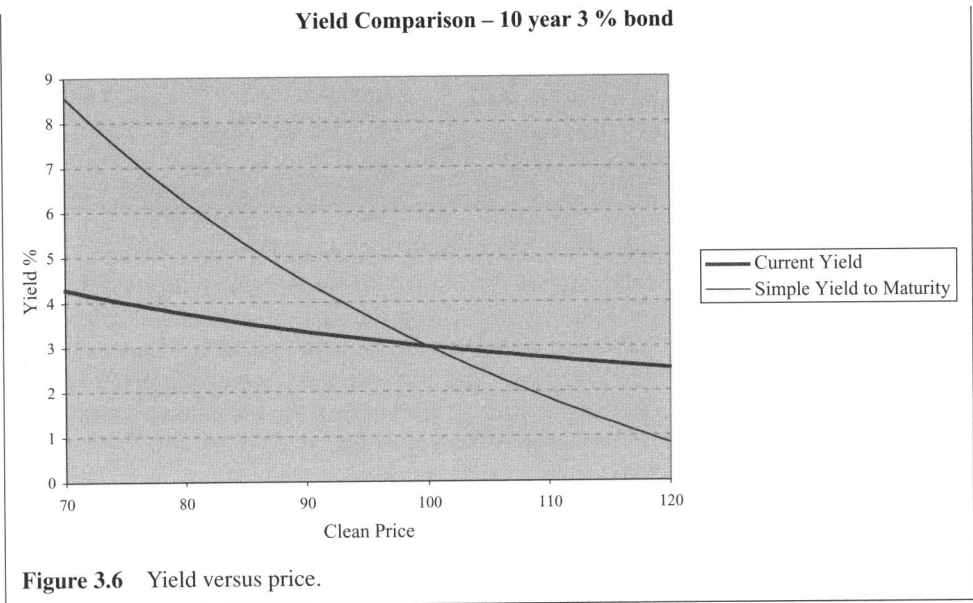

Figure 3.6 Yield versus price.

3.6.3 Redemption yield

The concept of a 'redemption yield' is one of the most common and useful calculations for valuing a fixed-rate bond. It has many attractions, but it also has a number of limitations.

As the redemption yield of a bond gives a much fuller picture than that of a current yield or simple yield to maturity, it is often just referred to as the 'yield' of the instrument. In the case of bullet or option-free bonds, which are bonds that can only be redeemed on one date (the maturity date), the redemption yield is often referred to as 'yield to maturity' (YTM).

As has been discussed before, bonds are priced so that their current value is equal to the sum of the discounted values of all the expected future payments. It will be seen that there is often some uncertainty to the exact future cash flow stream. This uncertainty can arise due to the terms of the bond (e.g. the issuer has an option to redeem the bond early if desired) or the issuer is unable to fulfil the terms of the issue (e.g. the issuer is now in liquidation).

The redemption yield of a bond is just the discount rate that makes the sum of all the assumed discounted future cash flows equal to the price of the bond. It uses the same discount rate for all the future cash flows irrespective of when they are being paid. Its calculation for a fixed-rate bond is dependent on:

- the dates and frequency of the expected coupon payments;
- the anticipated redemption date and amount; and
- the dirty price of the bond including the accumulated accrued interest.

The yield is not dependent on any other data item or external value or the state of the market in general. This makes the calculation both a robust and accepted value measure and is deceptively simple.

However, the elegance of the definition disguises some of its drawbacks. Even if we assume that all future cash flows can be discounted at the same rate, in practical terms what do you do with a coupon payment prior to redemption of the bond? There are various possible options:

- The coupon payment is required for immediate expenditure.
- Reinvest the coupon payment in the bond.
- Reinvest the coupon payment in another bond, e.g. a government security.
- Put it on deposit in a bank until there are sufficient funds to purchase another security.

If the *first* option is true then the redemption yield gives a good indication of the return on the bond but not the duration of the investment. The *second* option is often impractical due to the size of the coupon payment and the costs associated with buying small amounts. The *third* option is impractical for the same reason as the second and additionally gives a return that is now dependent on the yield of the other bond. The *fourth* option is what most fund managers adopt most of the time. However, there is little correlation between the return on the original bond and on the bank deposits and the possible subsequent bond.

The redemption yield definition assumes that it is possible to reinvest all the coupons that are received prior to redemption in the same security at the same rate of return and without any expenses. This is obviously a tall order. In essence it is the second option above. Figure 3.7 shows how the redemption yield of a 5 % bond compares with its current yield and simple yield to maturity for a range of clean prices. The bond pays coupons semi-annually and is redeemed in 5 years' time.

Another way of looking at a redemption yield is to say that it is just the current yield of the bond plus an amount (which may be negative) to allow for the capital appreciation/depreciation of the bond if held until redemption. The current yield of the bond is just the bond's current coupon divided by the clean price of the bond.

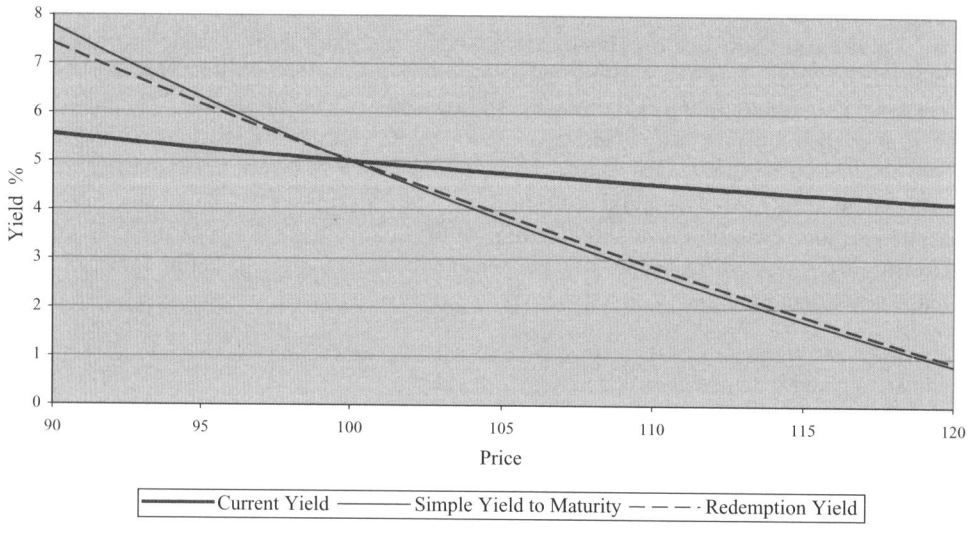

Figure 3.7 Comparison of current yield, simple yield to maturity and redemption yield.

How Do You Price and Value a Bond? 43

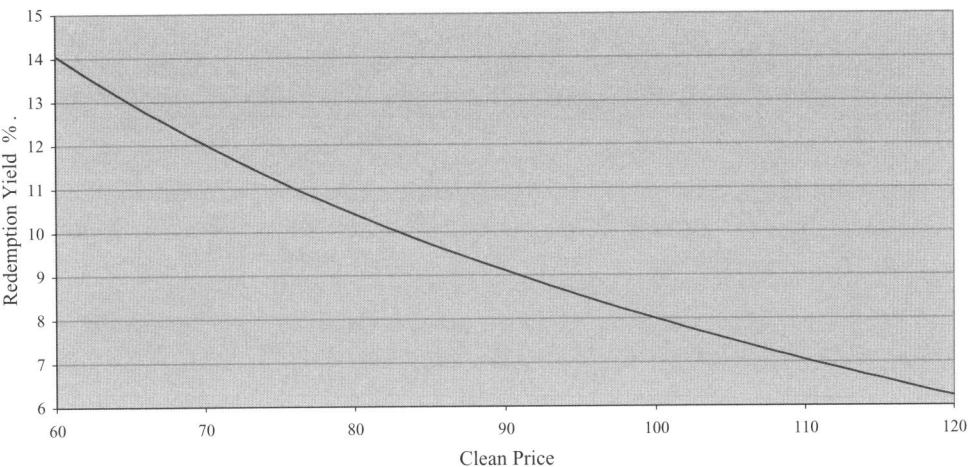

Figure 3.8 Redemption yield versus clean price.

As you would imagine, if the price of a bond is above its redemption value then you would expect the redemption yield of the bond to be less than its annual coupon, because of the capital loss at redemption. Similarly, if a bond's price is less than the redemption amount, the redemption yield will be above its annual coupon rate. If the price of a bond increases then its redemption yield decreases, and vice versa in a similar way to the current yield.

If you plot the calculation of the redemption yield of a 20 year 8 % bond paying coupons annually against its clean price you get a relationship as shown in Figure 3.8 below. It can be seen that the graph has a redemption yield of exactly 4 % (the coupon rate) when the clean price is 100. However, this is only true because the calculation:

- is compounded at the same rate as the coupon payment frequency and
- is for settlement on a coupon date, when there is no accrued interest.

Consider two otherwise identical 6 % bonds, where one pays coupons annually and the other pays them semi-annually, such that one of the payment dates coincides with the annual coupon payment date of the other bond. The relationship between the redemption yields on the two 6 % bonds that will both mature in 10 years' time is shown in Figure 3.9.

A bond that pays coupons semi-annually always yields more than an otherwise identical one that pays coupons annually, as the holder receives half the annual coupon early. You will notice that the difference in the yields increases as the prices of the bonds decrease and the yields increase. In the example, when the bonds are priced at 90, the difference between the yields is nearly 12 basis points, whereas when the price is 100 it is exactly 9 basis points and less than 7 basis points when the price rises to 110.

It is very easy to change from a redemption yield being compounded annually to one being compounded semi-annually, quarterly, monthly or even continuously. The calculations are described in Section B.18 of Appendix B.

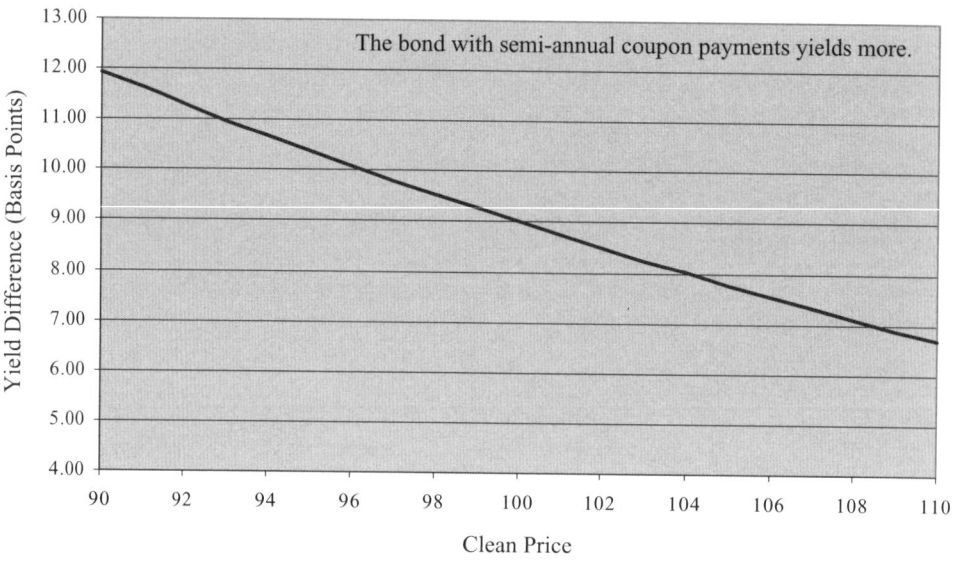

Figure 3.9 Difference in redemption yields between two 10 year bonds with 6% coupons, one semi-annual and one annual.

Program 3.1 Yield1

The program allows users to enter the basic terms of a fixed-rate bond issue together with either its price or yield. It then calculates the accrued interest, the clean and dirty prices, redemption yields compounded both annually, and semi-annually, and various associated calculations, such as Macaulay and modified durations and convexity, which are discussed later in this chapter.

Program 3.2 Yield2

This program is similar to Yield1 but in addition it allows users to specify the projected cash flow stream.

It has already been remarked that the redemption yield of a coupon-paying bond priced at its redemption price does not yield exactly the coupon rate between coupon payments. This is because accrued interest accumulates linearly and the time to the first coupon payment is less than the compounding period, assuming this agrees with the coupon payment frequency. This is illustrated for a 5% bond paying coupons annually in Figure 3.10.

Surprisingly, if you were instead to plot the yield of a bond paying annual coupons and priced at par, over time you would get a graph as shown in Figure 3.11. The downward sloping straight

How Do You Price and Value a Bond? 45

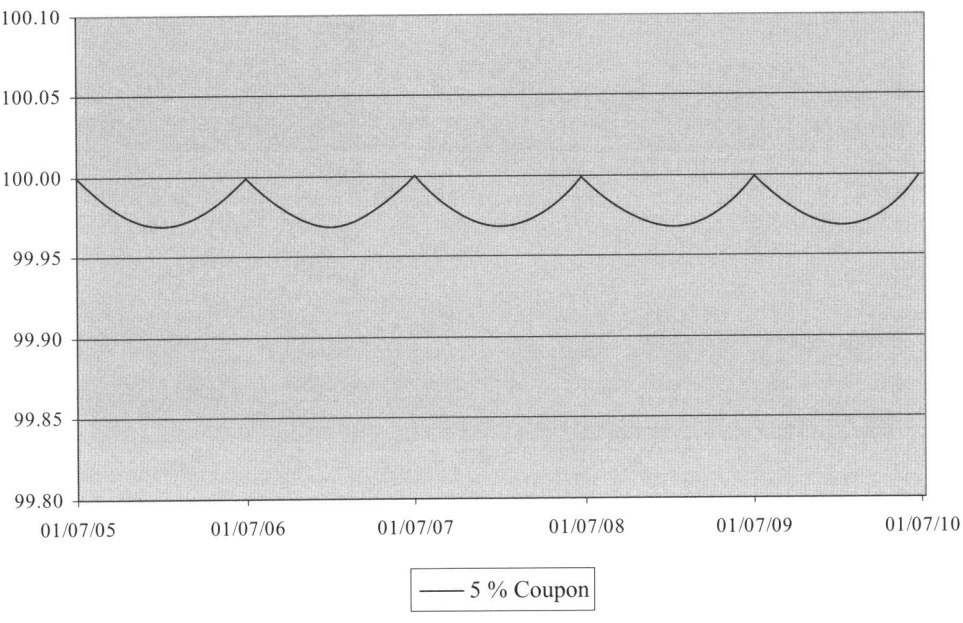

Figure 3.10 Price of a 5 % bond at constant yield = coupon.

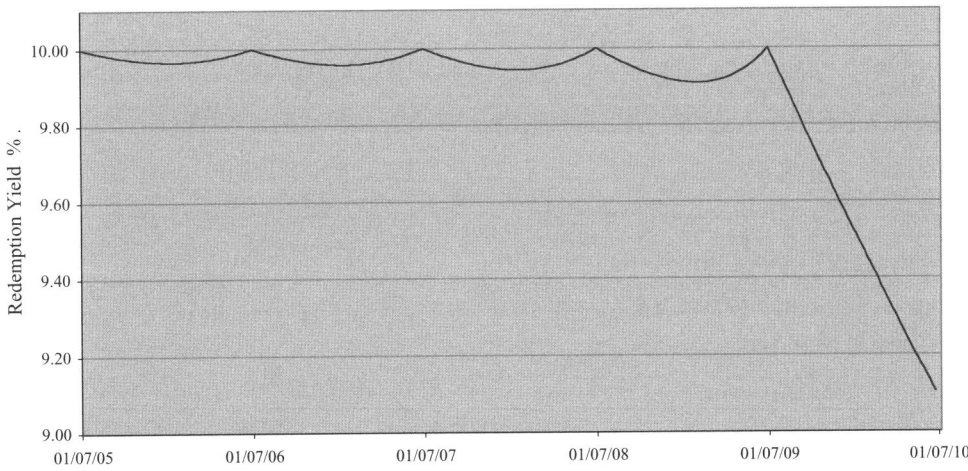

Figure 3.11 Yield over time of a bond priced at par.

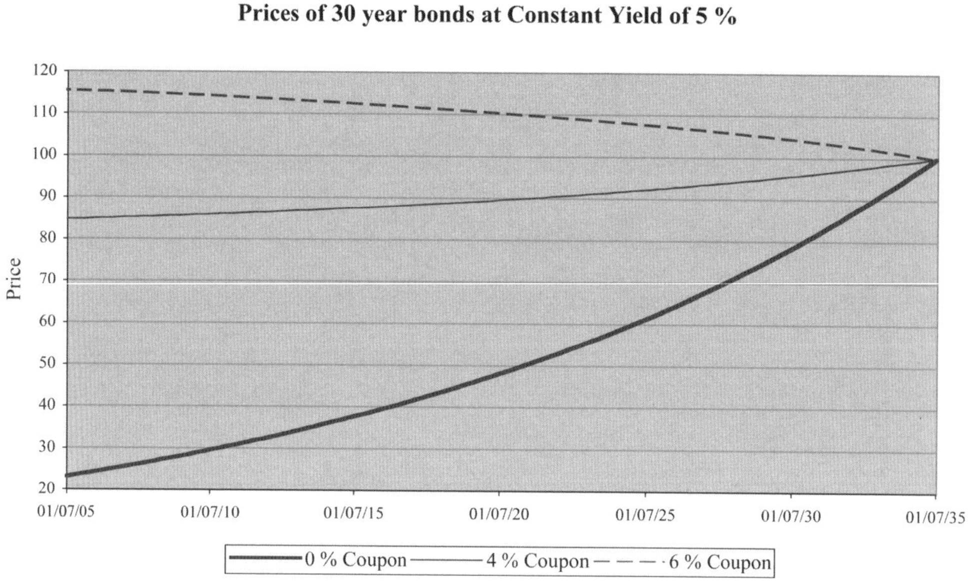

Prices of 30 year bonds at Constant Yield of 5 %

Figure 3.12 Prices for constant yields to redemption for three bonds.

line, when the bond has a life to maturity of less than one year, is caused by the compounding effect on the redemption amount, which is now less than one compounding period away.

Provided there are no unexpected events, such as defaults, the price of a bond will tend to move towards the redemption price over time. This is illustrated in Figure 3.12, which shows how the prices of three 30 year bonds with coupons of 0 %, 4 % and 6 % will move towards the redemption value of par assuming that the yields on all three bonds remain, albeit unlikely, at 5 % throughout the life of the bonds.

In practice yields on bonds vary over their lives. Figure 3.13 considers the price progression of a 10 year 2 % annual bond which is currently yielding 5 %. The constant yield price progression is shown together with lines that show what the prices would be if it were to yield 1 % more (i.e. 6 %) and 1 % less (4 %). The three yield lines converge, as you would expect over time.

Program 3.3   Price Progression

This program allows the user to specify the terms of a bond and to plot its price progression to maturity with various interest rate scenarios.

One often finds reference to the 'annual equivalent rate' (AER) or 'annual percentage rate' (APR) of an investment. This, at least in the UK, came about in an attempt by the government to standardize the claimed returns on financial products. The AER or APR is just the annualized return you would get on the investment if held for the appropriate period after allowing for all expenses. It is in effect just the redemption yield of the product compounded annually.

Comparison of Price Convergence over time for a 2 % Bond maturing in 2015

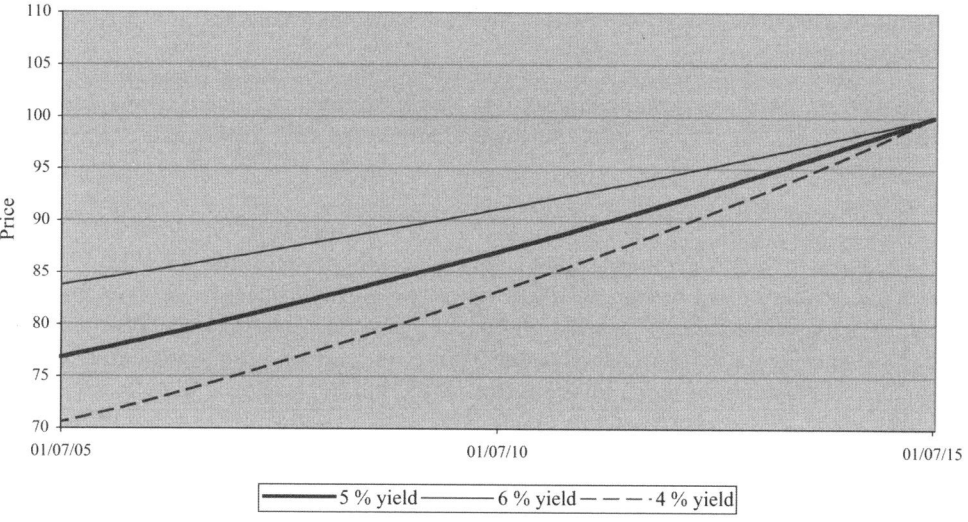

Figure 3.13 Constant yields of 4 %, 5 % and 6 % over time.

3.6.4 Life and duration

The terms of a bond issue may specify that it can be redeemed in a variety of ways. For example, the terms could specify that:

- It will be redeemed only on a specified date.
- It will be redeemed on a single specified date unless some specific event occurs beforehand, when it would be redeemed early.
- It will be redeemed at some time between two dates.

Example 3.9 $5\frac{1}{2}$ % UK Treasury Stock, 2008–2012

If not previously redeemed, the stock will be repaid at par on 10 September 2012, but Her Majesty's Treasury reserve to themselves the right to redeem the stock, in whole or in part, by drawings or otherwise, at par (100) on, or at any time after, 10 September 2008, on giving not less than three months' notice in the London Gazette.

- It will be redeemed in a series of specified tranches on specified dates.

Example 3.10

25 % of the bond will be redeemed on 1 September in each of the years 2015, 2016, 2017 and 2018.

- It will be redeemed in a number of tranches, depending on the life of the underlying assets. This can happen with mortgage backed securities.
- No final redemption date is specified. In this case there are usually specific circumstances under which the bond may be redeemed.

As a result the market uses several different measures for the life of a bond. If a bond is going to be redeemed in exactly 10 years' time then it is said, self-evidently, to have a 'life to maturity' of 10 years.

For bonds that specify in their description a range of maturity dates, where the issuer has the option to redeem the bond at any time between the two dates, an 'expected life' is often calculated. For such bonds it is assumed that the issuer will always act in his or her own best interest; i.e. the issuer will redeem the bond early if it can be refinanced for a lower cost. As a result the market calculates an expected life for the bond. For convenience, it is assumed that if the bond is being traded above par, then the issuer could reissue the debt at a lower cost and save money. In practice, the decision is not that simple, since this simplistic approach ignores the costs associated with issuing a new bond.

The expected life of such a bond is thus the period from the settlement date to the earliest possible redemption date if its clean price is over par and to the last date if it is below par.

Example 3.11

Use the above example of $5\frac{1}{2}\%$ Treasury Stock 2008–2012 (Example 3.9). During the summer of 2005, the price of the bond was over 100, with the result that the expected life of the bond was $3\frac{1}{2}$ years. However, if the price had dropped below 100, its expected life would jump to $7\frac{1}{2}$ years.

If a bond is going to be redeemed in several tranches, then an 'average life' to its weighted average maturity date is often calculated.

Example 3.12

If 25 % of a bond is redeemed on 1 July 2020 and the remaining 75 % on 1 July 2024, then the average life of this bond will be calculated up to the weighted average of these two dates, i.e. to 1 July 2023.

Other bonds instead give the holder of the bond the option to request repayment of the bond early. In such cases, it is assumed that the holder will act in his or her own best interest. However, redeeming the bond early just because the yield is greater is not always the correct action.

Example 3.13

Consider a bond that has an annual coupon of 6.00 %, is currently priced at 99 and the holder has the right to redeem it in 30 days' time at par (100). The bond will normally be redeemed in 5 years at par.

If a holder redeems the bond early, he or she will get a one-off bonus of 1%. On the other hand, if the holder then wants to reinvest the proceeds for a five year period, the question becomes one of whether more money can be made by redeeming the bond early and reinvesting or by not exercising the option to redeem the bond.

If you compare two 10 year bullet bonds with different coupons, the life to maturity does not tell the whole story as the timings of the monies an investor receives from the bonds will be different.

Example 3.14

Consider a 10 year zero-coupon bond and a bond that pays an annual coupon of 10%. Both bonds are redeemed at par on the same date.

With the zero-coupon bond the long-term investor will have to wait 10 years before receiving any return on the investment. On the other hand, the investor in the 10% bond will receive interest to the tune of 90% of the par value (9 years of coupon) before the redemption date and 110% (capital and income) on the redemption date.

The average time an investor has to wait to get a return on the investment is obviously shorter in the second case.

One way to compare these two bonds in a better way would be to compare the average time you have to wait for the income and capital repayments of each bond. In Figure 3.14, the

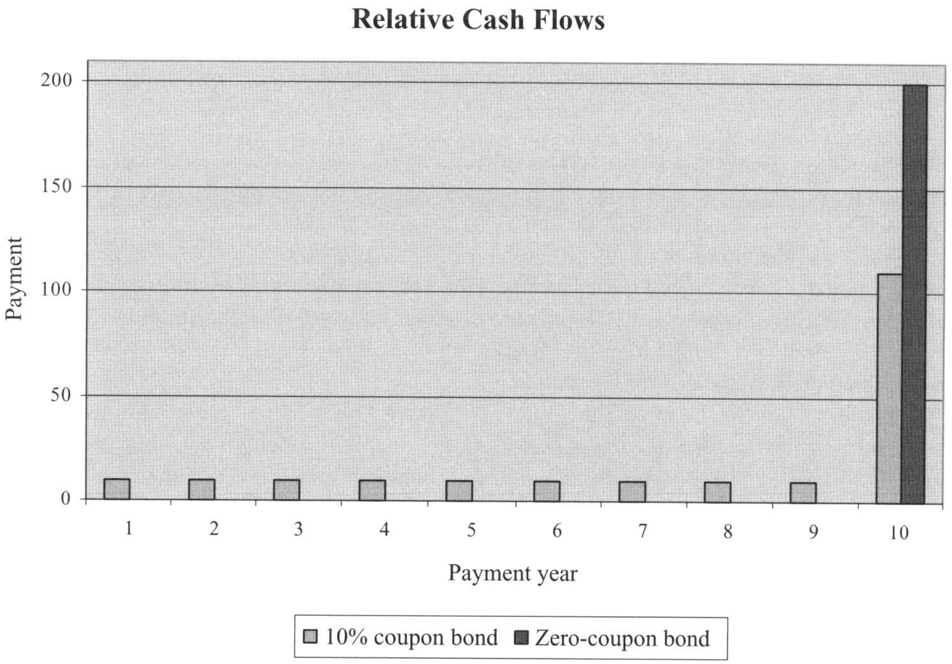

Relative Cash Flows

Figure 3.14 Relative cash flows.

redemption payment on the zero-coupon bond has been increased to make it compatible with the other bond.

Using the above examples, with the zero-coupon bond the average time to the payments is obviously 10 years as there is only one payment. However, with the 10 % bond the total coupon payments and the capital repayment are both 100. The average time to wait for the coupon payments is $5\frac{1}{2}$ years and the capital payment occurs in 10 years' time. Thus the average time for all the payments is $(5.5 + 10)/2 = 7.75$ years.

As investors normally require a return on their investment, an amount that you get back next week is regarded as more valuable than an identical one for which you have to wait 10 years. Unfortunately, the average payment time above does not allow for this.

However, in order to compare the average life of two investments, Frederick Macaulay in 1938 came up with the concept of 'duration'. Duration, or as it is sometimes called 'Macaulay duration' to distinguish it from other types of duration, gives you the average time to wait for each of the investments, weighted now by these sizes (as before) and now discounted by the redemption yield of the bond.

Example 3.15

Using the same examples as above, if both bonds have a redemption yield of 5.00 % per annum then, for the zero-coupon bond:

$$\text{Duration} = \frac{100/1.05^{10} \times 10}{100/1.05^{10}} = 10 \text{ years}$$

whereas for the 10 % bond:

$$\text{Duration} = \frac{10 \times (1/1.05 + 2/1.05^2 + \cdots + 10/1.05^{10}) + 100 \times 10/1.05^{10}}{10 \times (1/1.05 + 1/1.05^2 + \cdots + 1/1.05^{10}) + 100/1.05^{10}} = 7.270 \text{ years}$$

The formula for duration is given in Appendix B.

If you consider a bond that is priced at par, its duration will eventually reduce to zero as it approaches redemption. However, this progression is not smooth.

Figure 3.15 plots duration against life to maturity for a bond, priced consistently at par, that pays an annual coupon of 10.00 %. The sharp increases in duration over time occur when the bond goes ex a coupon payment. The payment that was removed from the duration calculations had a very small and diminishing life. Removing this payment increases the overall average of the time you have to wait for a payment.

Although as you would expect the duration of most bonds increases with life to maturity, surprisingly this is not always the case with some deeply discounted very long bonds. The graph in Figure 3.16 shows the durations of two bonds paying annual coupons and yielding a constant 10 % per annum as their life to maturity is increased up to 50 years with the plots being on their coupon payment dates. (This avoids the jumps in the calculations.)

Similarly, it can be shown that the duration of an undated bond is independent of its coupon (see the formulae in Appendix B). In fact, its duration reduces in the case of a bond that pays a constant annual coupon to just the inverse of its yield plus the fraction of a year to the first coupon payment.

How Do You Price and Value a Bond? 51

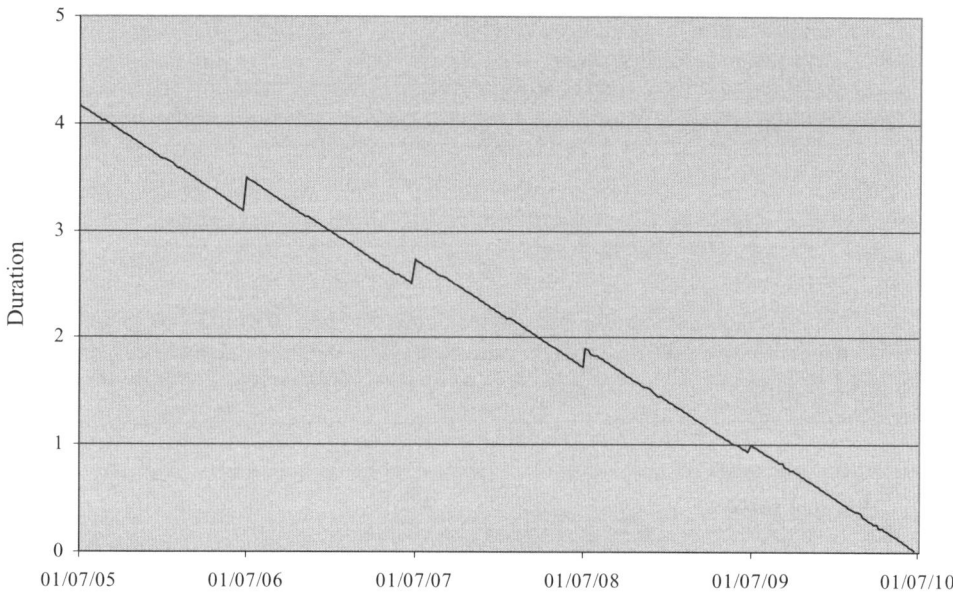

Figure 3.15 Duration versus life to maturity for a bond priced at par.

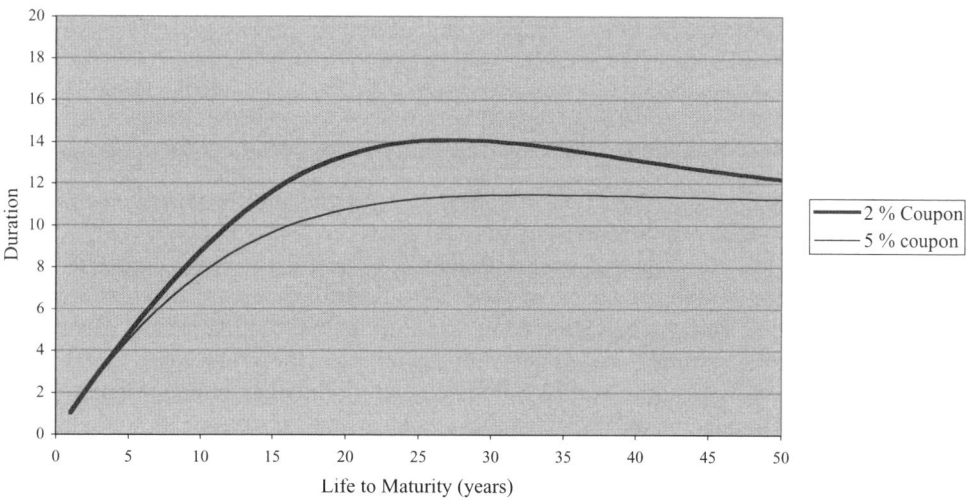

Figure 3.16 Durations of two deeply discounted bonds against life.

Table 3.1 Duration of an undated bond at different redemption yields

Redemption yield (%)	Fraction of year to first payment		
	0.0	0.5	1.0
2	50 years	$50\frac{1}{2}$ years	51 years
4	25 years	$25\frac{1}{2}$ years	26 years
5	20 years	$20\frac{1}{2}$ years	21 years
10	10 years	$10\frac{1}{2}$ years	11 years

If you look at the durations in Figure 3.16 for bonds that both have 50 year maturities and yield 10 % per annum, you will see that they are both over 10, but both lines are tending down to a value of 10 years. Hence some undated bonds have a duration that is shorter than similar long-dated ones.

3.6.5 Modified duration

In the equity markets much of modern portfolio theory is concerned with evaluating the 'alpha' and the 'beta' of a particular equity security or a portfolio of securities.[3] If the beta of a security is greater than 1.0 then it means that according to the analysis of its historic stock price movements, its price has been observed to be more volatile than that of its peer group. Similarly, if its beta is estimated to be less than 1.0, its price is regarded as not being as volatile as the market. Hence, one is interested in investing in securities with high betas if you expect the market to rise, and low ones if you expect it to fall.

In the bond markets, the volatility or beta of a bond's price is mainly determined by its structure (i.e. price, coupons, maturity date, options, etc.) and its issuer and associated credit risk. The structural part of the beta is called its 'modified duration' or price 'volatility'. Modified duration is defined to be the percentage change in price for a unit change in yield. It can be shown that, for a fixed-rate bond, it is related to the Macaulay duration by the formula:

$$\text{Modified duration} = \text{Macaulay duration} \times \text{discounting factor}$$

where the discounting factor is just $1/(1 + 0.05)$ for a bond yielding 5 % when compounding annually and $1/(1 + 0.06)$ for a bond yielding 6 %.

The derivation of this formula is given in Appendix B. Hence, as you would expect, the price volatility or modified duration of a bond increases as its duration increases and vice versa. The price of a bond that is going to be redeemed in the next few weeks, if there is no expectation that the issuer is going to default on it, is not likely to move very far from its redemption value.

Figure 3.17 shows how life to maturity, duration and modified duration are related for a bond that is priced throughout at 100 (par) and is paying annual coupons of 10 % over the last five years of its life.

---

[3] The expected price P of a security, at some time in the future, is given by a formula of the form:

$$P_{\text{Expected}} = P_{\text{Current}} + \alpha + \beta \times \% \text{ change in market}$$

where the values of α and β are mainly derived from an analysis of the previous volatility of the security relative to the market.

10 % 1 July 2010 Bond Priced at Par

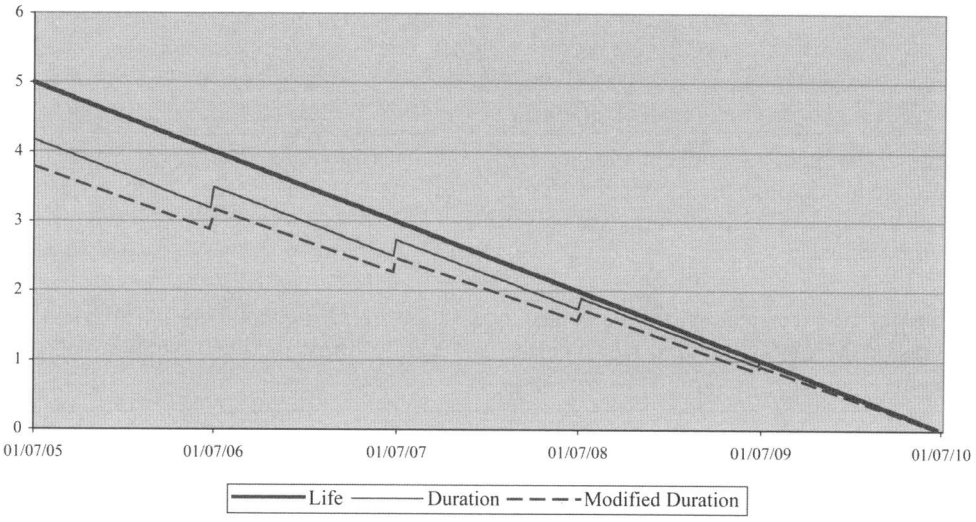

Figure 3.17 Life to maturity, duration and modified duration for bond priced at par.

Let us now examine some of the properties of the modified duration calculation. As you can observe in Figure 3.17 the modified duration of a bond decreases as it approaches maturity, although not in a continuous way. However, if you assume that the yield on the bond does not change during its life and only look at the modified duration calculations on coupon payment dates, it declines steadily towards zero at maturity. This is what you would expect as an investor is 'guaranteed' a fixed amount of money in an ever decreasing time period.

Example 3.16

Consider two zero-coupon bonds, one with a life of one year and the other with a life of two years. If they both currently yield 5 %, their current prices P are given by:

$$P_{1\text{year}} = \frac{100}{1+0.05} = 95.238$$

$$P_{2\text{year}} = \frac{100}{(1+0.05)^2} = 90.703$$

If the yield on both of them now changes to 6 %, the new prices become:

$$P_{1\text{year}} = \frac{100}{1+0.06} = 94.340$$

$$P_{2\text{year}} = \frac{100}{(1+0.06)^2} = 89.000$$

This gives percentage price changes of:

$$\frac{94.340 - 95.238}{95.238} = -0.943\,\%$$

$$\frac{89.000 - 90.703}{90.703} = -1.876\,\%$$

respectively. In other words, the longer dated bond has had, in percentage terms, a greater decrease in price than the shorter one. Conversely, if interest rates decrease, the longer dated bond will appreciate more in percentage terms.

Similarly, for fixed-rate option-free bonds, unless they are zero-coupon ones, if its yield decreases, its Macaulay duration will increase, and as a result its modified duration will also increase.

Example 3.17

Consider a bond with a duration of 5 years and a yield of 6 %. By definition this bond has a modified duration of:

$$5/(1 + 0.06) = 4.717$$

If the yield of the bond drops to 5.5 %, then unless it is a zero-coupon bond, when the duration will not change, its duration will increase to $(5 + n)$ years for some positive value of n.

The bond's modified duration is now given by:

$$(5 + n)/(1 + 0.055)$$

which is always greater than the 4.717 above as the numerator has increased and the denominator decreased.

Programs 3.1 and 3.2 (*Continued*)   Yield1 and Yield2

Both of these programs calculate Macaulay and modified durations for a user-entered bond or cash flow stream.

Now let us consider the effect of different coupon rates on modified duration. Figure 3.18 plots the calculated modified duration for option-free 20 year fixed-rate bonds all yielding 5 % per annum. The graph shows that not only does the modified duration increase as the coupon rate decreases but the increase is steeper for smaller coupon rates. If you apply this fact to a government bond market, where the bonds may be stripped, such as in the UK or France, their high durations mean that they are more volatile than the underlying securities, and as a result proprietary traders and hedge funds can take advantage of their greater volatility.

It is also possible to show that for an option-free fixed-rate bond the modified duration decreases as its yield increases. This is illustrated in Figures 3.19 and 3.20. As can be seen

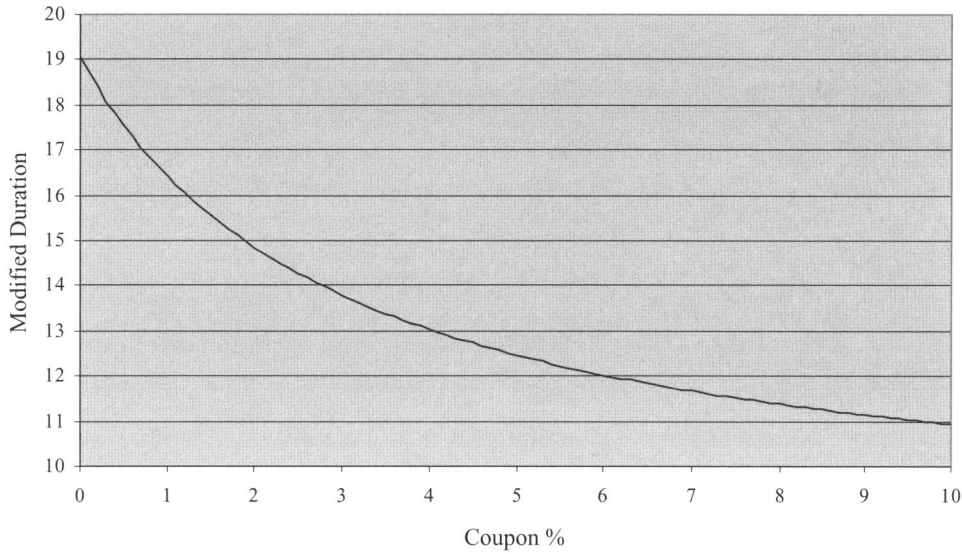

Figure 3.18 Modified duration versus coupon at constant yield.

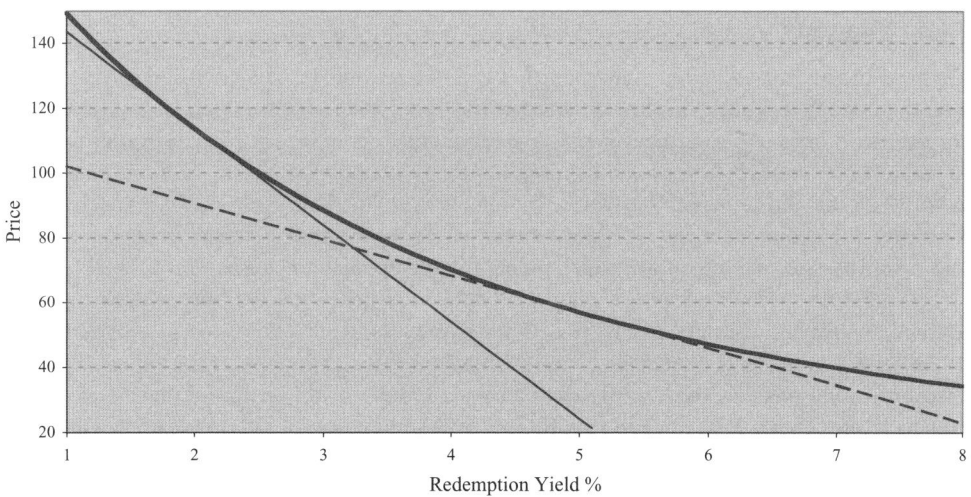

Figure 3.19 Price versus yield plus tangents (modified duration).

Five-year Fixed Rate Bonds

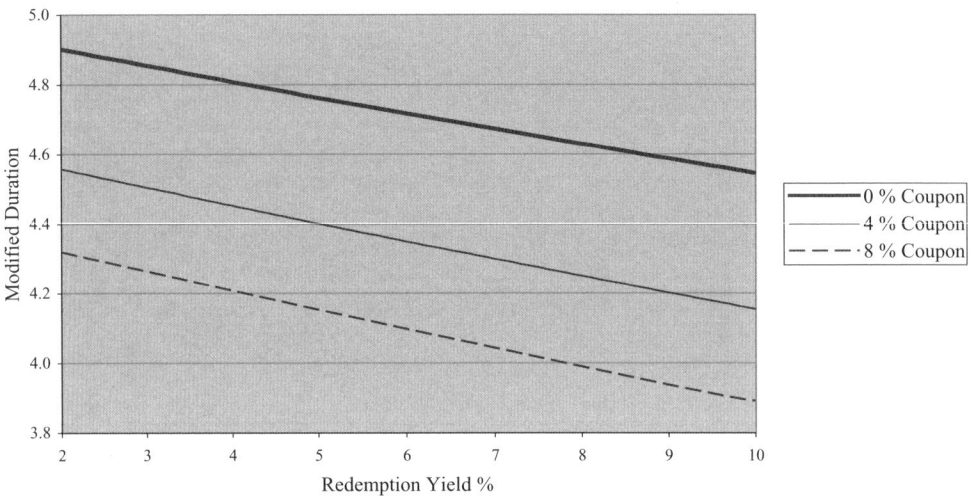

Figure 3.20 Modified duration versus yield.

in Figure 3.19, due to the convexity of the relationship between price and yield, the modified duration (i.e. the angle of the tangent to the x axis) decreases as the yield increases. Figure 3.20 shows the relationship between modified duration and yield for three different five year option-free fixed-rate bonds with different coupons. As you would expect the lower the redemption yield, the higher the modified duration.

3.6.6 Convexity

We have already seen that the relationship between a fixed-rate bond's price and its yield is not a straight line, but is curved. The curvature of this relationship for some bonds is greater than for others. 'Convexity' is a measure of this curvature. It is in effect a second-order measure of interest rate risk. Its formula and derivation are given in Appendix B. It can be seen from Figure 3.21 that the convexity (curvature) of the price/yield relationship increases as the life to maturity of the bond increases. It is also found that if you compare bonds with the same yields and maturity dates, then the lower the coupon, the greater the convexity.

If a bond has greater convexity than another similar bond that currently yields the same amount, then if interest rates rise its price will fall by less in percentage terms than that of the other bond. Similarly, if interest rates fall its price will rise by a greater percentage. From an investor's point of view, more convexity is a good thing. For this reason, bonds with greater convexity are often priced to yield slightly less than similar bonds with lower convexity. For a given yield and maturity, the convexity of a bond increases as the coupon rate decreases. This is shown in Table 3.2 of bonds with coupons of 0%, 5% and 10%.

If the convexity of zero-coupon bonds is plotted against their life to maturity, it is found that the convexity increases in proportion to almost the square of the remaining life and that the lower the yield the higher the convexity (see Figure 3.22). The derivation of the simplified zero-coupon convexity formula is given in Appendix B.

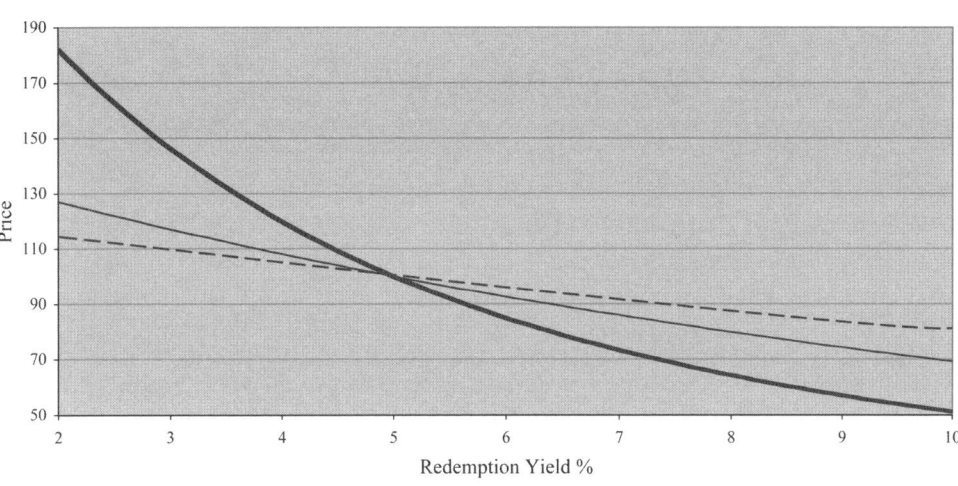

Figure 3.21 Price versus redemption yield for bonds with different maturities.

3.6.7 Dispersion

'Dispersion' measures the variance of the timing of the bond's cash flows around its duration. Its formula is given in Appendix B.

Let us consider a bond portfolio manager who has to match the returns on the portfolio against a specific future liability. In practice, pension fund managers will have a range of projected future commitments, but in the following example we will look at a single liability in four years' time. In order to reduce the chance of the portfolio failing to meet its objective due to changes in interest and associated reinvestment rates, it will be constructed in such a way that its aggregate duration is similar to that of the future liability, i.e. four years.

Figure 3.23 shows the expected cash flows from two possible portfolios, A and B, both with a duration of about four years. The distribution of the cash flows in portfolio A is much more pointed than those of portfolio B. Thus the dispersion calculation for portfolio A is less than that for portfolio B. This means that portfolio A is more likely to satisfy the future liability than portfolio B.

Dispersion is not widely used in the market.

Table 3.2 Convexity of bonds yielding 5 % per annum with different coupon rates

Coupon rate (%)	Life to maturity		
	5 years	10 years	40 years
0	27.21	99.77	1487.53
5	23.94	75.00	469.91
10	21.83	64.02	392.11

58 An Introduction to the Bond Markets

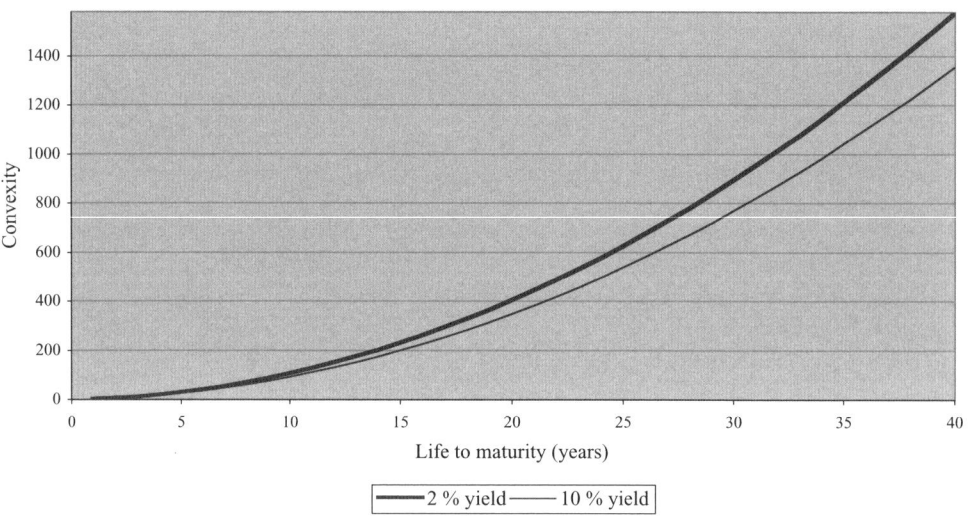

Figure 3.22 Zero-coupon convexity versus life to maturity.

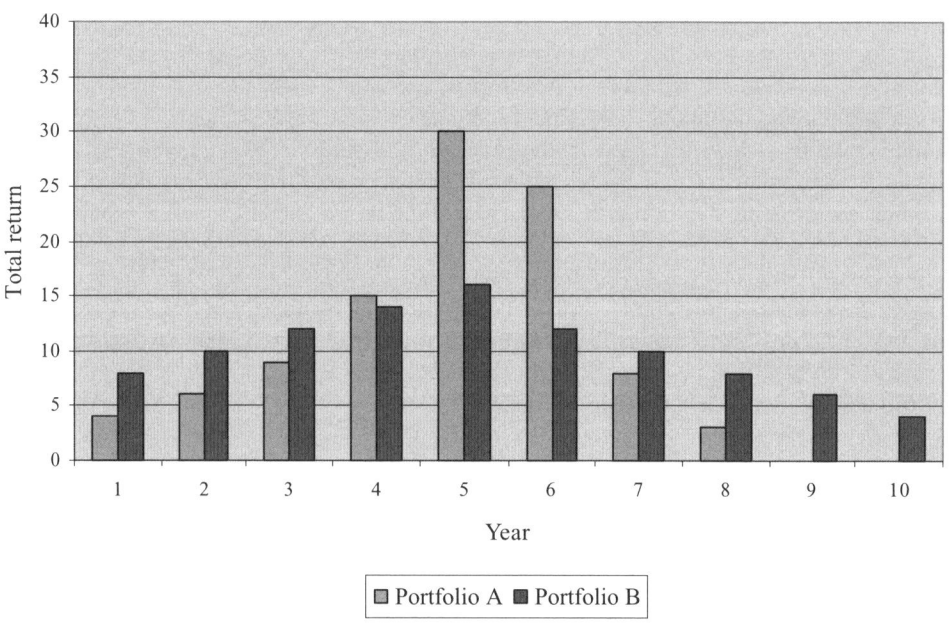

Figure 3.23 Total return versus year.

3.7 FLOATING-RATE NOTES

As has been pointed out, when a redemption yield is calculated for a floating-rate note (FRN), it is necessary to assume a future indicator rate, relative to which all future coupon payments are fixed. The market place as a result often likes to compare their projected future return relative to this indicator rate. This relative return is termed a 'margin'.

There are two different types of margin calculation: 'simple margin' and 'discounted margin'. These calculations are very similar to the simple yield to maturity and redemption yield calculations.

3.7.1 Simple margin (FRN)

The 'simple margin' calculation for a floating-rate note (FRN) measures the return that can be obtained on the FRN relative to its current indicator rate. The indicator rate is the interest rate relative to which the coupons are set. The simple margin calculation makes use of the note's known next coupon payment, the current indicator rate, its quoted margin relative to this indicator rate and its expected life. The calculation also assumes that the current market indicator rate will not change during the life of the bond.

The process of calculating a simple margin is:

- Take the current price and adjust it if necessary to reflect any changes in the indicator rate since the next known coupon was set. The following example shows how the price is adjusted.
- Calculate the required average annual gain or loss from the adjusted price to the redemption price.
- Add the note's quoted margin.

In other words, a simple margin is just the note's quoted margin plus the annualized price gain or loss to redemption.

Example 3.18

Consider a floating-rate note that was issued with semi-annual coupons equal to six month sterling LIBOR + 0.1 %. When the note was issued three months ago, the six month LIBOR rate was 4.5 %, but the current six month LIBOR rate is 4.0 %. Its indicator rate is the six month sterling LIBOR and the quoted margin is 0.1 %. The first coupon payment in three months' time was set at issue to be:

$$(4.5 + 0.1)/2 = 2.3\%^4$$

If the FRN is being traded on a clean price of 99 and it is redeemed in 4.75 years at 100, then to calculate the simple margin, you first adjust the trading price to allow for the fact that the indicator rate has dropped from 4.5 % to 4.0 % in the three months.

If the coupon rate were to have been set at today's rate, the next coupon would have been $(4.0 + 0.1)/2 = 2.05\%$, instead of $(4.5 + 0.1)/2 = 2.3\%$. This is a difference of 0.25 %. However, as we are now halfway through the coupon period, the difference in the payment would be half this amount, i.e. 0.125 %. The adjusted price is thus:

$$99 - 0.125 = 98.875\%$$

---

[3] This is not exactly true as the interest period will not be exactly 182.5 days.

60 An Introduction to the Bond Markets

> The difference between the adjusted price and the redemption price is $(100 - 98.875) = 1.125$, which will be made up over 4.75 years. In other words, at the rate of
>
> $$1.125/4.75 = 0.237 \text{ per year}$$
>
> The simple margin is the sum of this annual accretion and the quoted margin. Thus:
>
> $$\text{Simple margin} = 0.237 + 0.10 = 0.337\,\%$$

Figure 3.24 shows the simple margin calculation for a note with a life of three years and a quoted margin of 0.2 %. It can be seen that it is quite possible for the note to have a negative simple margin. This occurs when the average capital depreciation exceeds the quoted margin.

The margin calculations enable floating-rate notes to be compared with other floating-rate notes and money market instruments, which are based on the same indicator rate, but not with fixed-rate bonds or floating-rate notes based on other indicator rates.

3.7.2 Discounted margin (FRN)

The simple margin formula for floating-rate notes described in the previous section has two significant drawbacks when comparing how cheap or expensive the relevant security is. The calculation:

- Does not allow for the current yield effect on the quoted margin if the price of the note is above or below par.
- Assumes that any capital gain or loss occurs evenly over the life of the note, as opposed to being compounded at a constant rate.

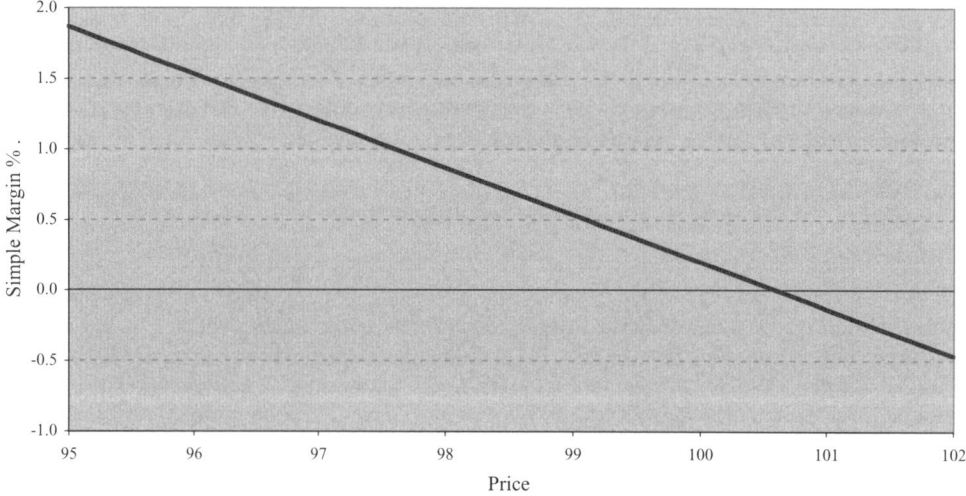

Figure 3.24 Simple margin versus price.

How Do You Price and Value a Bond? 61

Both of these problems are eliminated in the discounted margin calculation, which is described in Appendix B.

You will see that the formula is very similar to a redemption yield formula with the following modifications:

- The dirty price is now increased using simple interest to the first coupon payment at the current indicator rate for the period up to the coupon plus the required discounted margin. With the redemption yield formula compound interest is used.
- The first/next coupon is known, but all subsequent coupon payments are based on the current market indicator rate plus the quoted margin.
- All future payments, including the redemption amount, are discounted at a rate that equals the assumed market indicator rate plus the quoted margin.

Figure 3.25 shows the relationship between the clean price of a note paying quarterly coupons with 10 years to maturity, a quoted margin of 0.1 % and a current indicator rate of 4.0 %.

The relationship between the simple margin and the discounted margin calculations is similar to that between the simple yield to maturity and the redemption yield for fixed-rate bonds. Figure 3.26 illustrates this for the same 10 year note. This shows that the discounted margin changes more for a specified change in price than the simple margin.

It should be noted that, in practice, the discounted margin for a floating-rate note is often very close to its redemption yield minus its current indicator rate.

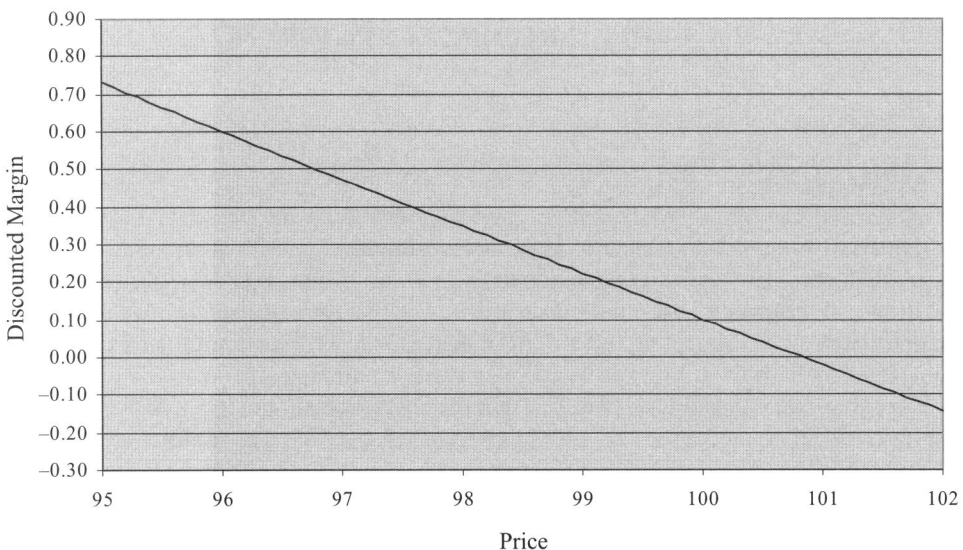

Figure 3.25 Discounted margin versus price.

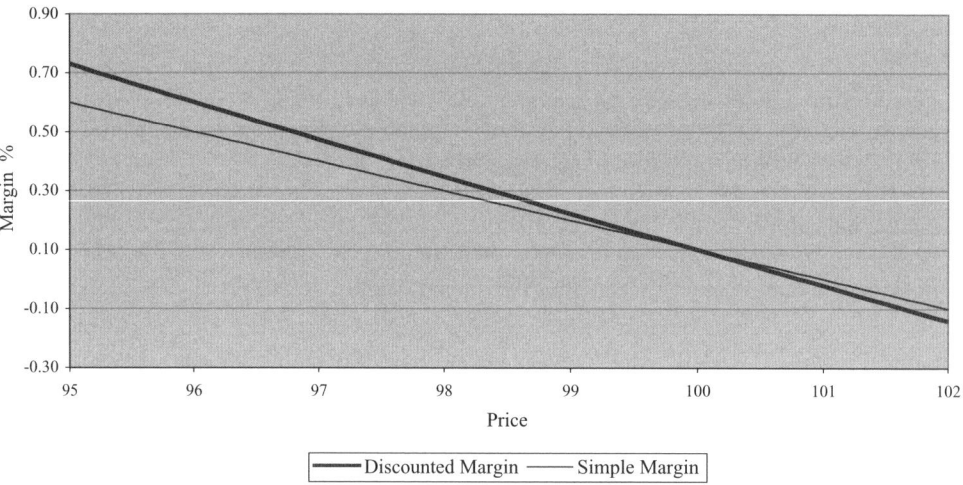

Figure 3.26 Simple and discounted margins versus price.

Program 3.5 FRN

This program allows the user to set up a floating-rate note and specify a price. It then calculates a simple margin, a discounted margin and a redemption yield for the note.

3.8 REAL REDEMPTION YIELD

Nearly all index-linked bonds have their coupons and final redemption value indexed to an index that is usually a proxy for inflation in the country of issue. For example, in the UK, Her Majesty's Treasury have issued bonds that are linked to the UK Retail Price Index. As a result, investors use such bonds as a hedge against future inflation. Historically, as you would expect, yields on fixed-rate bonds have been high when inflation is high and low when inflation is low.

In times of low inflation a yield of 10 % looks extremely high, but if you are investing in an environment where you expect inflation to be 15 % for the next year, then your expectation is that in real terms in a year's time your investment will have decreased in value. In such circumstances an investment of 100 will have increased to 110 in currency terms. However, the 110 is only worth $110/1.15 = 95.65$ in last year's currency. That is a loss of 4.35! An investment in index-linked bonds ensures that this cannot occur, unless of course the issuer defaults.

It is possible to calculate 'real' redemption yields on index-linked bonds, but this requires an inflation rate for the relevant index to be assumed for the life of the issue. The calculation is similar to that for an ordinary fixed-rate bond, but all future payments are grossed up, if appropriate, by the assumed inflation rate. Such calculations are unfortunately dependent on the assumption about future inflation. This is illustrated by the following extract from the FTSE UK Gilts Indices for UK index-linked stocks for 19 September 2005 (Table 3.3).

Table 3.3 FTSE UK Gilts Indices for index-linked stocks

	Inflation 0 %		Inflation 5 %	
Real yield	Yield (19 September)	Duration (years)	Yield (19 September)	Duration (years)
Up to 5 years	1.89	3.50	1.08	3.50
Over 5 years	1.60	12.00	1.36	12.12
5–15 years	1.70	8.92	1.38	8.97
Over 15 years	1.51	18.08	1.35	18.19
All stocks	1.61	11.33	1.36	11.46

Source: Copyright, FTSE International 2005. Reproduced by permission of FTSE group.

It can be seen from Table 3.3 that the differences in the real returns you get by assuming 0 % or 5 % inflation are still quite considerable. In addition, unlike the position with fixed-rate bonds, the duration varies according to the assumed inflation rate.

There is an alternative approach for the calculation of real yields on index-linked bonds that does not involve any assumptions about changes in the relative index. This approach can theoretically be applied to all index-linked bonds, but it is easier to understand if you just apply it to bonds that have a three month indexation lag, such as the 50 year UK $1\frac{1}{4}$ % Index-Linked Treasury Gilt 2055. This bond pays semi-annual coupons of 0.625 % index-linked to the UK Retail Price Index, and is redeemed at a real price of 100, which is again inflated by the change in the retail price index. The clean price quoted in the market place for this bond is relative to the real redemption price of 100. However, when you buy the bond you have to pay:

$$(\text{Real clean price} + \text{real accrued interest}) \times \text{index ratio}$$

where the index ratio measures the increase in the retail price index since issue and the real accrued interest is based on an annual coupon of $1\frac{1}{4}$ %.

The approach is simply to ignore the indexation completely. Thus for the above bond, the real redemption is calculated as if it were a fixed-rate bond with a coupon of $1\frac{1}{4}$ % paid semi-annually and redeemed at 100. In September 2005 the UK Debt Management Office issued £1250 million of such a bond at a price of £105.29 per £100 nominal on a real yield of just 1.112 % over a 50 year period!

3.9 MONEY MARKET YIELDS AND DISCOUNTS

Short-term money market instruments, such as Treasury bills, commercial paper and bankers acceptances, are often traded on a 'discount' or 'yield' as opposed to a price basis. The yield on short-term money market instruments is calculated using simple interest as opposed to compound interest, and as a result is not directly comparable with the redemption yields previously discussed.

It is conventional in the Treasury bills market to assume that a year has 360 days, unless it is denominated in sterling when it has 365 days, even in a leap year. Short-term money market instruments frequently do not have a specified coupon and as a result investors in them obtain a return by buying them at a discount to their face or redemption value.

Example 3.19

A 90 day US dollar Treasury bill is issued at 99% of its face value. It will be redeemed at its face value (100 %) 90 days after issue. It is traded on a discount basis. The discount is given by:

$$\text{Discount} = (100 - 99) \times \frac{360}{90} = 4\%$$

As in the US dollar money market a year is deemed to have 360 days.

The discount is often converted into a yield so as to make it comparable with other money market instruments. This yield is often called a 'money market yield'. Using the above example, the money market yield is just $4 \times 100/99 = 4.0404\,\%$.

The formulae for discounts and money market yields are given in Appendix B.

Program 3.6 Discount

This program allows the user to enter the price or discount, accrual basis and life of a money market instrument, and calculates its discount/price, money market yield and equivalent redemption yields compounded both annually and semi-annually.

4
Bond Options and Variants

When a bond is issued, especially if it is a long dated one, the issuer may want to have some flexibility about when it is repaid. This could arise, *inter alia*, because:

- the issuer's circumstances have changed in such a way that the loan is no longer needed or
- as interest rates have dropped, the issuer can refinance the loan more cheaply or
- the covenants on the loan prevent the issuer raising more capital in the most appropriate way.

Such an option that gives the issuer a right to redeem all or part of a bond early is called a 'call' option.

Another variant of this is when the issuer wants to redeem the bond in stages, instead of in one go, via a sinking fund. This may occur when the issue is relatively large compared to the size of the issuer.

In the case of collateralized mortgage bonds securitized with a pool of mortgages, the bond will be repaid according to when the underlying mortgages themselves are paid off. The bond is thus redeemed in a number of tranches of unknown size.

In a similar way, in order to make a bond more attractive to an investor, the issuer may grant the investor a variety of different options. These can vary from:

- a 'put' option, which gives the investor the right to request early repayment of the capital on a specific date or dates;
- having warrants to purchase other assets attached;
- automatically increasing the coupon rate, if the rating of the bond issue is reduced;
- having the right to convert the bonds at predefined rates into other instruments, usually the ordinary shares of the company issuing the bonds.

Bonds have been, and no doubt will continue to be, issued with a variety of unusual terms, e.g. reverse floating-rate notes, where the coupons rise as interest rates fall.

4.1 CALLABLE BONDS

A callable bond is a bond that gives the issuer the right to redeem or 'call' the issue early, or even sometimes in certain circumstances requires the issuer to call the bond, e.g. if the tax environment changes. (This did occur some years ago when the tax status of some eurobonds which were domiciled in the Netherlands Antilles changed.)

Example 4.1 UK Treasury $5\frac{1}{2}$ % 2008/2012

The UK Government has the right to call this bond at any time between 10 September 2008 and 10 September 2012 on 90 days' notice at par (100). In 2005 the redemption yields on UK gilt-edged stocks were below 5 %, with the result that the market priced this stock as if it were to be redeemed on 10 September 2008.

Example 4.2 Citigroup Inc. $6\frac{1}{2}$ % Notes 2011

In January 2001 the company issued $2.5 billion of the security at 99.724. The bonds will be redeemed on 18 January 2011 and pay interest semi-annually on 18 January and 18 July each year. If the tax status of the bonds changes then they may be called as a whole at any time on 30 days' notice from 16 January 2001 at 100.

Example 4.3 Santander Central Hispano Financial Services Fixed/Floating-Rate Subordinated Notes – Perpetual

£200 million of the notes were issued in June 2001 at 99.31. Unless previously called the bonds will pay interest each year on 7 December. The annual rate of interest will be $7\frac{1}{4}$ % until December 2011 and thereafter at 2.85 % above the London Interbank Offer Rate for three month sterling deposits.

The bond will be callable as a whole only on coupon dates on 30 days' notice from 7 December 2011 at 100.

For an option-free non-callable bond we have seen how the price of the bond increases at an increasing rate as its yield decreases. This relationship is not true with callable bonds (see Figure 4.1). With callable bonds, and for that matter with all investments, it is assumed that issuers will always act in their own best interest. This means that if it is advantageous to an issuer to call a bond, and then possibly reissue a new bond at a reduced rate, such that after expenses the total costs of servicing the debt have been reduced, then the issuer will do so.

It is often more expensive and difficult for a company to reissue a bond on better terms (from the issuer's point of view) than for a government or a supranational organization, which are issuing new bonds at regular intervals. The yield levels, at which the market prices of similar

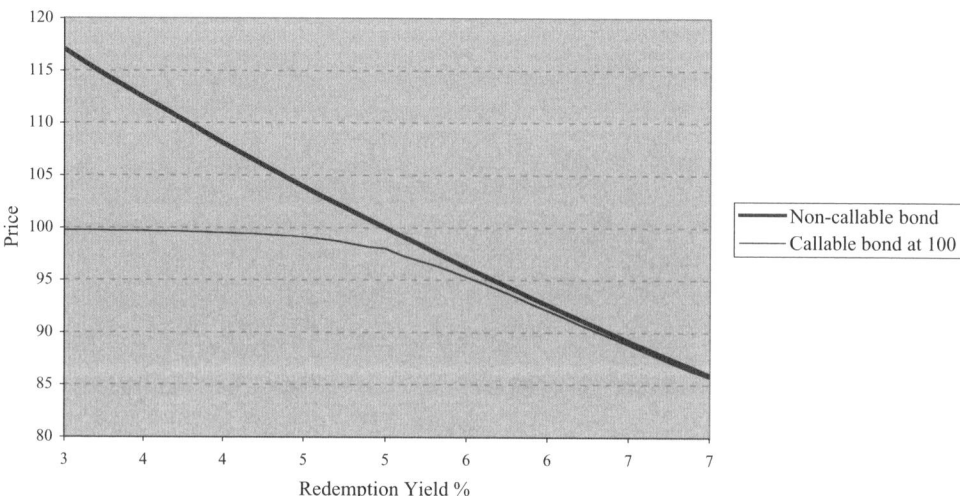

Figure 4.1 Price versus yield for callable/non-callable bonds.

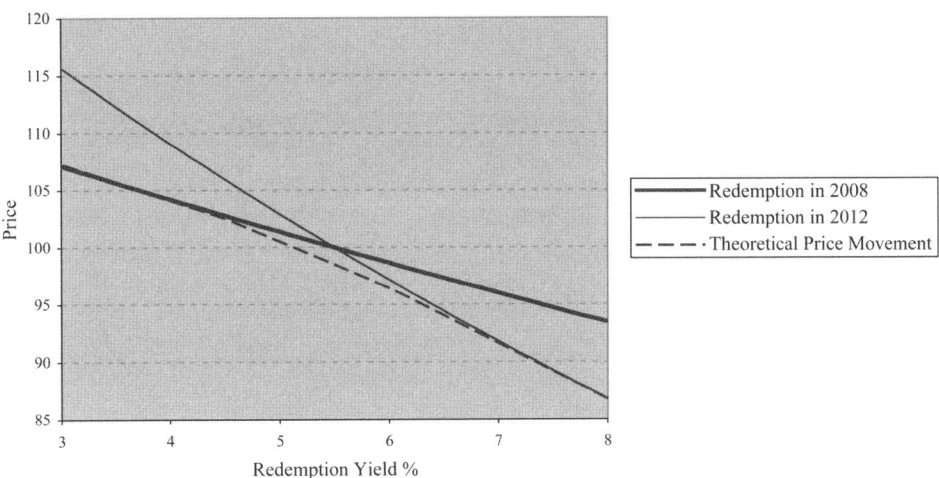

Figure 4.2 Price versus yield called and not called.

bonds with and without calls start to differ significantly, vary from bond to bond, based on the modified duration (volatility) of the bond and the expected volatility of the underlying interest rate.

Let us now consider the price performance of the UK $5\frac{1}{2}$ % Treasury 2008/2012. Throughout 2005 the price of $5\frac{1}{2}$ % Treasury has been consistently over par (100), at which price it can be called. As a result the market has assumed that the bond will be called at the earliest possible date, i.e. September 2008. Figure 4.2 shows approximately how the price of the security would vary against its yield as the market changes its assumption about the likely redemption date. The graph also shows the yield price relationship if the security did not have a call option.

The difference in the prices of the two lines for a specific yield is the value of the call option. There is no fixed, or accepted formula, for valuing the call option. Different market makers make different assumptions about the future volatility of interest rates and the implications for the issuer of calling the bond and possibly reissuing a new bond with different characteristics.

4.2 PUTABLE BONDS

Putable bonds are just the reverse side of callable bonds. A putable bond gives the holder the right to 'put' or request redemption at a predefined rate on specified dates prior to redemption.

Example 4.4 Republic of Panama $9\frac{3}{8}$ % Bonds 2029

$500 million of the bonds were issued in March 1999 at a price of 99.919. They will normally be redeemed at 100 on 1 April 2029 and they pay interest 1 April and 1 October each year. The holders of the bonds have the right on 30 days' notice to require early repayment of principal on 1 April 2006 at 100.

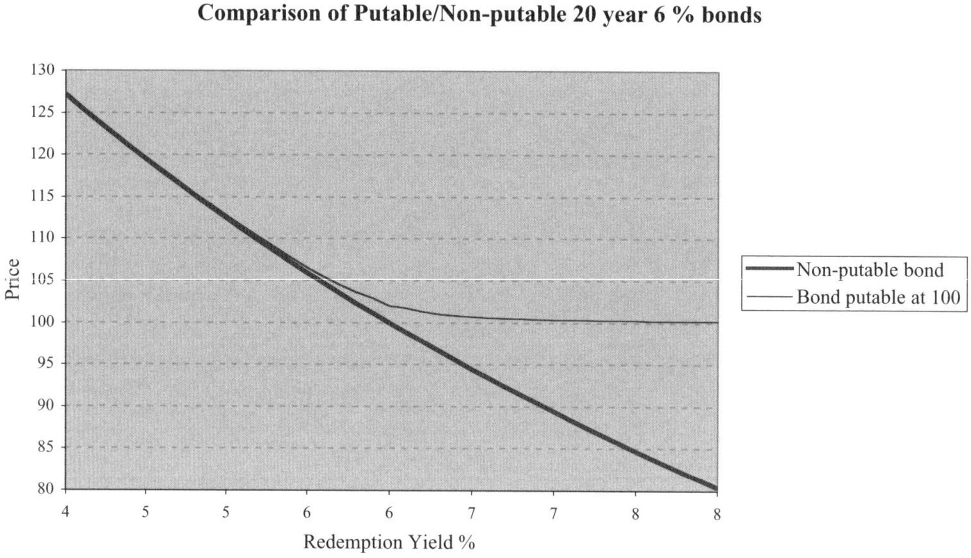

Comparison of Putable/Non-putable 20 year 6 % bonds

Figure 4.3 Putable and non-putable bonds.

A holder of a bond with a put option will exercise the option if the holder feels that the proceeds can be reinvested in investments that will give a greater return, and this extra return more than compensates for any greater risk.

Figure 4.3 shows the relationship between the yield and price of a 20 year 6 % non-putable bond and a similar one that is putable at par (100). Detailed mathematical models for calculating the value of the put option are outside the scope of this book. As you would expect, since the put option gives the holder the right to redeem the bond on certain dates at par, the expected price of the bond does not fall significantly below par, irrespective of the yield on an identical option-free bond.

From Figure 4.3 you will see that the put option increases the convexity (the curvature of the price/yield relationship). This in itself makes the bond more attractive than an equivalent option-free bond, since, assuming both bonds can be purchased for the same price, if interest rates rise, the bond price will fall by less than the option-free bond price.

It can be seen in the example below that some bonds are both putable and callable.

Example 4.5   Astra International PT $6\frac{3}{4}$ % Convertible Bonds 2006

The company issued $125 million in 1991. The bonds pay interest annually on 30 May and any outstanding bonds will be redeemed at 100 on 30 May 2006. Holders have the option to require early repayment on 30 May 1996 at 103.375 and 30 May 2001 at 100.

The bonds are callable on 30 days' notice as a whole or in multiples of $1 million at a variety of prices: from 30 May 1991 at 106.75, 1992 at 106.075, ..., 2000 at 100.675. The bonds are convertible into Astra International PT shares from 13 May 1991 at INR (Indian rupees) 23 850 each, 23 December 1993 at INR 23 035 each, etc.

4.3 CONVERTIBLE BONDS

Convertible bonds are usually normal straight bonds that, in addition, give the holder the option to convert the bonds into another security at predefined rates and dates. The conversion terms may be exercisable on specific dates, e.g. once a year, or continuously for part of the life of the bond. The conversion terms may also differ on different dates.

Example 4.6 Hammerson plc $6\frac{1}{2}$ % Subordinated Convertible Bonds 2006

The company issued £110 million of the bond in 1996. It pays interest semi-annually on 12 June and 12 December and will be redeemed at 100 on 12 June 2006, if not called or converted earlier. The holders may convert the bonds into Hammerson plc shares from 23 July 1996 to 5 June 2006, when the rights expire, at a cost of £4.356 each.

The bond is callable as a whole or in multiples of £5 million at any time on 30 days' notice from 26 June 2001.

Example 4.7 Hankyu Corporation $1\frac{1}{2}$ % Convertible Bonds 2006

JPY 10 billion of the bonds were issued in 1996 at 100. They pay interest semi-annually on 31 March and 30 September and will be redeemed on 30 September 2006 if they still exist. The holders have an option on 14 days' notice to require early repayment on 30 September 2003 at 101.5, unless the share price has been at least 120 % of the conversion price.

The bond is callable if its tax status changes. The bond is convertible into Hankyu Corporation common stock from 29 October 1996 at JPY 680 each, and then at JPY 510 each from 21 December 1999. The rights expire on 22 September 2006.

Convertible bonds have advantages for both issuers and investors, but at a cost. From the point of view of the issuer, a convertible bond enables:

- Capital to be raised at a slightly lower cost than would have been possible with a straight bond issue.
- It does not, at least initially, dilute the equity base by issuing more equity shares as an alternative to issuing a bond, as the terms of the convertible can postpone the possible issue of any new shares for several years.

From the investor's point of view, the purchase of a convertible means:

- The investor has bought an issue with an option to convert, usually into equity shares, at some stage in the future if circumstances make this desirable. For this option a small amount of interest is given up.
- The investor has acquired an investment with a fixed rate of interest, which is more secure and is, usually in the initial years, greater than the income that would have been received had the investor instead invested directly in the equity shares. However, it should be pointed out that, as you would expect, it normally costs more to purchase an equity via a convertible than directly. It is variations in this premium that some hedge funds attempt to exploit.

The following example illustrates the basic convertible calculations of 'conversion price', 'exercise cost', 'conversion premium/discount' and 'break-even period'.

Example 4.8

In 2005 Company A issues a convertible bond that is convertible into the ordinary shares of the company. The bond, which was issued at a price of £95, pays an 8 % annual coupon and will be redeemed at par in 2015 unless previously converted into ordinary shares. The holder has the option from 2008 onwards on each coupon payment date with one month's notice to exchange £100 nominal of the convertible bond into 40 ordinary shares.

The ordinary shares are currently priced in the market at 250 p and have a current dividend yield of 3 %. The current convertible price is £120.

There are several calculations that can be made on this example. The 'conversion price' is the nominal value of the convertible that may be exchanged for one share. Hence, in the above example the conversion price is:

$$100/40 = 250\,\text{p}$$

The 'exercise cost' of purchasing the ordinary shares via the convertible is therefore, as there is no accrued interest on a coupon payment date:

$$120/40 = 300\,\text{p}$$

since £100 nominal of the convertible issue costs £120 and can be converted into 40 shares. However, the price of the shares in the market is only 250 p. Thus the purchaser has to pay a 'convertible premium' of:

$$(300 - 250)/250 = 20\,\%$$

On the other hand, ignoring any tax considerations, the convertible has a current yield of $8/120 = 6.67\,\%$ compared with the equity yield of 3.00 %. Expressed another way, £100 of the convertible bond will yield £8.00 per annum, whereas the annual dividend on 40 shares (into which £100 of the bond can be converted) would be:

$$40 \times 3 \times 250/100 = £3.00\,\text{per annum}$$

Hence £100 of the convertible bond would each year yield £5.00 more than the ordinary shares into which it could be converted, assuming that the dividend on the ordinary shares is unchanged.

The extra cost of purchasing the equity via the convertible, assuming no change in the equity dividend, would thus be recouped in $(120 - 100)/5 = 4$ years. This is called the 'break-even period'.

In the above example and as is usual in the market place, it is possible to buy and sell both the convertible and the equity at any time, whereas conversion is only possible on certain dates. As a result, there is the possibility of an arbitrage trade between buying and selling the two issues, which a number of hedge funds have tried to exploit. Such arbitrage opportunities are obviously also open to long-term holders of the company's issues.

For a normal convertible bond the exercise cost of buying the equity via the convertible increases linearly with the price of the convertible, as shown in Figure 4.4. However, since buying a convertible and converting it into equity shares is an option and not an obligation,

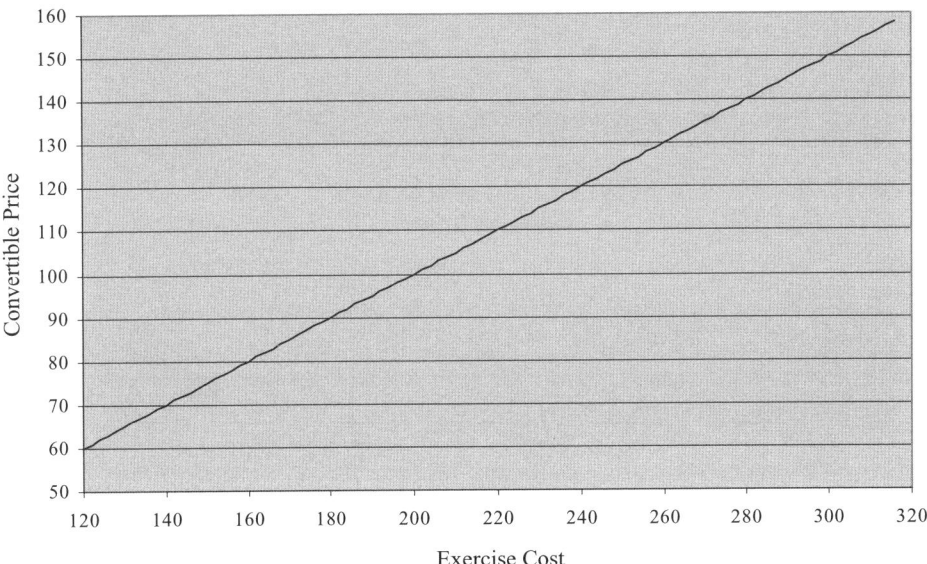

Figure 4.4 Price of convertible versus exercise cost.

the price of a convertible only tends to move linearly with the equity share price when its conversion price is below the current equity price. When the conversion price is considerably above the equity price, the convertible behaves as a bond. This is illustrated in Figure 4.5.

In the graph in Figure 4.5 the terms are such that a nominal quantity of 100 of the convertible is convertible into one equity share. Thus if the price of the equity rises to an amount considerably above 100, the price of the convertible will rise in approximately the same proportion. This is the straight line on the right-hand side of the graph. When the price of the equity drops below 100, the convertible starts to behave as a bond. As the equity price drops further, investors will demand a greater yield on the bond to compensate for the perceived greater risk of holding it. Eventually, if the equity price drops too much, the market factors in the possibility that the company may default on the convertible. As a result, the convertible price then drops more quickly.

In addition, the terms in the prospectus of a convertible issue usually protect the holders if there is a capital change that changes the value of the issues into which the shares may be converted.

Example 4.9

£100 of a convertible bond of Company A is convertible into, say, 20 ordinary shares of Company A. If Company A then has a one-for-one scrip issue, which has the effect of converting 100 shares into 200 shares at no cost to the holder, then terms of the convertible will also be changed so that £100 of the convertible is now able to be converted at the holder's option into 40 ordinary shares.

Comparison of Convertible and Equity Prices

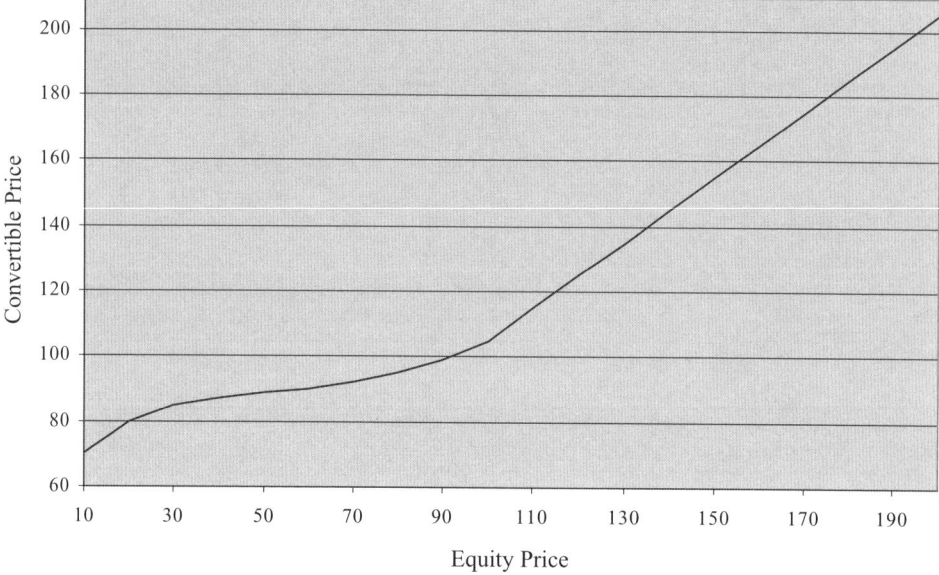

Figure 4.5 Price of convertible versus equity price.

Although convertible bonds are usually convertible into shares of the same issuer this is not always the case. Sometimes there may be the option to convert them into other bonds or even shares of a different company. When this occurs they are often called 'exchangeable' notes or bonds.

Example 4.10 Daily Mail and General Trust plc $2\frac{1}{2}$ % Exchangeable Notes 2004

£75 million of the notes were issued in June 1997 at 79.47. The bonds were redeemed on 5 October 2004 at 100 and paid semi-annual interest on 5 April and 5 October. The bonds were callable as a whole or in multiples of £1 million on 30 days' notice from 18 October 2002 at 100. The holders had the option to exchange the bonds for Reuters Group shares at the rate of £7.853 each from 11 August 1997 and £7.91149 each from 3 March 1998. The rights expired on 21 September 2004.

The trustees of the bonds were also able to perform the conversion at redemption, sell the resulting shares in the stock market and distribute the proceeds to the bond holders if they felt it was in their interests.

If a convertible option is not exercised, then the bonds are normally redeemed in the normal way.

4.4 DUAL CURRENCY BONDS

In order to take advantage of current differences in interest rates and projected changes in currency exchange rates, bonds have been issued with interest and capital repayments in different currencies. As you would expect, there are many variations in the terms of such instruments. Two variations are illustrated in the New South Wales Treasury issues below.

Example 4.11   New South Wales Treasury Corporation 3 % Dual Currency Issue 2001

JPY 23 billion of the bond was issued in 1997 at 100 with maturity on 20 August 2001. Bonds of JPY 500 000 were issued in bearer form. Interest is paid semi-annually on 20 February and 20 August in yen. However, each bond is redeemed at US $4444.44 based on a fixed exchange rate of $1 = JPY 112.5.

Example 4.12   New South Wales Treasury Corporation 5.15 % Dual Currency Issue 2005

JPY 15 billion of the bond was issued in 1995 at 96.5 for redemption on 31 January 2005 at 100 in yen. Interest, which is payable annually on 31 January, is paid in Australian dollars (AUD) at the fixed exchange rate of AUD 1 = JPY 75.11.

4.5 MORTGAGE-BACKED SECURITIES

Covered bonds or Pfandbrief are bonds issued by banks and are secured on a pool of mortgages or public loans. These bonds remain on the bank's balance sheet and behave as conventional secured bonds. This section, on the other hand, describes asset-backed securities or mortgage-backed securities, which have been taken off the balance sheet of the original company and put into a special-purpose vehicle.

'Mortgage-backed securities' (MBS) are conventional asset-backed securities, which have been secured on a pool of separate mortgages. However, there is often the provision that a proportion of the bonds will be redeemed early if the underlying mortgages are redeemed. Such securities are very common in the US. There are many reasons why the homeowner may wish to redeem a mortgage early. From the security point of view, any payments made in excess of the scheduled principal repayments are called 'prepayments'.

Thus at the end of any interest period (usually monthly) a payment may be made which consists of three parts:

- interest;
- scheduled capital repayment;
- capital prepayment.

The first two components behave in the same way as an annuity, but the third component is unpredictable. It is frequently assumed, if the mortgage pool, on which the security is based is sufficiently large, that a fixed proportion of the bonds will be redeemed each year. Hence a redemption yield and a valuation can be derived for the MBS. However, choosing the prepayment rate is not always that simple. If the current interest rates are at or above the prevailing interest rate when the MBS was created, then the prepayment rate caused by people wanting to sell their houses is fairly predictable. On the other hand, if the current interest rate is below the original interest rate, then many of the mortgagees may repay their loans early and refinance their debts at a cheaper rate.

4.6 COLLATERALIZED DEBT OBLIGATIONS

Many securities have been created that are classified under the generic heading of 'asset-backed securities' (ABS). These are frequently created by bundling, often non-marketable, assets together into a marketable security. This process is called 'securitization'.

The following lists a few of the many different types of assets that have been securitized:

- An institution's loan book. This enables the loan book to be taken off the institution's balance sheet.
- A pool of mortgages, creating a mortgage-backed security.
- Credit card debt.
- Car loan debt.

When the 'collateralized debt obligation' (CDO) has been created by the securitization process, investors have the guarantee of the underlying assets and are entitled to receive interest payments generated by them. When the underlying assets mature, the created security or securities are often redeemed by lot or proportionally according to the holding size.

Bundling the underlying assets together can create a security that is rated higher than would be the case for any of the individual assets. This process may be further enhanced by splitting the pool of assets into two, three or more securities with different risk profiles, the most secure tranche often being rated 'AAA'.

Example 4.13

A large pool of mortgages has been securitized as follows:

	Interest	Principal
Tranche A	Paid on principal outstanding	Receives all scheduled and prepayment of principal until completely paid off
Tranche B	Paid on principal outstanding	After tranche A, receives all scheduled and prepayment of principal until completely paid off
Tranche C	Paid on principal outstanding	After tranche B, receives all scheduled and prepayment of principal

---

In the above example, tranche A obviously has the shortest expected life and should be the most secure. Tranche C has the longest life and is the least secure, as any default on the underlying assets is met in the first case by tranche C. To compensate for this tranche A is often issued with a lower coupon than tranche B, whose coupon is less than that of tranche C.

There are, of course, many different methods of splitting the anticipated returns between the different tranches. For example, with a 'stripped mortgage-backed security' one tranche is entitled to all the interest payments, whereas the other tranche is entitled to all the principal repayments.

4.7 BONDS WITH CONDITIONAL COUPON CHANGES

In the late 1990s a number of companies wanted to raise very large amounts of debt relative to their size. In order to make the debt more palatable to the market they issued it with a coupon that would be automatically increased if the major credit companies downgraded the debt to below a specific rating. Most, but not all, of the companies issuing bonds with conditional coupon changes were in the telecoms sector, where the debt was used to buy 3G mobile telephone licences.

Example 4.14 **British Telecommunications plc $7\frac{1}{2}$ % Notes 2016**

In February 2001 the company issued £700 million of the notes at 99.113. The bonds if not previously called are redeemable on 7 December 2016 at 100. They pay interest annually on 7 December.

The coupon rate will be reset and increased by $\frac{1}{4}$ % for each reduction in the credit rating of the borrower made by Standard & Poor or Moody from their original ratings of A- and A3 respectively. Should there be any subsequent improvement in the rating then the coupon will be reduced by $\frac{1}{4}$ %, but in no circumstances will the coupon be reduced to below $7\frac{1}{2}$ %.

The bonds are also callable from 15 February 2001 at 100.

In a number of cases the bonds were downgraded, which automatically caused the coupons to be increased.

4.8 REVERSE FLOATERS

An interesting variation on floating-rate notes is the concept of 'reverse floating-rate notes'. From a technical point of view they behave in a similar way to ordinary floating-rate notes, except that now the coupon rate is set to a fixed amount less the reference indicator rate. However, this means that the reference coupon rate is no longer related to the current market rates, with the result that the price, unlike normal floating-rate notes, can and does move some distance from par.

Example 4.15

Consider a reverse floating-rate note that pays monthly coupons of 8 % minus the LIBOR rate for one month sterling deposits. Hence if the LIBOR rate is 5 %, it will pay interest at the annual rate of $(8 - 5) = 3$ %. If LIBOR decreases to 4 %, the payment will increase to $(8 - 4) = 4$ %.

It should be noted that if an investor holds equal amounts in both the above reverse floater and an ordinary floater which pays LIBOR plus 0.25 %, then together the investor has a fixed-rate bond which pays a combined coupon of:

$$(8 - \text{LIBOR}) + (\text{LIBOR} + 0.25) = 8.25\,\%$$

The following is an actual example of a bond that started life as a fixed-rate bond and then converted into a reverse floating-rate bond. Although it is denominated in Italian lire (ITL), the amounts are convertible into euros at the fixed conversion exchange rate.

Example 4.16   European Investment Bank 7.765 % Fixed/Floating Note 2010

ITL 200 billion of the security was issued in 1998. It will be redeemed at 100 on 26 January 2010. Until 26 January 1999 it pays an annual coupon of 7.765 %, when it is reduced to 7% until January 2001, when it becomes a floating-rate note with the interest set at $15\,\% - 2 \times 12$ month LIBOR. Thus after 2001 if LIBOR for 12 month deposits is 4 %, the bond will accrue interest at $(15 - 2 \times 4) = 7\,\%$ per annum.

Figures 4.6 and 4.7 show the effect of LIBOR changes on the coupon rate payable on the above security and for a date five years before maturity of the changes different LIBOR rates would

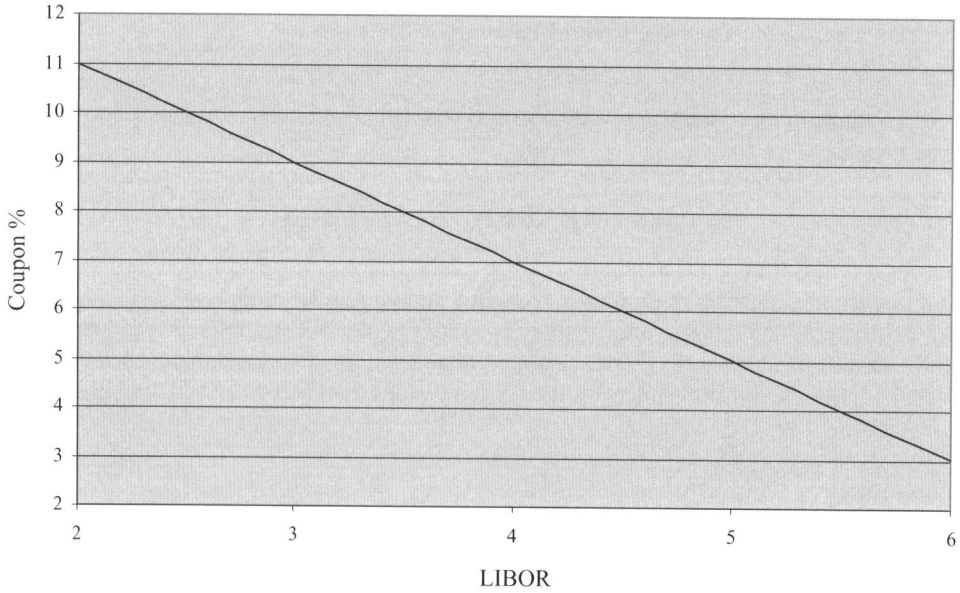

Figure 4.6   Coupon versus LIBOR.

European Investment Bank 7.765 % Fixed/Floating Note 2010

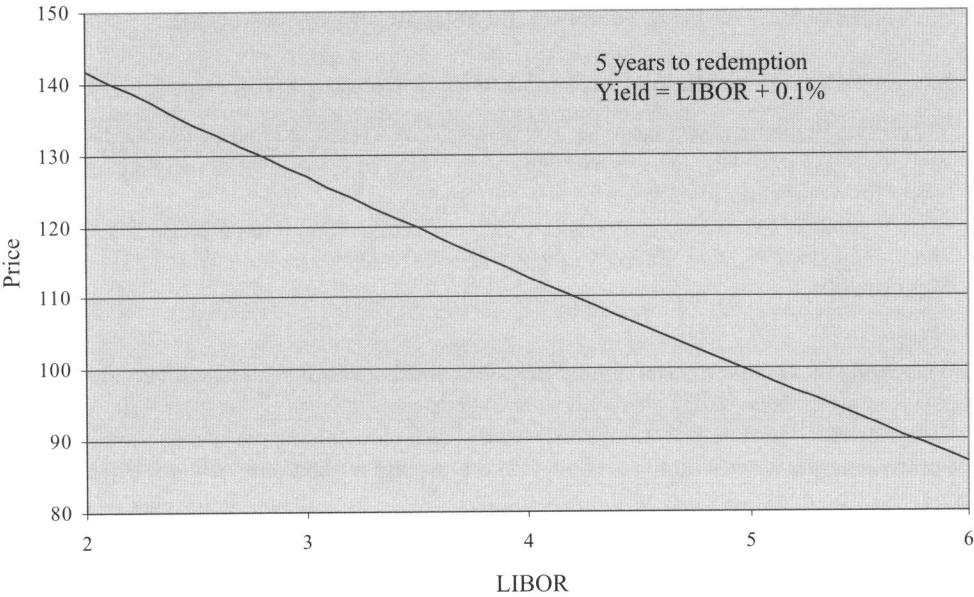

Figure 4.7 Price versus LIBOR.

have on the price of the security if one were to assume that a normal European Investment Bank five year floating-rate note would yield LIBOR plus 0.10 %.

4.9 BONDS WITH WARRANTS ATTACHED

In order to reduce the costs of raising capital, bonds have been issued with warrants attached. They used to be very popular with bonds issued by Japanese companies, although due to the lack of growth in the Japanese stock market, nearly all these have now matured. The warrants (options) give the holder the right to purchase an asset (usually an equity share) at a predefined rate at some time in the future. In exchange for this option, the purchaser of such bonds is prepared to give up a certain percentage of the interest on the bond. If, in return, the relevant share price rises above the sum of the cost of purchasing the share via the warrant and the loss of income, the purchaser will have benefited from the warrant.

Example 4.17 ONO Finance plc 13 % Notes with Warrants 2009

The company issued €125 million of notes with warrants attached in May 1999. The bonds are redeemable at 100 on 1 May 2009 and pay interest semi-annually on 1 May and 1 November. The bonds are callable at various prices from May 2004, and the holders have a put option in the event of a change of control of Cableuropa SA.

Each note was issued with one equity value certificate, which entitles the holder to receive a cash payment equal to the value of 0.002 244 131 6 shares of Cableuropa SA on the earlier of an initial public offering or a takeover of Cableuropa SA or 1 May 2009.

Example 4.18   Dow Mining Company Ltd $4\frac{5}{8}$ % Notes with Warrants 1997–2001

$50 million of the bond was issued at 100 in April 1997. It was guaranteed by the Industrial Bank of Japan and was due for redemption on 24 April 2001. The notes were issued in bearer form with a nominal value of $10 000.

Each note had two warrants attached, which entitled the holder to purchase JPY 633 750 of common stock of Dow Mining Company Ltd at JPY 395 per share from 8 May 1997 to 17 April 2001.

Bonds with warrants were often traded initially with the warrants attached, but after a short period the warrants were detached and were traded separately.

The warrant, which is just an option, usually has some value even if the 'exercise price' of purchasing the asset with the warrant is more expensive than purchasing it directly. This is because the market factors in the possibility that the price of the underlying asset might increase above the exercise price before the expiry of the warrant. If the warrant's exercise price is less than the current price of the relevant asset, then the difference is referred to as its 'intrinsic value'.

Example 4.19

If the warrant entitles the issuer to purchase one share at a price of 50 and the share is currently trading at 65, then its intrinsic value is 15.

5
Yield Curves

Unlike equity shares, many bond issuers issue a number of different instruments with the same guarantees, where only the entitlement to coupon payments and the maturity date differ. As the prices of similar bonds of the same issuer tend to move in line with each other, investors in the issuer's bonds will invest in the bond or bonds that meet their maturity and coupon requirements best. If one plots the yields on such a collection of bonds against their maturity dates, a yield curve is displayed (Figure 5.1).

Graphs similar to Figure 5.1 can be produced for issuers who have issued a significant number of similar issues. For example, they can be produced for many government issuers (e.g. Canada, France, Germany, Italy, Japan, US, to list just a few) and large supranational and corporate issuers (e.g. European Investment Bank, World Bank, General Electric Capital). Figure 5.1 in fact only shows fixed-rate gilt-edged issues, since the returns are not directly comparable with those of the UK Government's index-linked issues.

A yield curve not only shows the return an investor can get on a bond of a specific maturity but also, especially in the case of domestic government issues, the market expectation of future interest rates. This is because it is assumed that a government, in its own currency, will never default as it can always issue more bonds in that currency, although this may be disastrous from an inflation point of view. How this can be done is discussed below.

5.1 YIELD CURVE SHAPES

Although in theory the yield curve could be of almost any shape (see Figure 5.2), they can often be categorized as:

- *Normal*. The yields increase slightly as the bond's life to maturity increases. This compensates investors for taking on greater risk regarding the reinvestment rate of the coupons, potentially greater volatility in the bond's price in the short to medium term and even potential issuer default.
- *Rising*. The yields are considered by the market to be at a very low level and are expected to rise in the short to medium term.
- *Falling*. The short-term yields are considered to be historically very high and longer term yields are much lower. The market thus expects the short-term yields to reduce.
- *Flat*. The market discounts all issues from the issuer, irrespective of the maturity time horizon, at the same rate.
- *Bubble or humped*. The example above of the UK gilt yield in mid 2005 is an example of a bubble or humped yield curve. Such curve shapes are caused by supply and demand for the issuer's universe of bonds. Typically banks are interested in investing in short-dated bonds, whereas, on the other hand, pension funds use bonds to fund their future liabilities, which can extend over many decades. As a result pension funds like to purchase very long dated securities. This can leave the bonds with medium-term maturities not particularly wanted by either group. Hence they can sometimes tend to yield more than short- or long-dated bonds.

80 An Introduction to the Bond Markets

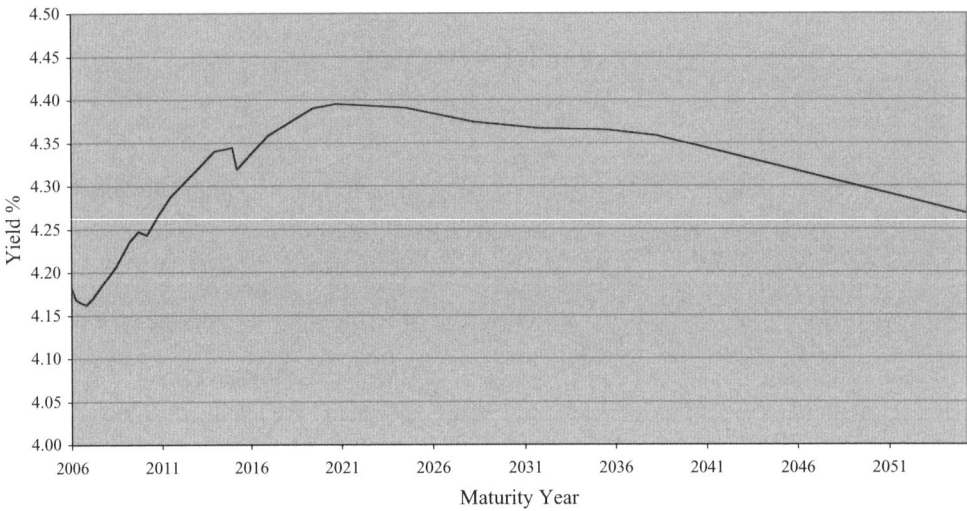

Figure 5.1 UK gilt-edged yield curve.

The standard yield curve calculation superficially shows the return an investor could get by investing in the bonds of the issuer for a specific maturity date. However, it may distort the real position, since the standard redemption yield calculation assumes that when a coupon payment is received, it can be reinvested in the same issue at the same rate as the original investment. The

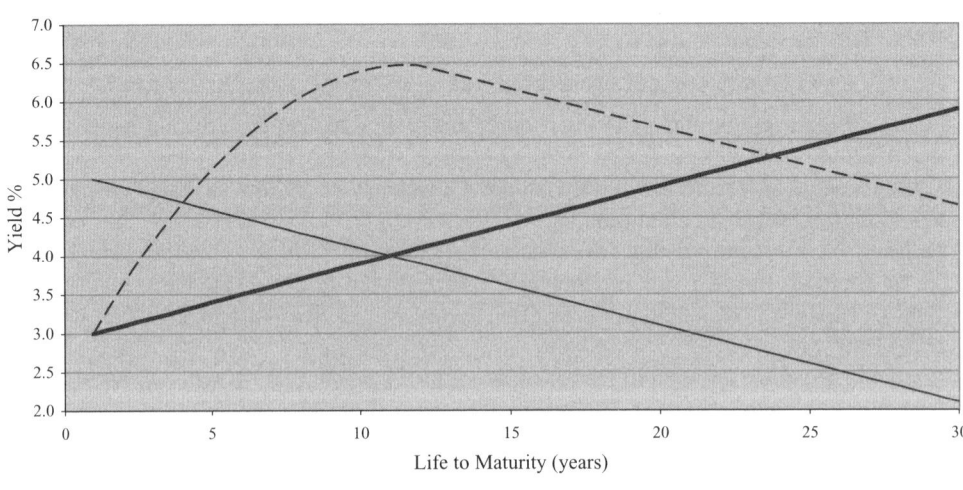

Figure 5.2 Yield curve shapes.

yield curve calculation does not allow for bonds with differing coupons, which have different durations for the same maturity date.

The coupon reinvestment problem can be illustrated by the following example with a slightly increasing yield curve, which is a fairly common shape.

Example 5.1

All the bonds of the issuer pay annual coupons and sit on the issuer's yield curve. This yield curve increases by 0.1 % for each year of life. The yield for a one year bond is 4.0 %. A five year bond paying an annual coupon sitting on the yield curve will thus yield 4.4 %.

If you assume, albeit unlikely, that the yield curve does not move over the life of the bond and ignore all transaction expenses, then we have the following scenario:

Life of bond	Reinvestment rate on coupon
5 years	4.4 %
4 years	4.3 %
3 years	4.2 %
2 years	4.1 %
1 year	4.0 %

The total return on a five year bond, assuming it is not a zero-coupon one, is thus obviously less than the expected 4.4 %, as the coupon cannot be reinvested at 4.4 %.

The position can be further distorted if the yield curve includes issues with significantly differing annual coupon rates.

Example 5.2

Consider an issuer who has two outstanding issues both redeemed in 10 years' time: one with a 10 % annual coupon yielding 5.00 % and the other a zero-coupon bond yielding 5.25 %. Superficially if you plot the yield against maturity for the two bonds the zero-coupon bond looks cheap. However, the duration (average time to getting one's money back in interest and capital repayments, after discounting the amounts by the redemption yield rate) of the 10 % bond is 7.270 years compared with 10 years for the zero-coupon bond.

It is then necessary to look at the shape of the issuer's yield curve to determine the expected reinvestment returns on the coupon payments of the 10 % bond, before it is possible to assess which of the bonds is cheapest.

This potential problem can be overcome by instead using the data of the individual bonds to construct a zero-coupon or spot yield curve. Such a curve measures the implied return you would get on a theoretical zero-coupon bond with each maturity date. From the spot yield curve, it is also possible to calculate both par and forward yield curves in a straightforward way. These are discussed below.

5.2 ZERO-COUPON OR SPOT YIELD CURVES

The problems of investors not being able to reinvest the coupon payments in the bond at the bond's original redemption yield and that of comparing bonds with different coupons can be removed if you only consider zero-coupon bonds. Unfortunately there are very few, if any, issuers who have issued a sufficient number of similar zero-coupon bonds with an adequate distribution of redemption dates or have bond strips of an appropriate size and liquidity.

It is not possible to calculate a spot (or zero-coupon) yield curve directly from a redemption yield curve as the calculation needs additional information about the individual bonds on which the curve is based. In particular, it needs to have details about the cash flows of all the bonds. In order to solve this problem, theoretical zero-coupon bonds are constructed for the issuer from the issuer's normal coupon bonds.

Each coupon bond can be regarded as a combination of several zero-coupon bonds with different maturity dates. This is simply the process that occurs when a bond is stripped.

Example 5.3

$1000 of a bond that is redeemed at par in 5 years' time and pays an annual coupon of 5 % can, if one ignores any tax considerations, be regarded as:

$50 of a zero-coupon bond that matures in 1 year
$50 of a zero-coupon bond that matures in 2 years
$50 of a zero-coupon bond that matures in 3 years
$50 of a zero-coupon bond that matures in 4 years and
$1050 of a zero-coupon bond that matures in 5 years

The method of constructing the zero-coupon or spot[1] yield curve is to consider in turn each of the relevant bonds in the order of their life to maturity.

With the shortest bond, all of its cash flows, including the redemption payment, are considered to yield the same as its redemption yield. We will call this y_1. The next shortest bond is then considered. It is first split into its constituent zero-coupon components. All those cash flows with a life of less than that of the shortest bond are assumed to have the same yield as the shortest bond, i.e. y_1. The remaining cash flows are then assumed to have a yield of y_2, where y_2 is calculated in such a way that the dirty price of the bond is just the sum of its future cash flows discounted now by a combination of y_1 and y_2. This is just a variation of the definition of a redemption yield, which states that the redemption yield is the discount rate that makes the dirty price equal to the sum of all the discounted future cash flows.

The process is then repeated for the third bond, using yields y_1 and y_2, calculating a new discount rate y_3 for the cash flows paid after the redemption of the second bond. Subsequent bonds are treated in the same way. As a result a series of yields $y_1, y_2, \ldots, y_n$ are created for different periods. These are just the components of the zero-coupon yield curve.

It is worthwhile pointing out that as the bonds that make up a yield curve may be traded on the open market and there is no restriction on what the investor does with the coupon payments, it is not possible for an investor to get a greater return from reinvesting the coupon payment

---

[1] A spot interest rate for a period n is the yield you get from investing in an instrument that does not give you any return until the end of the period n when it is redeemed, i.e. it is the yield on a zero-coupon bond of life n.

on a bond yielding 6 % to that of a similar one yielding 3 %, if they are paid on the same date. If this were possible, the market would automatically buy the cheaper instrument and sell the dearer one until the position was equalized.

Example 5.4 Constructing a zero-coupon yield curve

Consider an issuer who has only three bonds outstanding, all of which pay an annual coupon on the same date of 5 % and are repaid at par. The bonds have lives to maturity of 1, 2 and 3 years and redemption yields of 5 %, 6 % and 7 % respectively. The shortest bond has one cash flow of 105 % in one year's time. This cash flow yields 5 %.

The second bond, which has a redemption yield of 6 %, has two cash flows, one of 5 % in one year's time, which must be discounted at 5 %, and a second one of 105 % in two years' time. This second cash flow has to be discounted at a rate of y %, where y is given by solving the following formula:

$$\frac{5}{1+6/100} + \frac{105}{(1+6/100)^2} = \frac{5}{1+5/100} + \frac{105}{(1+y/100)^2}$$

$$y = 6.025\,\%$$

The yield on the final cash flow of the third bond z % is given by:

$$\frac{5}{1.07} + \frac{5}{1.07^2} + \frac{105}{1.07^3} = \frac{5}{1.05} + \frac{5}{1.06025^2} + \frac{105}{(1+z/100)^3}$$

$$z = 7.071\,\%$$

The relationship between the normal redemption yields and the calculated zero-coupon or spot yields is thus:

Maturity	Redemption yield	Spot yield
1 year	5.000 %	5.000 %
2 years	6.000 %	6.025 %
3 years	7.000 %	7.071 %

In practice, the calculation of zero-coupon yield curves is more complicated than the trivial example above.

Program 5.1 YieldCurve1

This program allows the user to either modify the shape of a normal yield curve or enter one's own yield curve and, based on the assumption that all the bonds forming the yield curve have the same coupon, which can be specified, automatically create a zero-coupon yield curve. It will be noticed that sharp changes in yield over time can make dramatic changes to the zero-coupon curve.

Figure 5.3 illustrates the relationship between a standard redemption yield curve and a zero-coupon yield curve for a theoretical issuer who has only ever issued bonds with an annual

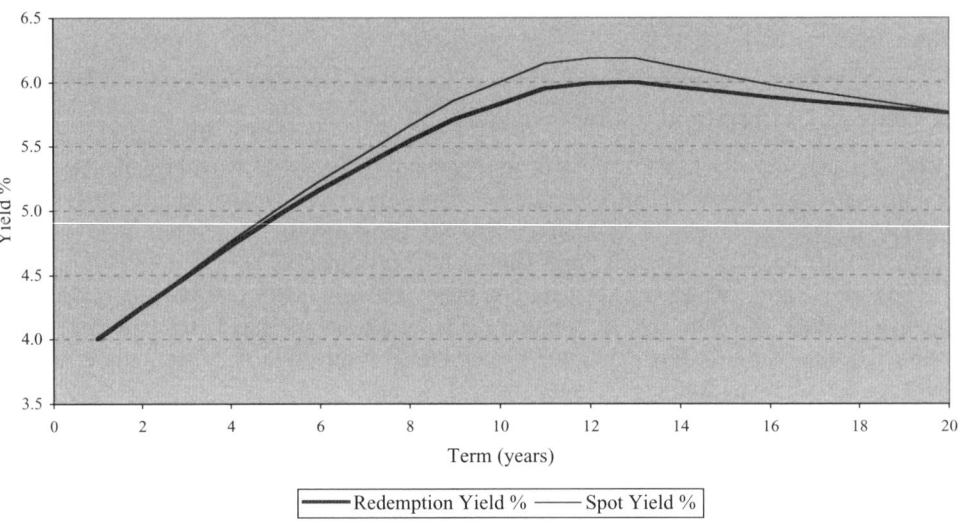

Figure 5.3 Standard and zero-coupon yield curves.

coupon rate of 5 %, which all pay coupons on the same day. The graph illustrates that if the redemption yield curve is steadily rising with maturity, the calculated spot yield will be greater than the corresponding redemption yield. This is what you would expect, as any received coupons are assumed to be reinvested at the original redemption yield rate, whereas in practice they are invested for a shorter period.

5.3 FORWARD OR FORWARD–FORWARD YIELD CURVES

A zero-coupon or spot yield curve allows you to calculate what the market expects forward or future interest rates to be in a fairly simple manner. A one year forward yield for a specified period is the expected spot rate for the specified period in one year's time. Similarly, a two year forward rate for a specified time horizon is the spot rate you would expect to see for the time horizon in two year's time.

Assuming that the market is efficient, you would expect to get the same return if, today, you were to invest in a one year instrument and commit to buy another similar one year instrument in one year's time with its proceeds, as that of investing today in a zero-coupon two year instrument. Similarly, if you were to invest in a two year zero-coupon instrument and commit to reinvest the redemption proceeds in a zero-coupon one year instrument, you would expect to get the same total return as initially investing in a three year zero-coupon instrument, assuming that the security of both investment strategies is identical.

This implies that if you know the spot yields for one year, two years and three years, it is possible to calculate the expected forward spot yields for one and two years in one year's time and the expected spot one year yield in two years' time.

In order to attempt to reduce the confusion over what forward rates are being considered, it is proposed to use the following notation in the example. The notation $y_{a,b}$ represents an anticipated forward yield in a years' time for a period of b years. It should be noted that a one-year forward rate for two years is *not* the same as a two year forward rate for one year.

Example 5.5

Consider the following situation where the spot yield for one year is 5.0%, for two years is 6.0% and for three years is 7.0%. The one-year forward yield for one year $y_{1,1}$ is given by:

$$(1 + 0.05) \times (1 + y_{1,1}/100) = (1 + 0.06)^2$$

$$y_{1,1} = 7.010\%$$

This equation just says that the value of an investment with interest at the two year spot rate for two years (the right-hand side) is equal to the value of the same capital increasing by the one year spot rate and the one year forward rate for one year:

$$(1 + 0.05) \times (1 + y_{1,2}/100)^2 = (1 + 0.07)^3$$

$$y_{1,2} = 8.014\%$$

This equation states that the value of an investment with interest at the three year spot rate for three years (the right-hand side) is equal to the value of the same capital increasing by the one year spot rate and the one year forward rate for two years:

$$(1 + 0.06)^2 \times (1 + y_{2,1}/100) = (1 + 0.07)^3$$

$$y_{2,1} = 9.028\%$$

This equation states that the value of an investment with interest at the three year spot rate for three years (the right-hand side) is also equal to the value of the same capital increasing by the two year spot rate for two years and the two year forward rate for one year.

It should be noted that $y_{1,2}$ (8.014%) is not the same as $y_{2,1}$ (9.028%).

Another way of expressing this relationship between spot and forward rates is to say that the value of an investment invested at the three year spot rate compounded for three years is after three years the same as investing it for one year at the one year spot rate, reinvesting the proceeds at the one year forward one year rate and then reinvesting the proceeds again at the two year forward rate for one year.

Figure 5.4 shows that, when the spot yield curve is rising, the one year forward rate is higher than the equivalent spot yield, and the two year forward rate is higher still. This is what you would expect.

5.4 PAR YIELD CURVES

The 'par yield curve' shows the coupon rate at which a new issuer could issue a bond at par for different maturities. Although it is not used significantly in the secondary market, it is a very useful tool in the primary market.

The par yield curve can be created in a straightforward way from the spot yield curve as the spot yield curve gives the discount rate at which to discount every coupon payment and the final redemption amount.

Spot and Forward Yield Curves

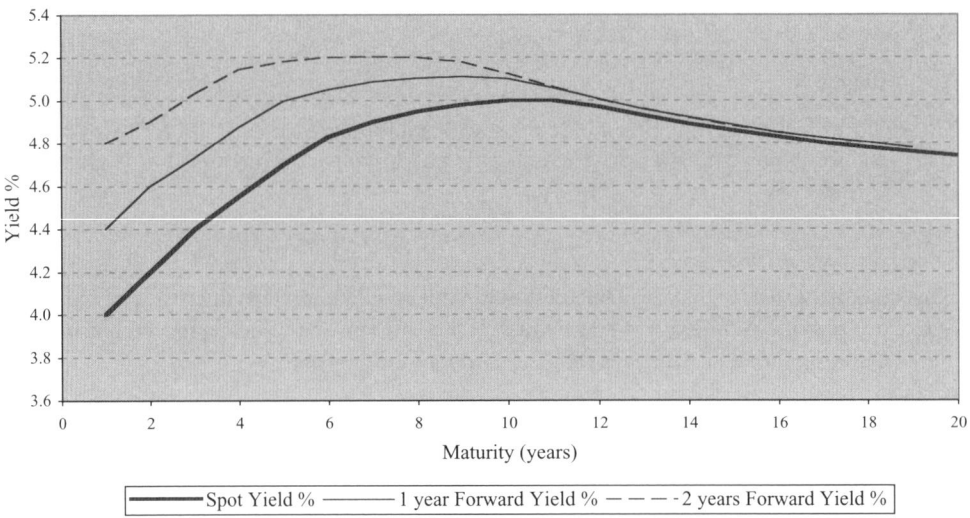

Figure 5.4 Spot and one year forward and two year forward yield curves.

Example 5.6 Calculation of a par yield curve

In order to simplify the calculations, it is assumed that the par yield curve is required for a bond that pays a coupon once a year. Suppose you calculate the point on the curve with a life of n years, i.e. for a bond with a life of n years. Assuming the bond is redeemed at par (100), it is necessary to determine its coupon rate g.

If the relevant spot yields for 1 year, 2 years, 3 years, ..., n years are $y_1, y_2, y_3, \ldots, y_n$ respectively, the coupon rate g is given by:

$$100 = \frac{g}{1 + y_1/100} + \frac{g}{(1 + y_2/100)^2} + \frac{g}{(1 + y_3/100)^3} + \cdots + \frac{g + 100}{(1 + y_n/100)^n}$$

The above equation can then be solved for $n = 1, 2, 3$, etc. In the special case of $n = 1$, the equation reduces to:

$$100 = \frac{g + 100}{1 + y_1/100}$$
$$g = y_1$$

In other words, the one year par yield is the same as the one year spot yield.

It is very easy to show that if the spot yield curve is completely flat then so is the forward yield curve and the par yield curve; they all have the same value. On the other hand, if the spot yield curve is increasing slightly each year then so will the forward and par yield curves, but they will now have different values. Similarly, if the spot curve continually decreases, so will the forward and par curves.

Table 5.1 Comparison of spot, par and forward rates with annual coupons for gradually increasing spot yields

Term (years)	Spot yield (%)	Par yield (%)	1 year forward yield (%)	2 years forward yield (%)	3 years forward yield (%)
1	5.0000	5.0000	5.2001	5.4003	5.6006
2	5.1000	5.0975	5.3001	5.5004	5.7007
3	5.2000	5.1932	5.4002	5.6005	5.8009
4	5.3000	5.2871	5.5002	5.7006	5.9010
5	5.4000	5.3790	5.6003	5.8007	6.0011
6	5.5000	5.4688	5.7003	5.9008	6.1013
7	5.6000	5.5566	5.8004	6.0009	6.2014
8	5.7000	5.6421	5.9004	6.1009	
9	5.8000	5.7254	6.0005		
10	5.9000	5.8063			

Table 5.1 illustrates the relationship between spot, par and one, two and three year forward rates for annual paying bonds for gradually increasing spot yields. You will notice that with this scenario the par yields do not increase as much as the spot yields, which is what you would expect as coupons are paid before maturity. On the other hand, the forward rates are actually higher than the par rates. If the spot rates had been decreasing then the position would have been reversed. If the spot yield curve is humped, as in Table 5.2, the par and forward rates can diverge significantly from the spot rates.

Table 5.2 Comparison of spot, par and forward rates with annual coupons for a humped spot yield curve

Term (years)	Spot yield (%)	Par yield(%)	1 year forward yield (%)	2 years forward yield (%)	3 years forward yield (%)
1	4.0000	4.0000	4.4004	4.8012	5.0013
2	4.2000	4.1959	4.6006	4.9012	5.1516
3	4.4000	4.3885	4.7340	5.0347	5.2618
4	4.5500	4.5310	4.8757	5.1464	5.2766
5	4.7000	4.6706	4.9968	5.1813	5.2814
6	4.8300	4.7894	5.0508	5.2012	5.2712
7	4.9000	4.8543	5.0864	5.2039	5.2582
8	4.9500	4.9007	5.1031	5.2010	5.2259
9	4.9800	4.9294	5.1117	5.1786	5.1607
10	5.0000	4.9491	5.1005	5.1247	5.0895
11	5.0000	4.9527	5.0586	5.0633	5.0240
12	4.9700	4.9332	5.0079	5.0054	4.9753
13	4.9300	4.9060	4.9588	4.9619	4.9295
14	4.8900	4.8785	4.9217	4.9203	4.8859
15	4.8600	4.8581	4.8856	4.8803	4.8562
16	4.8300	4.8376	4.8502	4.8527	4.8276
17	4.8000	4.8172	4.8261	4.8261	4.8001
18	4.7800	4.8034	4.8024	4.8002	
19	4.7600	4.7898	4.7791		
20	4.7400	4.7764			

An Introduction to the Bond Markets

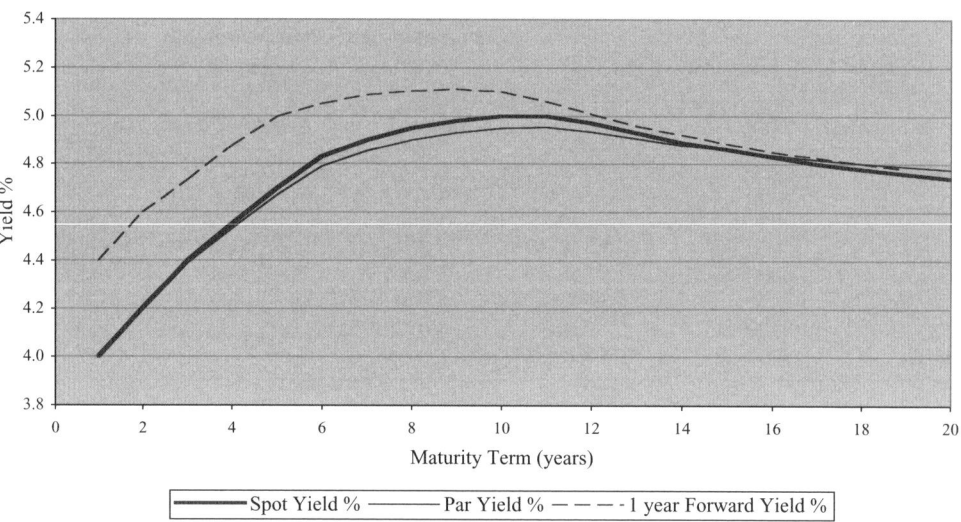

Figure 5.5 Spot, par and one year forward yield curves.

As illustrated in Figure 5.5, when interest rates are rising the forward rates are higher than the corresponding spot rate. Similarly, when the spot yield curve flattens out the par yield curve drops below the spot curve.

Program 5.2 YieldCurve2

This program allows the user to specify the annual spot rates, and calculate the resulting par and one, two and three year forward yield curves. The results are shown in both tabular and graphical form.

5.5 INVESTMENT STRATEGIES FOR POSSIBLE YIELD CURVE CHANGES

It is frequently possible to calculate a yield curve for a homogeneous group of fixed-rate bonds of similar credit rating, in which you are happy to invest. Assuming that these bonds remain either on or remain the same distance away from the yield curve, then the shape of the yield curve and its expected shape at your specified time horizon determine the part of the market you should consider buying and conversely the maturity range you should consider selling.

This is illustrated in the following example, with an investment time horizon of one year. In other words, we want to make investment decisions that should be valid for a year. However, it should be pointed out that although this is our aim, if something unforeseen occurs then an earlier change of strategy may be considered.

If we assume that the shape of the yield curve in one year's time will be identical to now, then we should only invest in securities of a maturity where there is a positive yield curve. Consider a market that consists solely of bonds which pay a 5 % annual coupon on the same

Table 5.3 Current yield curve details

Life (years)	Yield (%)	Price of 5 % bond on curve
1	4.00	100.9615
2	4.40	101.1252
3	4.78	100.6016
4	5.16	99.4348
5	5.45	98.0757
6	5.67	96.6710
7	5.80	95.5022
8	5.90	94.3890
9	5.97	93.3937
10	6.00	92.6399
11	5.98	92.2630
12	5.94	92.0932
13	5.89	92.0702
14	5.81	92.3817
15	5.69	93.1607
16	5.52	94.5673
17	5.35	96.1552
18	5.20	97.6982
19	5.10	98.8013
20	5.00	100.0000

day, and the investment decision is being made on the coupon payment date. The current yield curve for this market is shown in Table 5.3 and Figure 5.6.

If you consider a bond on the yield curve, with a 5 % annual coupon, then if it has a life of 15 years, it currently has a yield of 5.69 % with an associated price of 93.1607. In a year's

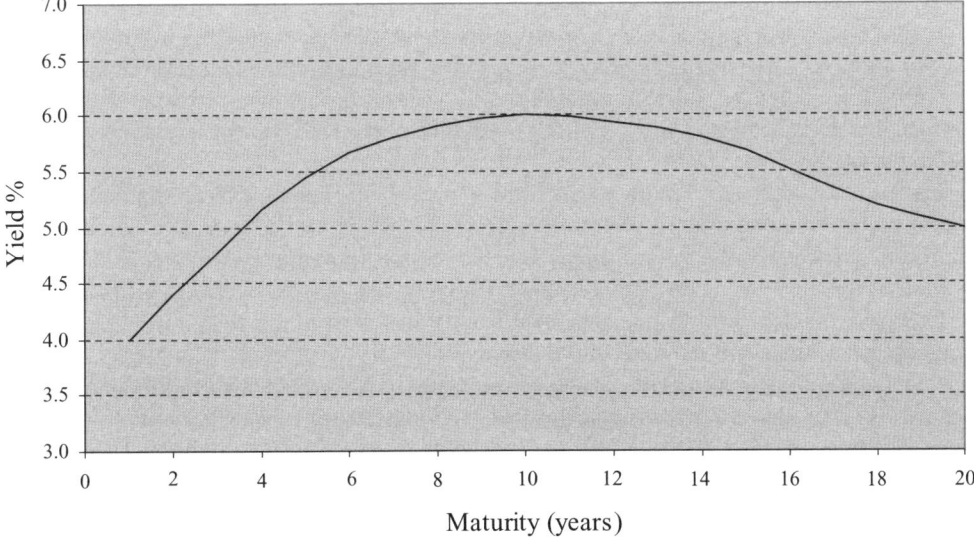

Figure 5.6 Yield curve.

90 An Introduction to the Bond Markets

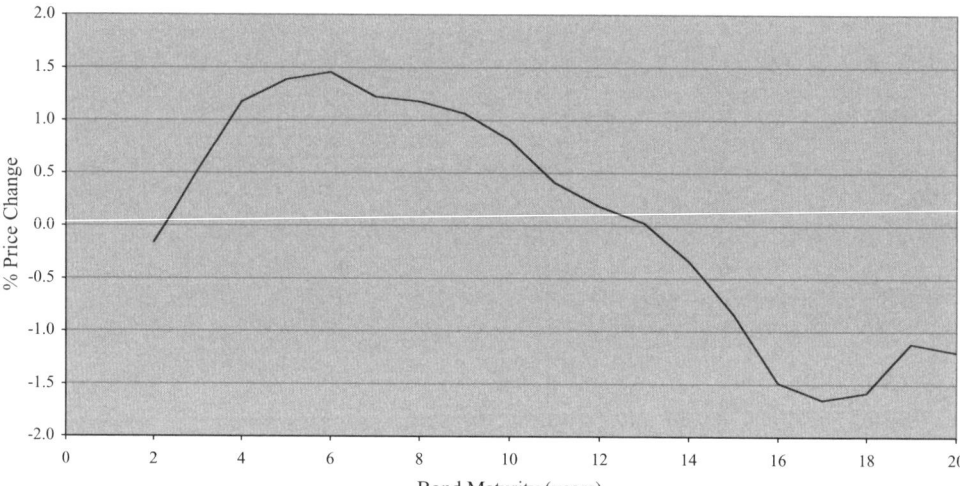

Figure 5.7 Expected capital changes over one year.

time, it will have a life of 14 years and an expected yield of 5.81 %, with an associated price of 92.3817, i.e. a price fall of 0.7790 (0.8361%) or, taking into account the income received on the investment and the capital depreciation, a total return of 4.1638 %.

However, if you consider a similar 5 % annual bond with a current life to maturity of six years, which is yielding 5.67 % (with an associated price of 96.6710), this is almost the same yield as the 15 year bond's. In one year's time it will have a life of five years and an expected yield 5.45 %, which gives an expected price of 98.0757. This is a capital gain of 1.4047 (1.4530 %) and a total return of 5.4530 %.

It can be seen in Figure 5.7 that it is still possible to make a capital loss if you move to a part of the yield curve that is yielding less, and vice versa, due to the reduction in the bond's maturity. It is obviously better to invest in the six year bond than in the 15 year bond, if you assume that over the next year the yield curve will be unchanged. However, the market is not as simple as this.

It is possible that one's liabilities match the returns (both coupon and redemption amount) on the eight year bond exactly, with the result that the shape of the yield curve in one year's time, and in particular the price of the eight year bond, assuming the obligation is honoured, is irrelevant. Hence from a risk point of view, the eight year bond is the safest investment.

Now let us look at what happens if there is a parallel shift in the yield curve. Let us first consider what happens if the yield curve increases by 1.0 % throughout its maturity range. If we were to use the same example as above, we would have the results given in Table 5.4 and Figure 5.8. This shows fairly graphically that the longer the life of the security, as they all have the same coupon, the greater the decrease in the value of the holding for a 1 % increase in yield. It can be shown that this decrease is proportional to the duration of the security.

Such a graphic illustration shows that if a portfolio is being actively managed and the investment manager expects interest rates to increase in the near future then he or she should

Table 5.4 Old and new yield curve details

Life (years)	Old yield (%)	Old price	New yield (%)	New price	Change in price (%)
1	4.00	100.9615	5.00	100.0000	−0.9523
2	4.40	101.1252	5.40	99.2604	−1.8440
3	4.78	100.6016	5.78	97.9065	−2.6789
4	5.16	99.4348	6.16	95.9952	−3.4591
5	5.45	98.0757	6.45	93.9661	−4.1902
6	5.67	96.6710	6.67	91.9581	−4.8751
7	5.80	95.5022	6.80	90.2313	−5.5191
8	5.90	94.3890	6.90	88.6104	−6.1220
9	5.97	93.3937	6.97	87.1486	−6.6868
10	6.00	92.6399	7.00	85.9528	−7.2183
11	5.98	92.2630	6.98	85.1378	−7.7226
12	5.94	92.0932	6.94	84.5418	−8.1997
13	5.89	92.0702	6.89	84.1051	−8.6511
14	5.81	92.3817	6.81	83.9888	−9.0850
15	5.69	93.1607	6.69	84.3017	−9.5094
16	5.52	94.5673	6.52	85.1730	−9.9339
17	5.35	96.1552	6.35	86.2050	−10.3481
18	5.20	97.6982	6.20	87.1998	−10.7457
19	5.10	98.8013	6.10	87.8215	−11.1130
20	5.00	100.0000	6.00	88.5301	−11.4699

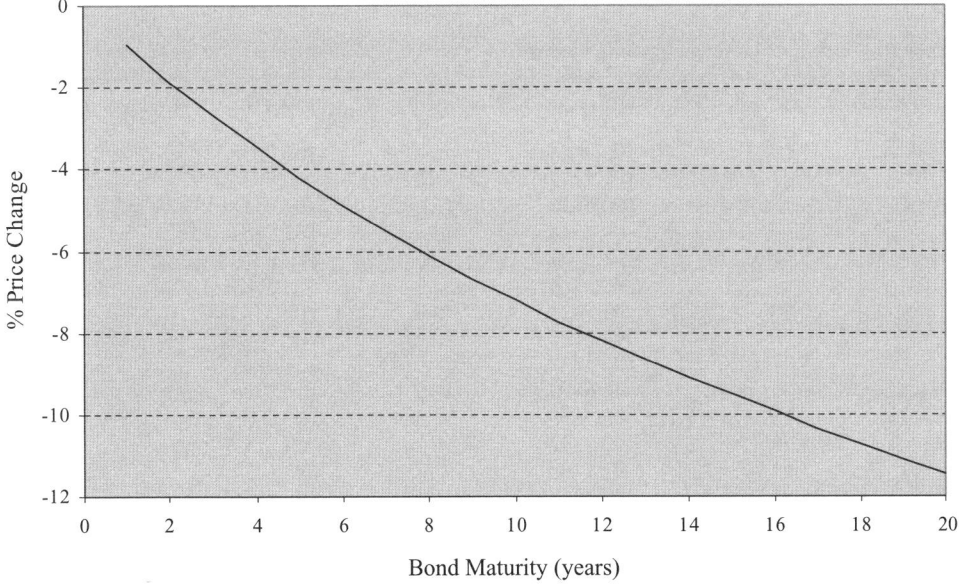

Figure 5.8 Change in price for a 1 % increase in yields.

consider either reducing the average life of the portfolio or even converting the portfolio into cash. In practice this is not always easy to achieve for several reasons:

- There is often insufficient liquidity, except in the government bond markets, to enable a large holding to be sold, without significantly changing the price in an unfavourable direction.
- Similarly, it is often not possible to buy enough of the shorter security at an appropriate price.
- There may be other transaction charges associated with the deals.
- Such structural changes to the maturity profile of the portfolio may not be appropriate for the portfolio's obligations.

Conversely, as you would expect, if the investment manager expects redemption yields to decrease across the board then moving to longer dated securities should be considered.

As we have discussed previously, sometimes the shape of the yield curve changes. This can be for many reasons, but they all boil down to one of supply and demand. For example, in the Summer of 2005 the UK gilt-edged yield curve was humped, at least partly because a significant proportion of the securities are held by UK pension funds, who have an obligation to attempt to match their liabilities with their assets. Since some of the current contributors to the pension fund will want to receive a pension in at least 50 years' time, they want to invest their funds in assets that will still be giving a return in 50 years' time. To this end the UK Government has issued 50 year conventional and index-linked gilts. These have a life considerably longer than any of their current bonds other than the undated gilts that were issued over 50 years ago. In future, if sufficient of the 50 year securities are issued, the humped shape of the yield curve could disappear.

Table 5.5 Old and classic yield curve details

Life (years)	Old yield (%)	Old price	New yield (%)	New price	Change in price (%)
1	4.00	100.9615	4.00	100.9615	0
2	4.40	101.1252	4.10	101.6951	0.5635
3	4.78	100.6016	4.20	102.2117	1.6004
4	5.16	99.4348	4.30	102.5231	3.1057
5	5.45	98.0757	4.40	102.6413	4.6551
6	5.67	96.6710	4.50	102.5789	6.1114
7	5.80	95.5022	4.60	102.3485	7.1687
8	5.90	94.3890	4.70	101.9627	8.0239
9	5.97	93.3937	4.80	101.4343	8.6093
10	6.00	92.6399	4.90	100.7759	8.7824
11	5.98	92.2630	5.00	100.0000	8.3859
12	5.94	92.0932	5.10	99.1187	7.6286
13	5.89	92.0702	5.20	98.1437	6.5966
14	5.81	92.3817	5.30	97.0866	5.0929
15	5.69	93.1607	5.40	95.9582	3.0028
16	5.52	94.5673	5.50	94.7689	0.2132
17	5.35	96.1552	5.60	93.5287	−2.7315
18	5.20	97.6982	5.70	92.2470	−5.5796
19	5.10	98.8013	5.80	90.9323	−7.9644
20	5.00	100.0000	5.90	89.5927	−10.4073

Yield Curves

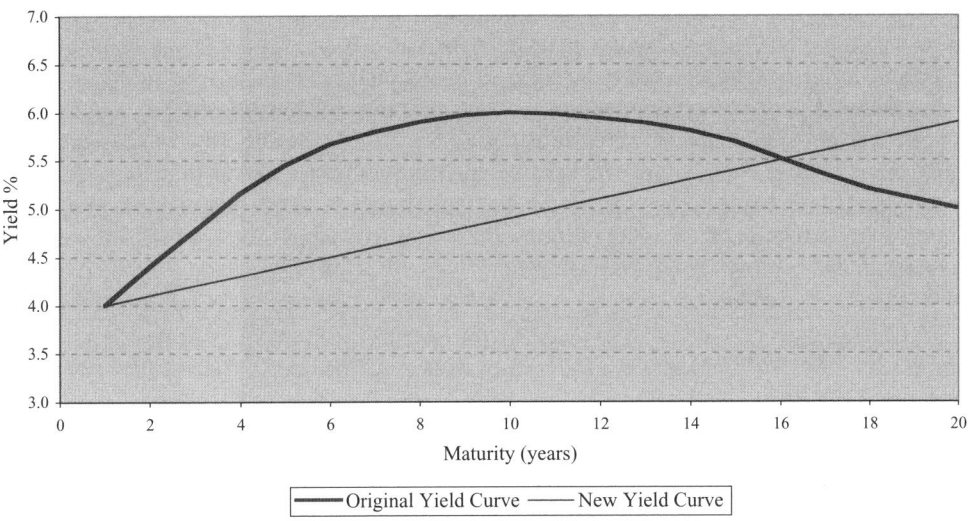

Figure 5.9 Two yield curves: humped and classical.

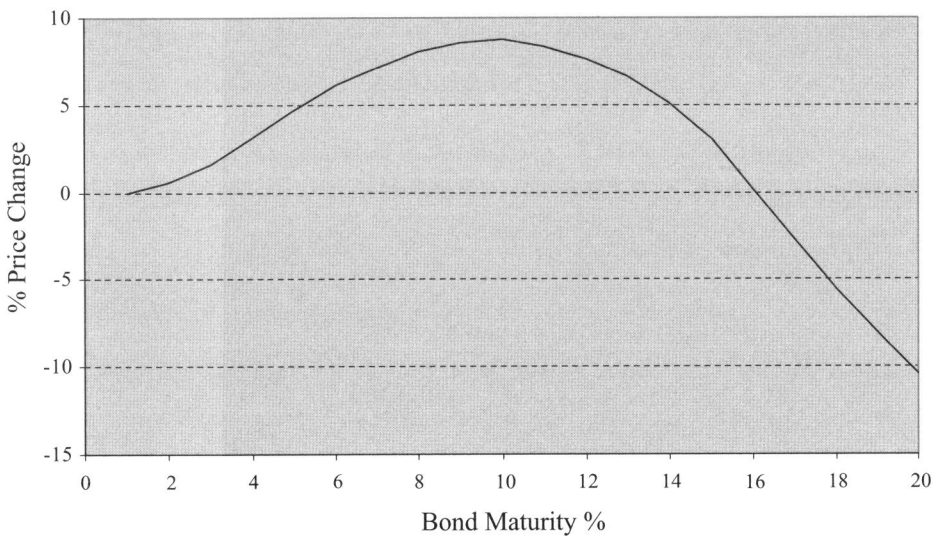

Figure 5.10 Change in prices in moving from one yield curve to another.

Why would an investor who does not need to be protected against long-term liabilities want to buy 30 year securities that yield less than 10 year securities with the same guarantees? The investor could of course be taking a punt on long-term interest rates dropping in the short term. In such a case, a 30 year bond will appreciate more than a 10 year bond. Other than that, such a decision has to be based on other expected structural changes to the market.

In principle, as we have discussed, we would expect over the long term for a yield curve to revert to the classical shape of increasing slightly over its life. Let us now consider the same yield curve we discussed before, but assume that the yield curve moves to the classic shape shown in Table 5.5 and Figures 5.9 and 5.10. This shows, as you would expect, that if you predict that the hump in the middle of the yield curve is to disappear then it is best to invest in bonds with the same maturity as the hump.

Program 5.3   YieldCurve3

This program allows the user to enter the current yield curve in the market, make assumptions about its change in shape or enter a projected yield curve at a specified date in the future. It then displays the two yield curves and, for a specified coupon rate and payment frequency, the expected change in prices.

6
Repos

A 'repo' is a form of secured short-term lending, usually between banks. A repo, or to give it its full title a 'sale and repurchase agreement', is a two-part transaction whereby one party agrees to sell securities to another and at the same time commits to buy back identical securities on a specified date at a specified price. The buyer of the securities provides cash to the seller at a predefined rate, the 'repo interest rate'. On the second date the transaction is effectively unwound, with the original seller getting the securities back and the cash provider getting the cash back together with the agreed interest. In effect, a repo is a short-term secured loan – the securities acting as collateral.

In Figure 6.1, Bank A is said to have executed a repo, whereas Bank B has executed a 'reverse repo'. Sometimes banks prefer, instead of going directly to another bank, to go via a third party when arranging a repo. Such arrangements are called tri-party repos (Figure 6.2). The tri-party repo agent takes a commission from both parties for arranging the trade.

There are basically two types of repos, 'classic' and 'sell/buy-back'. In addition, 'stock borrowing and lending', which functions in a similar way, is often carried out by the same department in the bank and as a result is often grouped with it. These types are described later in the chapter.

As with many financial innovations the European financial markets have tended to follow those in America. This was certainly true with the European repo markets. In Europe, the repo market did not emerge until the 1980s when dealers started to look at an efficient way to cover their short positions and finance their long inventory. Up to that time, short positions were covered through Cedel (now Clearstream) and Euroclear and long positions were financed with bank loans. Sale and repurchase agreements, or repos, had by this time been a major market in New York for many years, using US Treasury bonds as collateral.

By 2005, the repo markets on both sides of the Atlantic were significant well-established financing mechanisms in their own right. This is illustrated by recent research carried out by

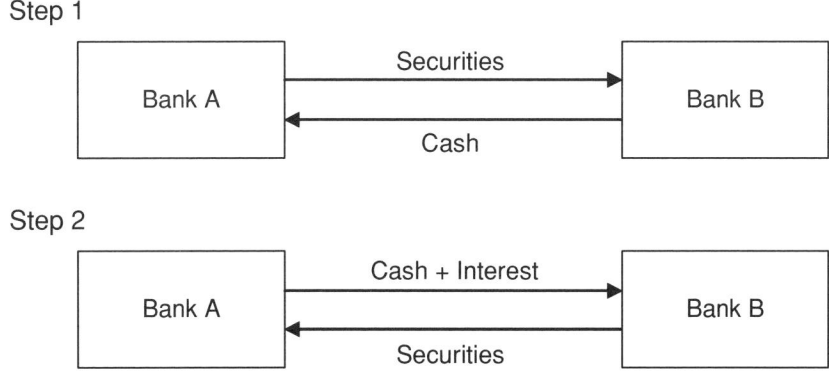

Figure 6.1 Standard repo.

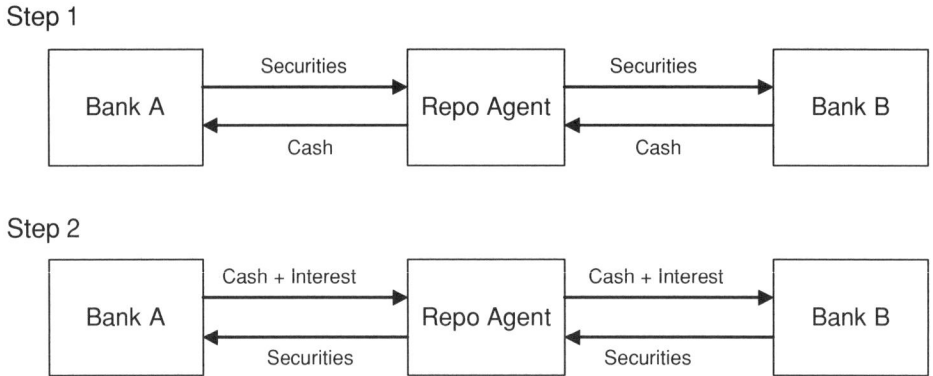

Figure 6.2 Tri-party repo.

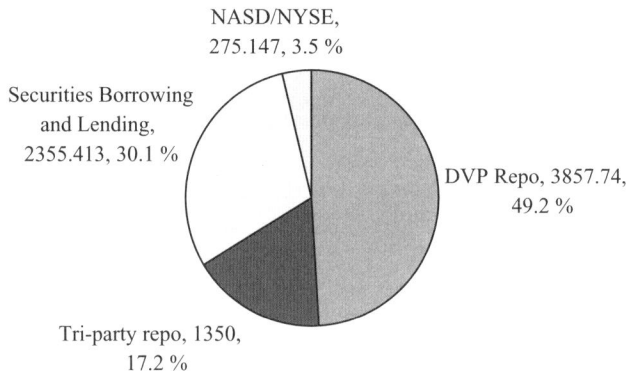

Figure 6.3 US repo product breakdown.

the Bond Market Association (TBMA) in the US[1] and by the International Capital Market Association (ICMA) with the support of ICMA's European Repo Council in Europe[2] on the size of the repo market and that of securities borrowing and lending.

According to the US survey, the outstanding volume of transactions as at 30 June 2004 was $7.84 trillion ($7 840 000 000 000). This was divided between the DVP (delivery versus payment) repo, tri-party repo, securities borrowing and lending and NASD/NYSE margin lending, as shown in Figure 6.3.

The latest ICMA European survey, which is carried out every six months, shows that at 8 June 2005, there were outstanding repo transactions to the value of more than €5.3 trillion (€5 300 000 000 000). This figure was based on 74 European financial institutions (e.g. see

---

[1] Repo and Securities Lending Survey of US Markets Volume and Loss Experience, The Bond Market Association, January 2005.
[2] International Capital Market Association, European Repo Market Survey Number 9, conducted June 2005.

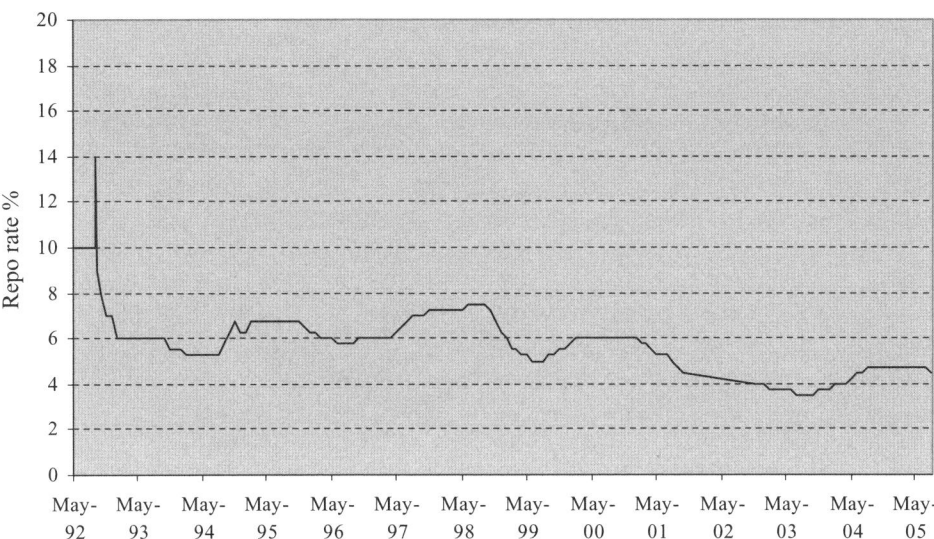

Figure 6.4 Bank of England repo rates.
Source: Bank of England.

Figure 6.5) who responded to the survey, and excluded stock borrowing and lending transactions, and transactions undertaken with central banks as part of their official money market operations. The survey showed that there had been an increase in the value of repo trades of about 19 % over the previous year, which was similar to the increase in the previous year. The survey broke down the repo transactions in a number of ways, including the type of repos, whether they were fixed, floating rate or open, the currency of the cash used, the outstanding period, etc.

The types of repo that have been split into classic, documented sell/buy-back and undocumented sell/buy-back are shown in Figure 6.5. The documented sell/buy-backs often use the sell/buy-back annexes of the TBMA/ISMA Global Master Repo Agreement (see below).

The European survey showed that 10.4 % of the outstanding transactions were tri-party ones, with the main European tri-party repo agents, namely Bank of New York, Citigroup, Clearstream, Euroclear, JP Morgan Chase and SegaInterSettle, contributing data. This figure contrasts with the US survey where the tri-party market share, excluding securities borrowing, was 24.6 %.

Similarly, the majority of the repo transactions were at a fixed rate (86.6 %), compared with a 7.6 % floating rate, most of which were indexed to EONIA,[3] and 5.6 % open (Figure 6.6). An open repo contract is one with no final maturity date, but it is terminable by either counterparty on demand. About 70 % of the transactions were executed with the cash element in euros. Of the remainder, 11.8 % were in sterling and 11.1 % in US dollars (Figure 6.7). The majority of repo transactions are for a very short period with some 37.8 % being for a week or less (Figure 6.8). A forward–forward transaction was defined as one where the first leg was at least five days in the future.

---

[3] Euro OverNight Index Average – the effective overnight interbank interest rate.

An Introduction to the Bond Markets

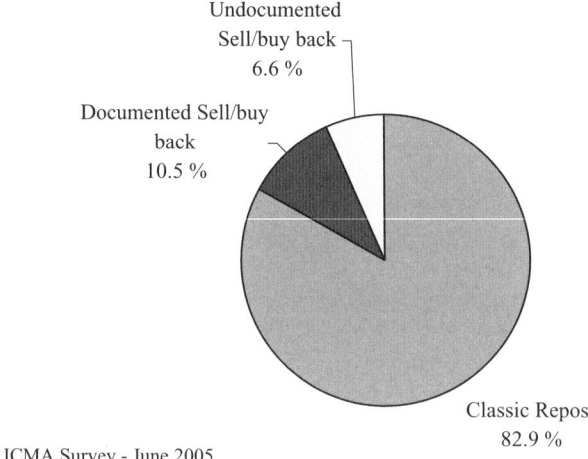

Figure 6.5 Types of European repos. Reproduced by permission of ICMA.

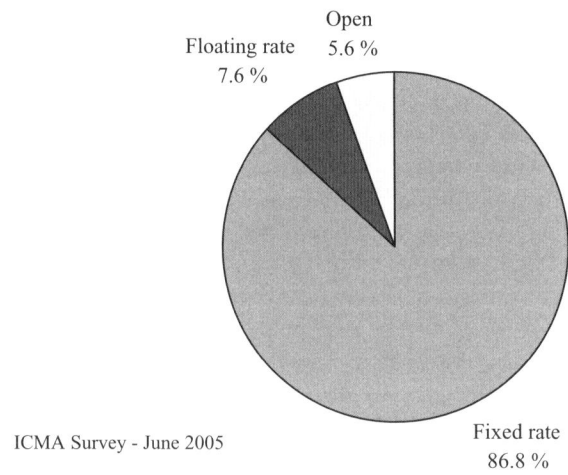

Figure 6.6 European contract types.

The above analysis shows that the size of the repo transactions, which dwarfs that of the cash markets, amounts in Europe to over €1 trillion per day. This is supported by the fact that, for several years, over 80 % of all bond trades by value reported to ICMA's TRAX[4] system were repo transactions. Although the value of the repo trades is large, the number of transactions is relatively small, as individual transactions of $100 million or more are fairly common.

---

[4] Nearly all bond trades transacted in London, and a large proportion of those transacted in Continental Europe, are reported to TRAX.

European Repo Currency Distribution

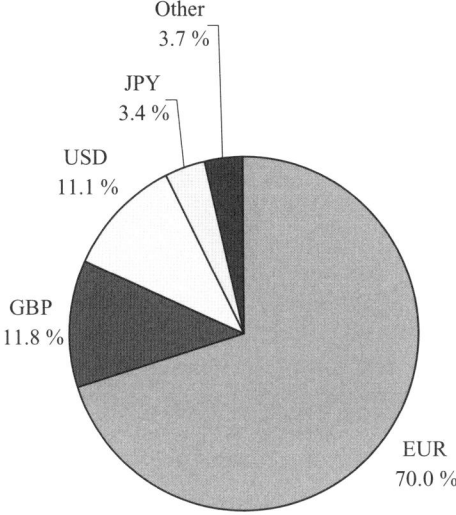

ICMA Survey - June 2005

Figure 6.7 Currency distributions.

The collateral given on a repo is usually, but not always, provided by high-quality bonds. As a result the repo desk in a bank often sits in the Treasury or the bond trading areas. This analysis is supported by the ICMA survey which shows that the collateral for 70.4 % of repo transactions was provided by European Union central government bonds (see Figure 6.9).

Outstanding European Repo Maturities

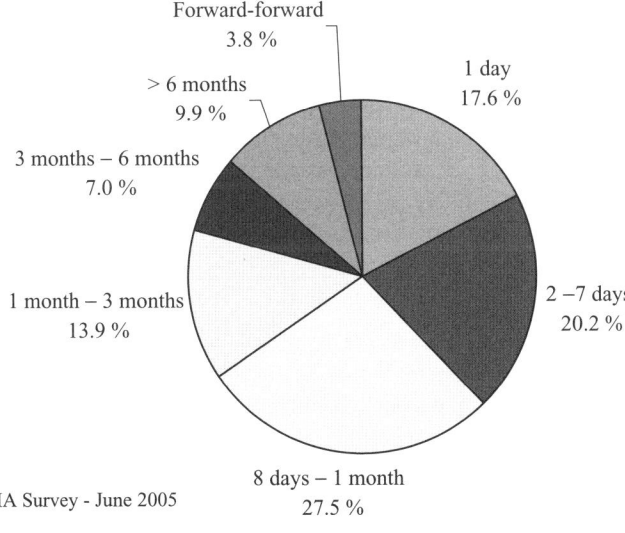

ICMA Survey - June 2005

Figure 6.8 Outstanding repo maturities.

European Repo Collateral

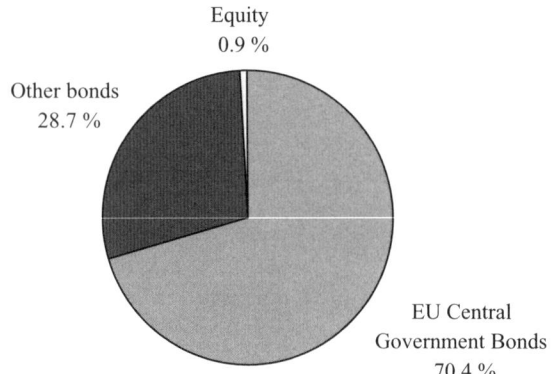

ICMA Survey - June 2005

Figure 6.9 Repos collateral.

The European survey figures above have excluded stock borrowing and lending, which amounted to some 23.8 % of the repo figure. Unsurprisingly, with stock borrowing and lending, the percentage of transactions involving equity shares has increased by 11.4 %.

During the period of the repo transaction, the legal title of the securities has been transferred, but the market risk and economic benefits of owning them remains with the seller of the securities. For example, if the value of the collateral provided drops considerably during the life of the repo then the cash provider can often demand that the seller provides more collateral. This is called 'variation margin'. Similarly, the original seller is still entitled to any interest that accrues or is paid out during the repo period.

6.1 CLASSIC REPOS

Classic repo transactions are conducted according to a repo contract that has been signed in advance by both parties. A repo legal contract was drafted initially in the international arena by the US Bond Market Association (TBMA) and the International Securities Association (ISMA) in 1992. This contract, the Global Master Repo Agreement (GMRA) has been modified over the years to allow for market developments, and various annexes have been added to it so that it is now acceptable in a number of countries. For example, the GMRA was extended, in Annex 1, to allow for gilt repo transactions. The Bank of England is keen for participants to abide by the agreement.

The GMRA provides for the following:

- Absolute transfer of the title of securities.
- Daily marking-to-market. In other words, the securities used as collateral are valued each day to see if there has been a material change in their value. If this occurs the lender of the money can demand extra collateral.
- The possible provision of an initial margin and the maintenance of a variation margin throughout the life of the repo transaction, if the mark-to-market value of the collateral changes significantly.
- Defines the rights and obligations of the parties in the event of a default.
- If a default occurs, there is a full set-off of claims between the counterparties.

- Defines how collateral can be substituted and how to treat coupon payments.
- The terms are subject to English law, or another agreed jurisdiction.

A classic repo transaction involves one party A selling a security of an agreed quality to another party B, and agreeing to buy it, or equivalent securities, back from B frequently at a specified date for the same dirty (gross) price. Party B will charge party A interest for lending the cash. Normally, party A is not interested in the specific collateral, provided it is of an appropriate quality, with the result that it is lent at the current general collateral (GC) repo interest rate. However, sometimes party B wants specific securities to meet a commitment. In this case, the demand for the bond may cause the interest rate to be cut below that of the GC repo rate. Such a bond is said to be 'special'. Sometimes a classic repo transaction is executed without a specified date for the final leg. When this occurs, the transaction is said to be 'open', and it may be terminated by either party on demand.

The following examples show the calculations involved in two different classic repo transactions. The first one shows a straightforward repo transaction in a liquid government bond, where the lender of the money felt it was not necessary for there to be any initial margin. In the second example, initial and variation margins are required.

Example 6.1   Classic repo

On 27 July 2005 for settlement on 28 July 2005, Bank A agrees to sell £10 million of 5 % Treasury 2012 to Bank B and to buy it back again on 4 August 2005. The transaction is constructed to give a repo interest rate of 4 %. As it is a high-quality liquid security, Bank B does not demand any additional collateral.

The clean price of 5 % Treasury 2012 on the 28 July is 104.49 to which must be added accrued interest of 1.94 %, giving a dirty price of 106.43 %. Bank B thus lends Bank A £10 643 000. For doing this Bank B wants interest of 4 % for seven days:

$$= 10\,643\,000 \times 4 \times 7/36\,500 = £8164.50^5$$

The transactions are as follows (see Figure 6.10):

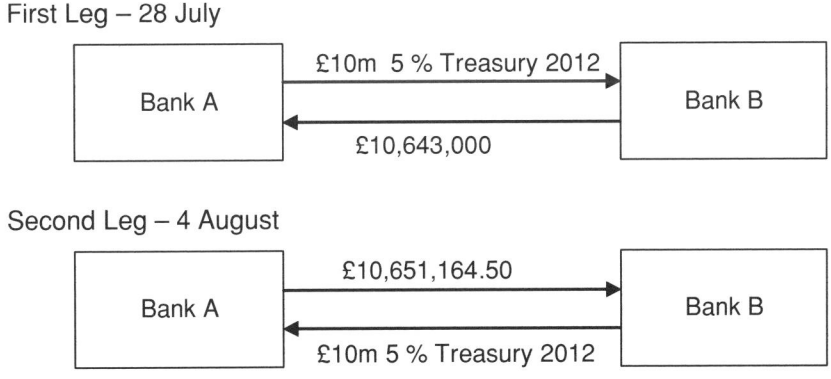

Figure 6.10   Classic repos.

---

[5] As the transaction is in sterling the interest is calculated on a 365 day year.

First leg on 28 July
Bank A sells £10 million of 5 % Treasury 2012 to Bank B for a payment of £10 643 000.

Second leg on 4 August
Bank A buys back the securities for the same price of £10 643 000 plus accrued interest of £8164.50 = £10 651 164.50.

In the above example if the repo transaction had been conducted over 7 September, a coupon payment date, the interest would have been sent to Bank B, who would have had to forward it to Bank A. In other words, although the securities had been legally transferred to Bank B between the two legs, Bank A is still entitled to the coupon payments.

Example 6.2

On 31 August 2005 for settlement on 1 September 2005 Bank A sells $10 million of security X to Bank B, with an agreement to buy it back after 30 days for the same price plus interest at 3.5 % per annum. As security X is not very liquid, Bank B demands initial collateral of 2 % as protection in the case of a default.

Security X is priced at 90 % and has accrued interest of 0.90 % on 1 September. On the 15 September, the price of security X has dropped to a clean price of 85 % plus accrued interest of, say, 1.15 %; as a result Bank B demands extra collateral from Bank A to make up the deficit (see Figure 6.11). We will assume that there are no further demands for variation margin.

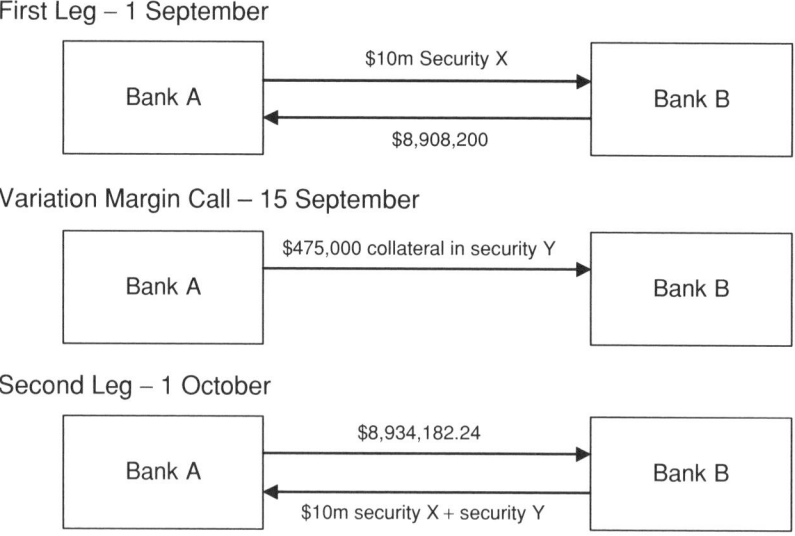

Figure 6.11 Variation margin repo.

First leg on 1 September
The dirty value of the $10 million of security X is $10\,000\,000 \times (90 + 0.90)/100 = \$9\,090\,000$. As Bank B is requiring a margin of 2 %, it is prepared to lend $9\,090\,000 \times 0.98 = \$8\,908\,200$ in exchange for the securities.

Call for variation margin on 15 September
Bank B would like to have the loan backed by securities worth at least $9 090 000. On 15 September the securities are worth $10\,000\,000 \times (85 + 1.15)/100 = \$8\,615\,000$, i.e. a shortfall of $475 000. Under the terms of the agreement, Bank A has to provide Bank B with a further $475 000 in collateral. Suppose this collateral is in security Y.

Second leg on 1 October
Bank A buys back the $10 000 000 of security X and the additional collateral in security Y for:

$$8\,908\,200 \times (1 + 3.5 \times 30/36\,000) = \$8\,934\,182.24$$

6.2 SELL/BUY-BACKS

A sell/buy-back transaction is very similar to a classic repo, insofar as one party agrees to sell securities to another party for an amount of money, and simultaneously agrees to buy them back at a specified later date for an agreed amount. The cash provider can require an initial margin in the same way as for a classic repo, but there is no provision for a variation margin.

The main differences are:

- Generally with sell/buy-backs there is no legal agreement.
- No repo interest rate is specified. The interest rate is implicit in the price of the second leg of the repo.
- If the collateral provided pays a coupon during the period of the sell/buy-back then the seller is entitled to it. This coupon payment will be reflected in the price of the second leg. The seller will thus have to wait until the end of the repo agreement to receive the payment.

Example 6.3 Sell/buy-back

On 27 July 2005 for settlement on 28 July 2005, Bank A agrees to sell £10 million of 5 % Treasury 2012 to Bank B and to buy it back again on 4 August 2005. No initial collateral is demanded.

The clean price of 5 % Treasury 2012 on the 28 July is 104.49, to which must be added accrued interest of 1.94 %, giving a dirty price of 106.43 %. Bank B thus lends Bank A £10 643 000. On the 4 August, 5 % Treasury 2012 will have an extra seven days' accrued interest, amounting to $5 \times 7/365 = 0.096\,\%$, giving a total accrued interest of 2.036 %.

As with the first classic repo example, Bank B wants interest of 4 % for seven days:

$$= 10\,643\,000 \times 4 \times 7/36\,500 = £8164.50$$

Thus the total proceeds of the second leg are:

$$= 10\,643\,000 + 8164.50 = £10\,651\,164.50$$

The dirty price of 5 % Treasury 2012 in the second leg is thus 106.511 645, giving a clean price of $106.511\,645 - 2.036 = 104.475\,645$.

The transactions are as follows (see Figure 6.12):

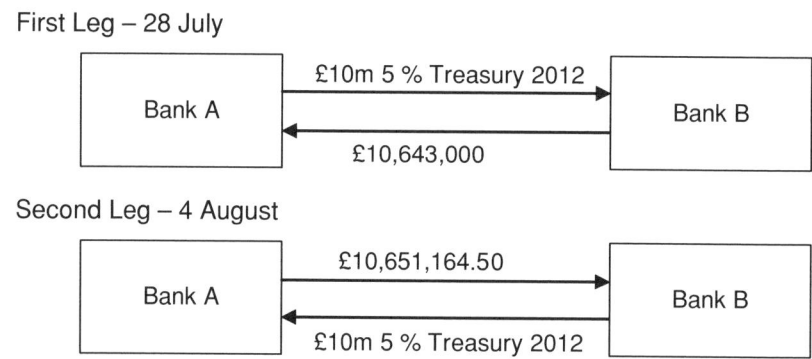

Figure 6.12 Sell/buy-back repo.

First leg on 28 July
Bank A sells £10 million of 5 % Treasury 2012 at a price of 104.3 plus accrued interest to Bank B for a payment of £10 643 000.

Second leg on 4 August
Bank A buys back £10 million of 5 % Treasury 2012 at a price of 104.475 645 plus accrued interest for a total consideration of £10 651 164.50.

It can be seen that the cash flows of this sell/buy-back repo are identical to those for the classic repo.

In volatile markets, sell/buy-backs are regarded as more risky than classic repos because there is no provision for variation margin.

6.3 STOCK BORROWING/LENDING

Some institutional investors such as pension funds and insurance companies prefer to lend out their securities for a fee, instead of getting involved in repos. The effect is very similar, although frequently no final date will be specified. The final date is said to be 'open'.

The parties to the stock lending will agree a 'rebate' interest rate, which will be lower than the 'general collateral' interest rate. (The rebate interest rate is equivalent to the special repo interest rate.) The profit to the institutional investor arises because of the difference between these two rates.

Example 6.4

A pension fund lends $10 million worth of security X, of which it is a long-term holder, to a market maker, who is short of the security. The market maker provides the pension fund with cash of $10 million as collateral, on which the market maker charges the pension fund interest at a rebate rate of 3.5 % per annum.

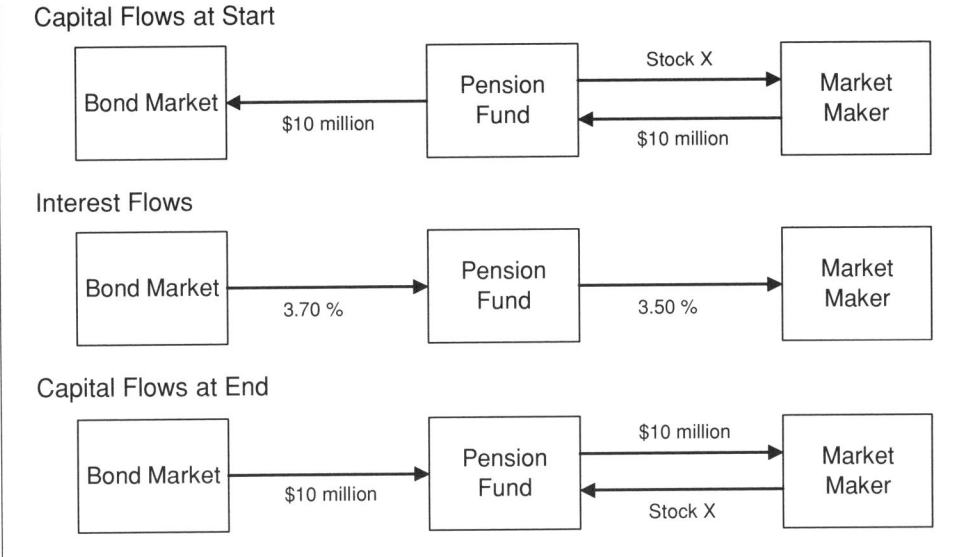

Figure 6.13 Stock borrowing/lending.

The pension fund then reinvests this cash at the higher interest rate of 3.7 % per annum in the bond market for the term of the stock borrowing. Thus the pension fund is able to make an additional 0.2 % (see Figure 6.13).

7
Option Calculations

An option is an agreement whereby the purchaser of the option has the right, but not the obligation, to buy or sell from the writer (or seller) of the option a specified instrument at a specified price within a specified time period. The writer of the option grants the buyer this privilege for a sum of money called the 'option price' or 'option premium'. The buyer of the option may exercise the option at the 'strike price' at or at any time up to the 'expiry date'.

If the buyer can exercise the option at any time up to the expiry date of the option, it is called an 'American option'. If the buyer can only exercise the option at the expiry date, it is called a 'European option'. There is no geographical significance to the designations of American and European.

When the option grants the buyer the right to purchase the instrument from the writer, it is called a 'call option'; when it grants the buyer a right to sell an instrument it is called a 'put option'. These two basic types of options may then be combined together, possibly with other instruments, to form a variety of investment strategies. Such combinations are often called 'exotic' options.

A party to a call or a put option can thus:

- buy a call option;
- buy a put option;
- write (sell) a call option; or
- write a put option.

The financial implications of buying and writing (selling) put and call options are obviously different. If you buy an option the maximum you can lose is your initial stake, whereas if you write an option, if it is not covered by another transaction, the loss can be very large.

7.1 BUYING A CALL OPTION

Buying a call option is also referred to as acquiring a 'long call position'. Unless it is to protect some other position, an investor will buy a call option if the price of the asset is expected to increase. If the asset on which the option is based is a bond the investor will buy it if the interest rates are expected to fall.

Consider the following call option.

Example 7.1

The writer of the option has granted the buyer the right to purchase security A during the next three months for 85 for a fee of 5. From the point of view of the buyer of the option, the buyer will make a profit if the price of the security rises above 90 ($= 85 + 5$). However, the buyer will make a loss if it does not. There is theoretically no limit to the profit that the buyer can make, although this is dependent on the nature of the security on which the option has been written. On the other hand, the potential loss is limited to the cost of the option, i.e. 5.

The profit and loss to the buyer is shown in Figure 7.1.

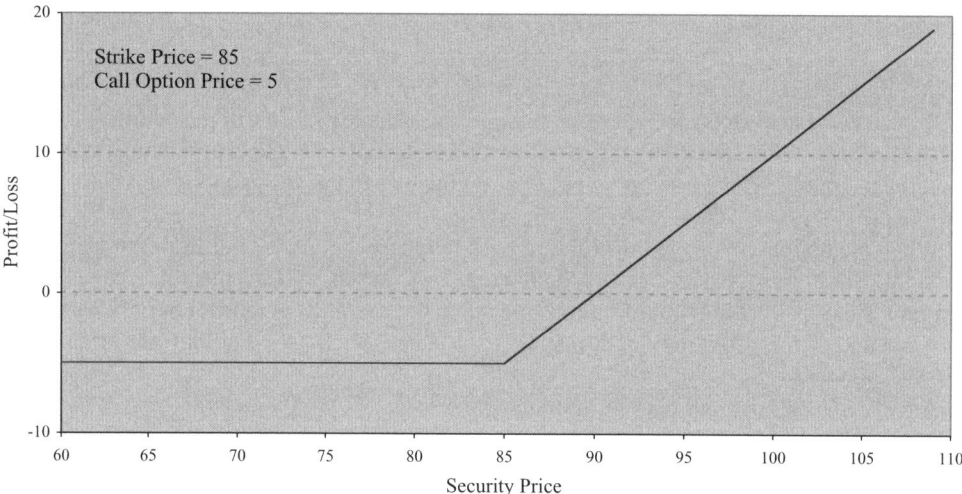

Figure 7.1 Profit/loss on buying a call option.

7.2 WRITING A CALL OPTION

Whenever a party buys a call option, another party has to write, or sell, it. The writer of a call option is said to have acquired a 'short call position'.

The seller of the option makes a profit if the price of the security in question either falls or rises by less than the call option price. However, now the potential loss is unlimited as the value of the underlying asset may rise considerably. In the case of writing a call option on a bond, the seller will want the interest rates to either rise or not change significantly.

Figure 7.2 illustrates the potential profit and loss of writing and buying a call option with a strike price of 85 for a payment of 5.

7.3 BUYING A PUT OPTION

Buying a put option is also referred to as acquiring a 'long put position'. An investor will purchase a put option if there is a need to be protected from the possibility of a fall in the value of the underlying asset. The put option gives the buyer the right to sell the underlying asset for an agreed amount (the strike price) depending on the type either before or on the expiry date. If the value of the underlying asset falls by more than the cost of the put option then the

Profit/Loss on Buying and Writing a Call Option

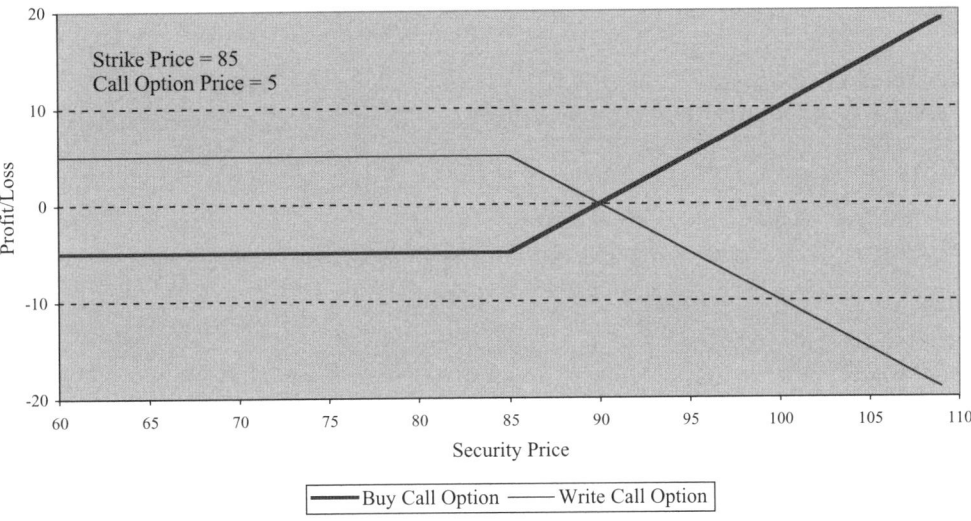

Figure 7.2 Profit/loss on buying and writing a call option.

buyer makes a profit. If, on the other hand, it does not then the loss is limited to the cost of the option. If the option is on the price of a bond, then an investor will only buy a put option if the interest rates are expected to rise.

Figure 7.3 shows the profit and loss of buying a put option with a strike price of 85 at a cost of 5.

Profit/Loss on Buying a Put Option

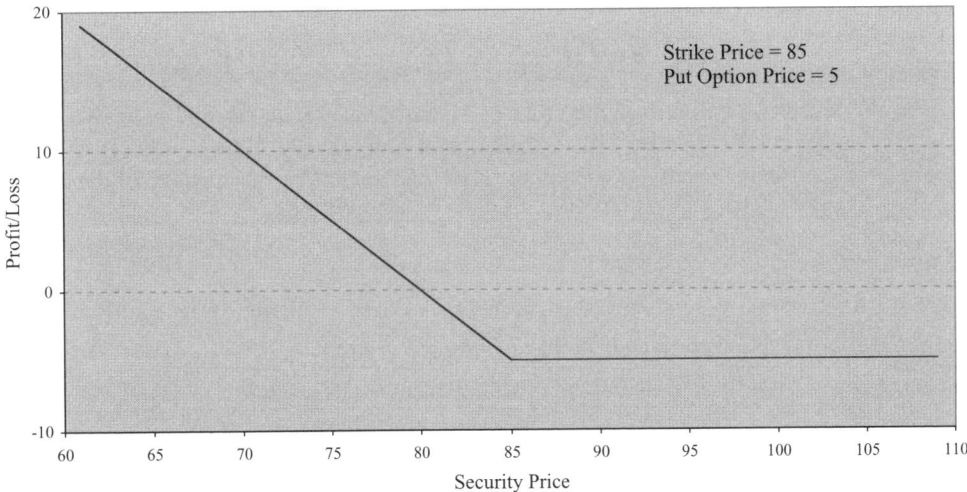

Figure 7.3 Profit/loss on buying a put option.

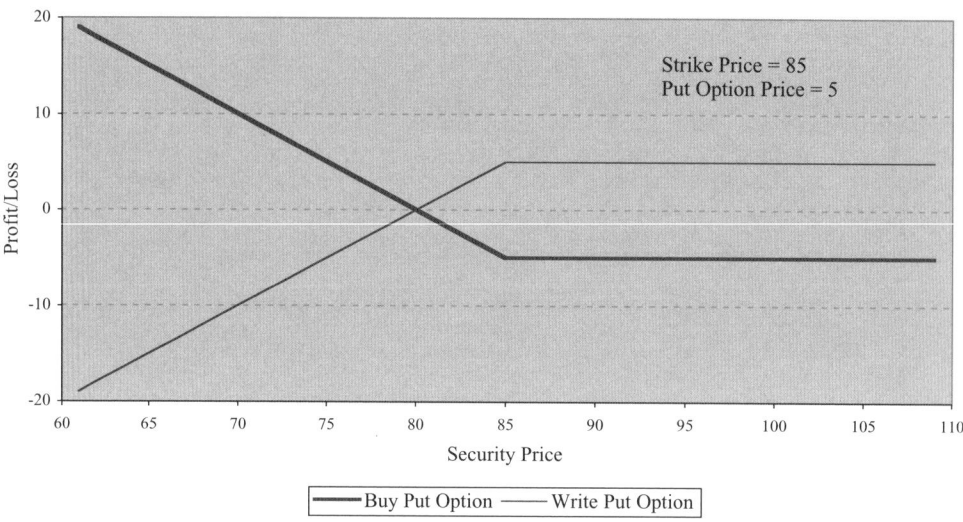

Figure 7.4 Profit/loss on buying and writing a put option.

7.4 WRITING A PUT OPTION

Writing a put option is also referred to as acquiring a 'short put position'. The writer of a put option guarantees, up to the expiry date, to buy the underlying asset at the agreed strike price, if required to do so, by the buyer of the put option in return for the payment of the put option price. Thus an investor will only write a put option on a bond if interest rates are expected either to fall or stay approximately the same.

Using the same example as above, Figure 7.4 shows the profit and loss to the buyer and writer of a put option according to the value of the underlying asset at the expiry date.

7.5 THEORETICAL VALUE OF AN OPTION

In an earlier chapter we discussed the profit or loss associated with call and put options, and how many bonds can be regarded as a combination of a bullet bond and an option. If an option is to be exercised immediately, its economic value is called the 'intrinsic value' of the option.

Example 7.2

There is a call option to purchase a security at a strike price of 90. If the price of the security is currently 110, then the intrinsic value is $110 - 90 = 20$. However, if the price is below the strike price the intrinsic value is zero.

For a call option, if the current security price is above the strike price then:

- The intrinsic value is the difference between the current security price and the strike price.
- The option is said to be 'in-the-money'.

If the current security price is at the strike price then:

- The intrinsic value is zero.
- The option is said to be 'at-the-money'.

If the current security price is below the strike price then:

- The intrinsic value is zero.
- The option is said to be 'out-of-the-money'.

The intrinsic values for a put option can be similarly defined. However, now a put option has an intrinsic value of zero unless the security price is less than the strike price.

If there is some time before an option expires, then even if the option is currently at or out-of-the-money, it often still has a value. This value is called the 'time value of the option'. More generally, it is given by the formula:

$$\text{Time value of an option} = \text{option price} - \text{intrinsic value}$$

There are several factors that influence the option price. They are:

- current price of the underlying security;
- the strike price;
- the time to the expiration of the option;
- the expected volatility of the price of the underlying security.

More particularly, if the underlying security of the option is a bond, the expected volatility of the underlying security can be expressed as a function of:

- the coupon rate of the bond;
- the short-term risk-free interest rate over the life of the option; and
- the expected interest rate volatility over the life of the option.

Many models have been developed to estimate the theoretical fair price of an option. These models are dependent on whether the option is a call or a put, and as to whether it is an American (exercisable at any time up to and including the expiry date) or a European (exercisable only on the expiry date) type. An American option gives the purchaser more options than the holder of a European option, and so is likely to be more expensive than the European one. The difference in price is, in part, dependent on the time to the expiry date and the volatility of the underlying instrument, but there is nothing to stop a holder of a European option locking in the profit by writing an opposite put or call option in the same instrument prior to the expiry date.

Figure 7.5 illustrates a typical theoretical fair price and the intrinsic value of a call option on a bond with a strike price of 100. If the volatility of the price of the underlying instrument and the time to expiry increase then the time value of the option will rise.

7.6 COMBINING OPTIONS

As mentioned above, it is possible to combine options together and so protect the investor from a variety of risks. A few examples of the possible options are illustrated below.

If an investor buys a call and a put option in the same security at the same strike and expiry date, he or she is said to have purchased a 'straddle'. An investor would only do this if there is a need to be protected from a movement in the price in either direction. The effect of this

112   An Introduction to the Bond Markets

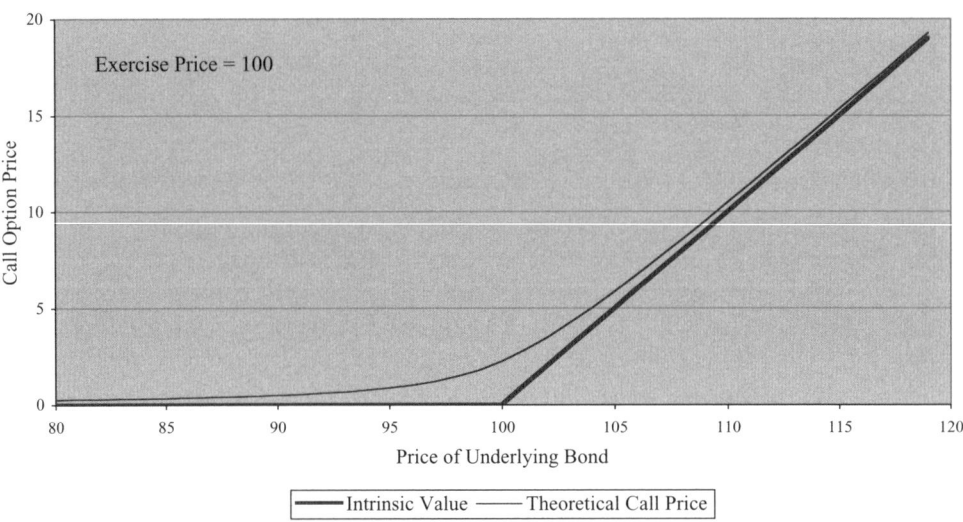

Figure 7.5 Theoretical call price of an option.

approach is shown in Figure 7.6, where the cost of purchasing a call option at 85 is 5 and that of purchasing the put option at 85 is also 5.

Sometimes an investor will buy a call option in an instrument, which then rises in price. The investor would then like to ensure that at least some of the profit is secure, in exchange for limiting the profit. One option would be to then write a call option in the same instrument at a higher price. The effects of this are shown in Figure 7.7, where the original call option at

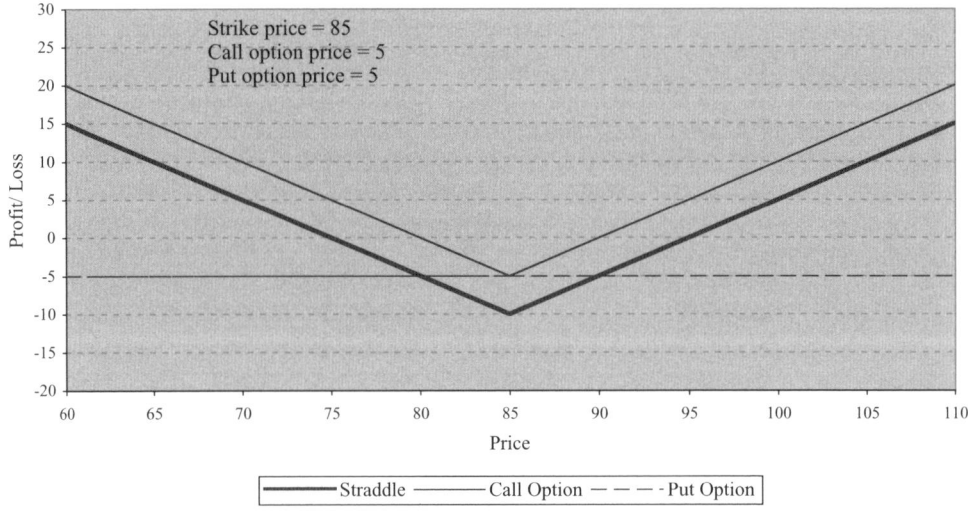

Figure 7.6 Straddle of a call and put option.

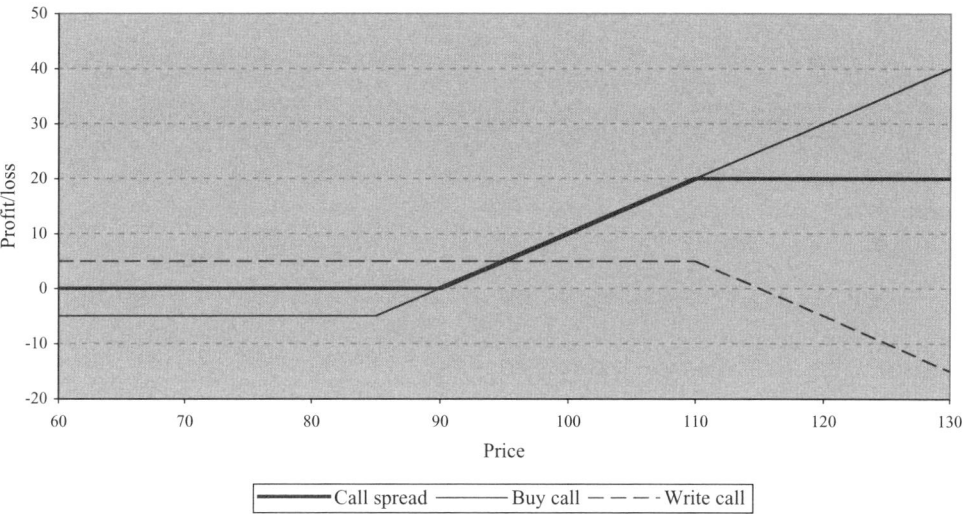

Figure 7.7 Call spread option.

85 cost 5, and the investor wrote the second call option for 5 with a strike price of 110. Such a strategy is called a 'call spread'.

If an investor is a long-term holder of a bond, he or she may wish to be protected from any significant loss of value in the future. The investor can do this by buying a protective put in the bond. Figure 7.8 shows the effect of this strategy on the profit and loss on a bond, where a long put has been purchased with a strike price of 90 for 5.

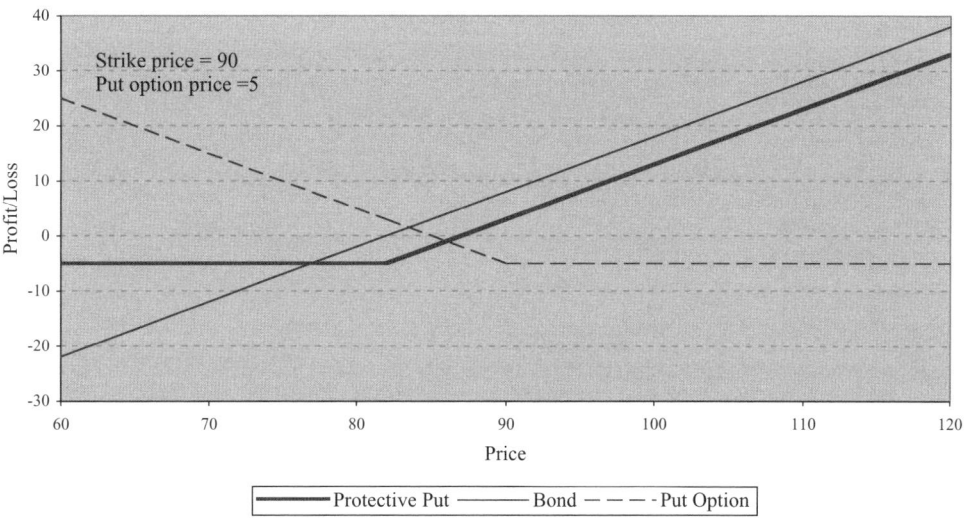

Figure 7.8 Protective put.

8
Credit and Other Risks and Ratings

This chapter discusses some of the reasons why bonds with the same structures, with regard to coupons, maturity, currency and embedded options, often yield significantly different amounts. In particular, it looks at the way both credit risk and liquidity effect the market valuation of bonds.

Both borrowers and investors are interested in bonds being rated and for them to have reasonable liquidity. From a borrower's point of view the higher the rating and increased liquidity of existing issues, the easier and possibly cheaper it is to raise new debt.

8.1 CREDIT RISK

Investors like to purchase securities where there is virtually no credit risk, unless they are adequately rewarded for the risk. This presents the user with a dilemma. There is a need to assess which securities in the universe are 'risk free' and how risky are other securities that provide a greater return.

As has already been discussed, the market traditionally treats domestic government issues denominated in the currency of the country as risk free. Thus US Treasury dollar bonds and UK sterling gilt-edged securities are regarded as risk free, but is this a sensible assumption if the security will not be repaid for some time and the country is politically unstable? Even in the eurozone, in late 2005, the market required a yield premium of between 15 and 20 basis points for euro ten year bonds issued by Italy and Greece over those issued by Germany. This premium was in fact very similar to that of 10 year euro Pfandbrief issues, which are issued by banks and are usually secured on property. A similar yield premium occurs in the US dollar short-term commercial paper market. In December 2005, AA (see Table 8.1) rated commercial paper yielded in the order of 25 to 40 basis points more than the equivalent three and six month Treasury instruments.

Luckily for the investor there are now a number of companies that assess the credit risk of individual bond issues, which helps in assessing whether issues are cheap or dear. Several of these credit rating companies only assess bonds in one or two domestic markets, but there are three credit rating companies who dominate the international bond markets. They are Standard & Poor, Moody and Fitch. Each of these rating companies, *inter alia*, produces assessments for companies and short-term and long-term debt (i.e. at least 12 months). It is the long-term debt assessments that we are interested in.

Unfortunately not all bond issues are rated. This does in turn provide investment opportunities for investors who are prepared to do their own research into the expected credit rating of the issue, provided that they are allowed to invest in such issues. In fact, some fund managers are not allowed to invest in any bond securities that have not been rated by at least one and sometimes two of the major rating companies. This has enabled other fund managers, without such restrictions, to purchase unrated secured corporate bonds cheaply and as a result outperform the others. However, the fact that a corporate bond has been rated does not in itself

Table 8.1 Commercial paper market

Term	Commercial paper discount rates		Treasury yields
	AA financial	AA non-financial	
1 day	3.99	3.99	—
7 day	4.10	4.06	—
15 day	4.17	4.15	—
30 day	4.23	4.21	3.84
60 day	4.29	—	—
90 day	4.32	—	4.03

Sources: Commercial paper rates – Depository Trust Company, 8 December 2005; Treasury yields – US Treasury: treasury yield curve based on quotations obtained from the Federal Reserve Bank of New York, 7 December 2005.

Table 8.2 Allied Domecq example

	Price 01/04/05	Price 28/04/05	Yield 01/04/05	Yield 28/04/05
Allied Domecq $6\frac{5}{8}\%$ 2011	105.015	100.790	5.712	6.567
Allied Domecq $6\frac{5}{8}\%$ 2014	105.525	98.840	5.827	6.727

give an investor a long-term view of how secure the investment is. Consider the following two examples.

In April 2005, Allied Domecq had a takeover approach from Pernod Ricard. As a result of this approach, the equity share price of Allied Domecq rose substantially, but the prices on its outstanding bonds, rated BBB, dropped significantly, as it was perceived by the market that the takeover would result in a downgrading of the rating of the bonds (see Table 8.2).

In another example, the Danish cleaning company ISS was taken over by a private equity group following a leveraged buyout in March 2005. As a result of the buyout, which was unexpected, the value of the bonds, which did not have a change of ownership clause, dropped by 20 % and ISS was downgraded by six notches to below investment grade. This angered the major bond holders, who hired lawyers in an attempt to stop the private equity company and ISS issuing more debt. Eventually an agreement was reached by the parties about the nature and guarantees of any proposed new financing by the companies.

These problems can often be reduced by adding a number of covenants to the bond prospectus.

8.1.1 Covenants

The concerns of the investment industry were such that in 2003 an industry working group was set up to report on how market standards could be improved in the European fixed income markets.[1] They felt that the problem was not as great in the US dollar market, where there is a certain amount of discipline due to the SEC registration and disclosure requirements.

Covenants can protect corporate bond holders in a number of ways. There are various ways that investors could be protected in the case of a change of control from asset stripping and

---

[1] 'Improving market standards in the sterling and euro fixed income credit markets', October 2003.

give some bite to the often near meaningless negative pledge statement. A change of control could, in certain circumstances, give bond holders a put option to demand redemption at, say, the greater of:

- par (100) and
- a yield that would give the same return as the original reference government bond, or an appropriate substitute, plus the issue yield spread.

This put option might only be exercisable if the change of control results in a downgrading of, say, at least two notches or from investment grade to speculative grade. Similar change of ownership clauses are now often included in the terms of new corporate bond issues.

Similarly, a borrower should not be allowed to dispose of company assets or restructure the company in such a way that is detrimental to the instrument's integrity. For example, a clause stopping a company from deposing of more than, say, 20 % of the debt of the company in any one year, unless it is used for reinvestment in the company or for repurchasing bonds of a higher or similar ranking. Failing this, the holder could demand that the bonds are bought back at par.

Bonds are often issued with a 'negative pledge' clause. This basically says that the issuer will not issue any debt that has a prior claim on assets. Unfortunately, there are a number of ways such a clause can be circumnavigated. In fact, in the European capital markets such clauses often exclude bank debt, thus making it virtually meaningless. In addition, the negative pledge clause often does not restrict the company from securitizing assets or entering into sale and leaseback agreements on assets.

Covenants do not have to be all in favour of the investors. For example, in the sterling market bonds sometimes have a 'Spens clause' that allows the borrower to redeem the bonds early at the greater of par and the price that gives a yield that is the same as the current redemption yield on the reference UK Government gilt-edged issue. A Spens clause, requiring early redemption, can sometimes even be invoked as a result of a corporate action, which is deemed to be detrimental to the bond holders. This occurred in 2000 with Stagecoach when it sold a subsidiary resulting in a ratings downgrade. As a result, an outstanding sterling bond with a Spens clause had to be redeemed early, but a shorter bond denominated in euros without a Spens clause did not. Redeeming a bond with a Spens clause is very expensive for the borrower, as the bonds were usually issued and are trading at an appreciable yield premium to the relevant gilt. As a result, companies seldom exercise the option, although they may try to circumvent the bond covenants. A less onerous standard could be fairer to both parties.

8.1.2 Ratings

As has been discussed above, if bonds have been rated by the rating agencies, the process of pricing the issues is made easier. Bonds are frequently priced relative to the interest rates of so-called 'risk-free debt'[2] in the relevant currency and maturity range.

On the other hand, issuers are interested in having their bonds rated, since they hope it will reduce the cost of borrowing. In recent years the majority of large international issues have been rated by at least one of the three major credit rating agencies. However, there are a few

---

[2] Domestic debt issued by a government in its own currency is often referred to as a risk-free debt, since at least theoretically it can always print more money to repay the loan, albeit sometimes in a depreciated currency.

Table 8.3 Relative bond credit ratings for three agencies

Standard & Poor	Moody	Fitch	Description
AAA	Aaa	AAA	Bonds are judged to be of the highest quality, with a minimal credit risk
AA+ AA AA−	Aa+ Aa Aa−	AA+ AA AA−	Bonds are judged to be of high quality, with a very low credit risk
A+ A A−	A+ A A−	A+ A A−	Bonds are judged to be of upper medium grade, with a low credit risk
BBB+ BBB BBB−	Baa+ Baa Baa−	BBB+ BBB BBB−	Bonds are judged to be of good credit quality, with a moderate credit risk
BB+ BB BB−	Ba+ Ba Ba−	BB+ BB BB−	Bonds are judged to have speculative elements and are subject to a significant credit risk
B+ B B−	B+ B B−	B+ B B−	Bonds are judged to be speculative and are subject to a high credit risk
CCC+ CCC CCC−	Caa+ Caa Caa−	CCC+ CCC CCC−	Bonds are judged to be of poor standing and are subject to a very high credit risk
CC	Ca	CC	Bonds are highly speculative, with a default of some kind probable
		C	Default is expected imminently
D	C	DDD DD D	Bonds in default With Fitch ratings, DDD indicates an expected recovery rate of 90 %–100 %, DD a recovery rate of 50 %–90 % and D less than 50 %

major exceptions. Neither US Treasury dollar issues nor UK gilt-edged sterling securities are rated, although the UK Government did get an AAA rating for their non-sterling bonds.

The bond credit ratings for all three rating agencies go from AAA or Aaa for the most secure debt to D for debt that is in default. Some of the major rating categories are further subdivided into three sections to denote their standing within the category. This is shown by adding a plus (+), no suffix or adding a minus (−). The relative ratings are shown in Table 8.3. It should be noted that bonds rated BBB− or Baa− or above are considered to be investment grade investments, whereas bonds rated below this are regarded as 'speculative grade'. Speculative grade bonds are also called 'junk bonds' or 'high-yield bonds'.

Bond ratings are obviously reviewed on a regular basis. Table 8.4, compiled by Moody, shows how over a 30 year period the different corporate bond rating categories have changed over a five year time horizon.[3] The table shows that on average over a five year period, 56.0 % of originally Aaa rated bonds are still rated Aaa, but that 23.3 % have been downgraded to Aa

---

[3] Since this survey is based on bonds rated by Moody, it is heavily biased to US securities.

Table 8.4 Five year corporate bond rating / default transition rates 1970–2001

From rating	To rating								
	Aaa	Aa	A	Baa	Ba	B	Caa–C	Default	Withdrawn*
Aaa	56.0	23.3	5.0	0.5	0.5	0.2	0.1	0.1	14.4
Aa	4.5	52.0	23.3	3.6	0.9	0.3	0.0	1.3	15.1
A	0.3	8.2	58.3	13.7	3.0	0.8	0.1	0.4	15.3
Baa	0.2	1.6	15.8	47.1	9.6	2.4	0.3	1.6	21.4
Ba	0.1	0.3	2.9	12.6	33.0	10.6	0.7	8.2	31.7
B	0.1	0.1	0.5	2.9	13.3	30.4	1.6	19.6	31.6
Caa-C	0.0	0.0	0.0	2.2	6.1	7.7	16.2	41.9	25.9

* A bond that has been withdrawn will usually have matured, been called or brought private.
Source: Moody (2002). © Moody's Investors Service, Inc and/or its affiliates. Reprinted with permission. All Rights Reserved.

and a further 5.0 % to A, but only 0.1 % have defaulted. On the other hand, of those bonds that were rated B, less than 1 % have been upgraded to A or better and 19.6 % have gone into default.

As you would expect, the strength of the economy affects the default rates in a significant way. Figure 8.1 illustrates this very well. Over the 20 year period, the average one year default rate is 1.5 %, but it has been below 0.5 % and over 4 %.

8.2 LIQUIDITY

Liquidity should not be confused in any way with market risk. For example, there are AAA rated products with very little liquidity and speculative grade securities that are very liquid. Defining liquidity is not a precise science, with many people having different definitions. However, one definition from a public market issuer covers many of the relevant points:

> A liquid issue is one in which two way markets are made available to investors in reasonable size over an extended period without undue disruptions or difficulties in establishing fair value.

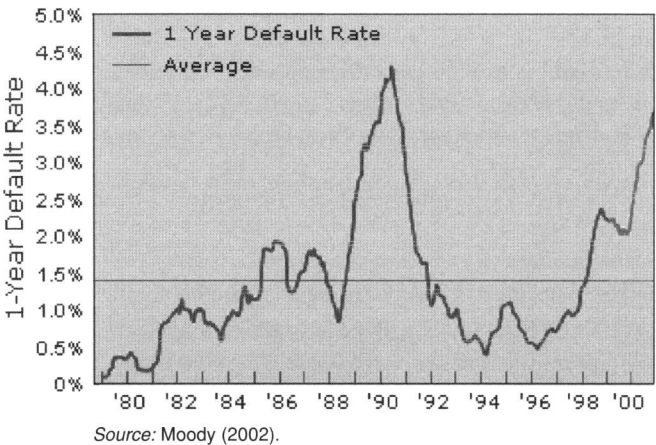

Figure 8.1 Default rates varying over time. © Moody's Investors Service, Inc and/or its affiliates. Reprinted with permission. All Rights Reserved.

This definition obviously has many caveats. However, in principle it should mean that if investors hold liquid bonds then, if they want to sell them before maturity, they can do so at a fair price. As you would expect, investors are prepared to pay for liquidity, because it gives them an option, which is not available with an illiquid issue.

Let us now consider some of the positive and negative factors that determine liquidity:

- *Name of issuer.*
  If the issuer is either a well-known company or a government, then the issue is more likely to be liquid. In a previous chapter, we discussed the type of collateral used for repo transactions. In Europe, the majority of the collateral was provided by central government debt, and partially as a result, such debt is likely to be among the most liquid.
- *Size of issue.*
  Usually the larger the issue the more liquid.
- *Denominations.*
  Some bonds are only issued with denominations of at least €100 000 or equivalent in another currency. Such bonds, where the minimum trading size is the minimum denomination, are not designed to be liquid. In Europe most domestic government debt is now tradeable in units of €1.00 or less.
- *Currency of issue.*
  The holders of a bond issue are no longer just from one country. For example, look at the Chinese investment in US Treasury issues. If an investor predicts that the currency of a bond issue is likely to depreciate against another currency, then the investor will not want to invest in it even if it is relatively cheap compared with other bonds denominated in the same currency.
- *Credit rating.*
  Although above it was stressed that liquidity and credit rating are two separate measures, the credit rating of a bond does have an effect on its liquidity, as some fund managers are not allowed to hold bonds that are rated below a certain level. This level is often set at whether they are rated as investment grade (at least BBB− or Baa−) or not, but sometimes it is set higher.
- *Complexity of structure.*
  If a bond does not include any embedded options, e.g. it is a fixed-rate option-free bullet bond, then as it makes it very easy to value and compare with other similar bonds, it tends to be more liquid than bonds with embedded options. Similarly, the more complicated the embedded option, the less liquid it is likely to be. In fact, some options are designed for specific investors, who are expected normally to hold the bond until maturity. Bond investors like to have certainty about future cash flows when evaluating how much a bond is worth, with the result that even a straightforward call option that is exercisable imminently can reduce its liquidity.
- *Number of market makers.*
  In the eurobond markets, over a number of years it has been observed that the most liquid securities are those with five or more committed market makers. However, this measure may be regarded as a 'chicken and egg' situation – which came first?
- *Bid/offer price spread.*
  The smaller the market maker's bid/offer price spread, the more liquid the bond is likely to be, since the market maker believes that he or she will be able to transact the other side of the trade at a profit. As a word of caution, except in some regulated mainly domestic

government markets, the market maker can instantaneously drastically increase the quoted spread.

- *Benchmark status.*

  Bonds that have benchmark status and/or are included in bond market liquid indices are likely to be more liquid than similar bonds that are not.

- *Initial number of bond holders.*

  If, when the bond is initially issued, the majority of the bonds are placed with only a handful of investors, the bond is unlikely to be very liquid. In such cases, the bond may even have been constructed to meet their specific needs, and as a result there is a high expectancy that they will be long-term holders.

- *Years since issue.*

  Except in the case of government and similar issues, which are used for stock lending and collateral and which may be increased in size by new tranche issues, the longer it is since the bond was issued the less liquid it is likely to be. This is partly due to the fact that after a while a significant proportion of the bonds end up in the portfolios of pension funds and insurance companies, who are long-term holders.

9
Swaps, Futures and Derivatives

The global capital markets have considerably increased their use of derivatives over the last twenty years or so. It is the flexibility of derivative instruments, which can be created to allow for almost any financial activity or credit risk, that has helped to make them so popular. Derivatives come in many forms: swaps, forward rate agreements, futures, credit default swaps, options and many combinations of the above such as swaptions.

9.1 SWAPS

The swap market over recent years has grown considerably, with the result that it is now very large and very flexible. According to a survey, conducted by the Bank for International Settlements (BIS),[1] of the OTC (over-the-counter) derivatives market activity in the second half of 2004, the notional amounts outstanding at the end of December 2004 of interest rate contracts amounted to some $187 trillion with a gross market value of $5.3 trillion. Of these, the majority were interest rate swaps (see Figure 9.1).

Interest rate OTC contracts tend to have a much longer life than repos, which frequently have an initial maturity of under one month. Of the outstanding OTC interest rate contracts, over 25 % of them had an outstanding life to maturity of over five years and about two-thirds over one year (see Figure 9.2). Similarly, the most popular currency is now the euro, where the activity represents 8.4 % more of the total activity than the US dollar (see Figure 9.3).

The majority of swaps include synthetic securities that are often constructed in part from cash market securities and may include currency exchange rates. In addition to 'interest rate swaps', which are the most important, there are several other types of swaps, e.g. 'asset swaps', 'basis swaps', 'cross-currency swaps' and 'forward rate agreements'.

9.1.1 Interest rate swap

There are in the main two different types of debt, fixed-rate and floating-rate. The value of fixed-rate debt changes if interest rates change, but the interest payments remain unchanged. If interest rates rise then its price drops and vice versa. On the other hand, the value of floating-rate debt normally remains close to par irrespective of the changes in the interest rates, which are usually reset near the beginning of each coupon period. A holder of a fixed-rate bond may feel that interest rates are going to rise over the next few years, or the income from this bond has to service an obligation where the payments vary with the short-term interest rate. In either case the holder would like to switch the income flow from fixed to floating. An interest rate swap enables this to be done.

An interest rate swap between two parties involves one party exchanging a stream of fixed-rate coupon payments, frequently from a cash bond market instrument, for floating-rate coupon

---

[1] The official website of the Bank of International Settlements is www.bis.org.

124   An Introduction to the Bond Markets

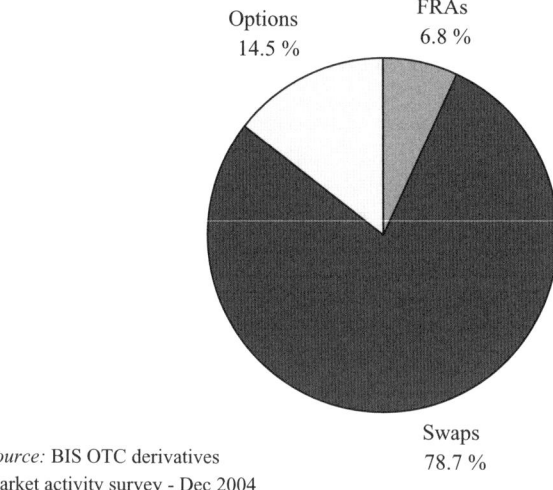

Figure 9.1 Interest rate contract types. Reproduced by permission of the Bank for International Settlements.

payments from the other party. In some currencies it is possible to agree such swaps for periods of up to 30 years. The fixed-rate payer is said to have 'received' (the floating-rate interest) or 'bought' the swap, and is also referred to as being 'long' in the swap. The floating-rate payer, as you would expect, is referred to as having 'sold' or being 'short' in the swap.

If, during the life of the swap, interest rates rise, the buyer who pays a fixed rate of interest will make a profit. Similarly, if they fall, the buyer will make a loss.

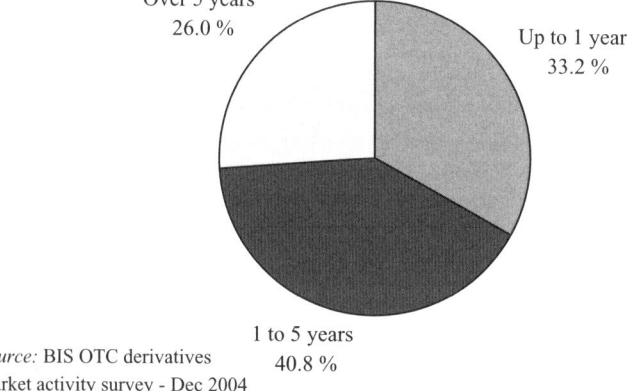

Figure 9.2 Interest rate contracts – residual life. Reproduced by permission of the Bank for International Settlements.

OTC Interest Rate Contracts
Currency distribution

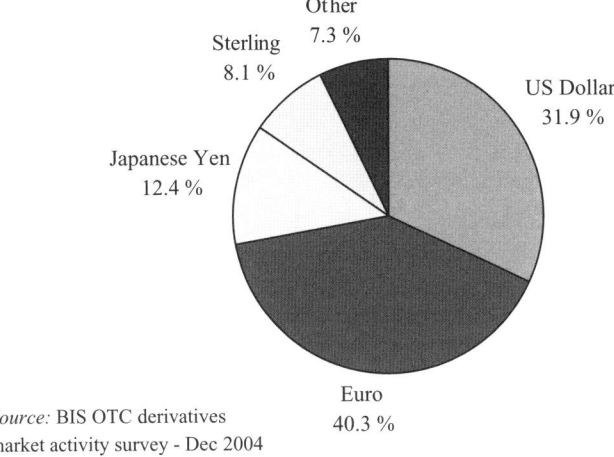

Source: BIS OTC derivatives market activity survey - Dec 2004

Figure 9.3 Interest rate contracts – currencies. Reproduced by permission of the Bank for International Settlements.

Example 9.1

An interest rate swap has been agreed between two parties A and B, whereby party A agrees to give party B semi-annual payments at an annual rate of 4.2 % on a nominal amount of CHF 10 million, in exchange for party B giving a six month LIBOR plus 50 basis points for a period of three years based on the same nominal amount. The six month Swiss franc LIBOR rates are to be set at the current rate two business days before the start of each six month period.

The interest payments agreed by the parties are:

Six month period	A receives	B receives
1	(LIBOR + 50)/2	2.1
2	(LIBOR + 50)/2	2.1
3	(LIBOR + 50)/2	2.1
4	(LIBOR + 50)/2	2.1
5	(LIBOR + 50)/2	2.1
6	(LIBOR + 50)/2	2.1

Using this example, if the LIBOR rates for each of the six semi-annual periods are 4.1 %, 4.5 %, 4.0 %, 3.5 %, 3.2 % and 3.8 % respectively, then the individual payments each party would receive will be as shown in Figure 9.4.

As can be seen in the above example, one party pays a fixed annual amount of 4.2 %, whereas the other pays LIBOR + 50 basis points. In order to standardize the quotations that market makers provide, the floating rate is set equal to the base floating-rate index and the fixed rate is adjusted appropriately. For example, sterling rates are quoted against LIBOR and euro ones

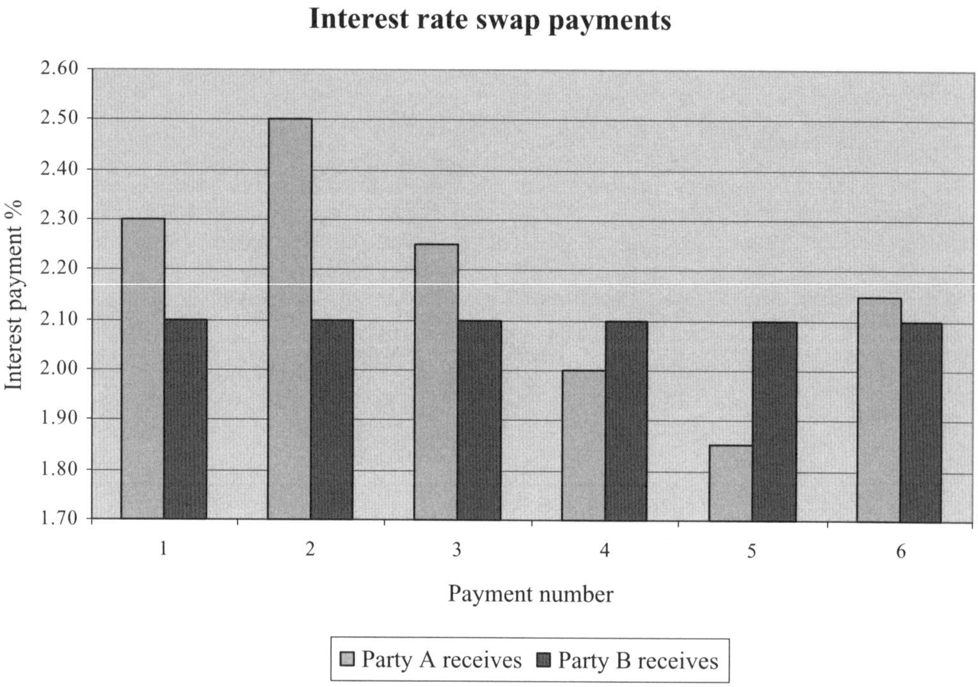

Interest rate swap payments

Figure 9.4 Swap agreement payments.

against either EURIBOR or LIBOR. Thus, in the example, the deal was struck at a swap rate of $(4.2 - 0.5) = 3.7\%$.

Program 9.1 Swap

The program enables the user to enter the details of an interest rate swap, together with details of the projected yield curve of the floating-rate indicator-rate. It then calculates and displays the projected cash flows, and calculates the returns for both parties.

Table 9.1 shows an extract from a table of quoted interest rate swap rates in October 2005. On screen services, this quotation is often followed by the spread in basis points of the swap rate over the government benchmark security for that maturity date.

Short-dated swap spreads are influenced by the yields in the cash markets and the yield on futures. Longer-dated swaps are regarded as a combination of a long position in a fixed-rate corporate bond and a short position in a floating-rate note. Thus the swap spread is highly influenced by the credit spread on fixed and floating corporate debt. Table 9.2 shows the relationship between benchmark US Treasury bond yields and the US dollar swap yields in October 2005. As you can see the dollar swap curve is some 40 to 50 basis points above the US Treasury curve. The curves are shown graphically in Figure 9.5.

Table 9.1 Quoted interest rate swap rates

	Euro €		£ sterling	
27 October 2005	Bid	Ask	Bid	Ask
1 year	2.54	2.57	4.64	4.66
2 years	2.74	2.77	4.62	4.66
3 years	2.88	2.91	4.66	4.70
4 years	2.98	3.02	4.67	4.72
5 years	3.08	3.12	4.69	4.74
....				
10 years	3.50	3.53	4.71	4.76
....				
20 years	3.87	3.90	4.55	4.68
25 years	3.93	3.96	4.50	4.62
30 years	3.95	3.98	4.44	4.57

Source: International Swaps and Derivatives Association Inc., (ISDA®).

Table 9.2 Relationship between benchmark US Treasury bond yields and US dollar swap yields in October 2005

Period	Bid yield on benchmark US Treasury	Swap bid yield (US $)	Swap spread (basis points)
2 years	4.36	4.76	40
5 years	4.44	4.89	45
10 years	4.57	5.04	47
25 years	4.78	5.26	48

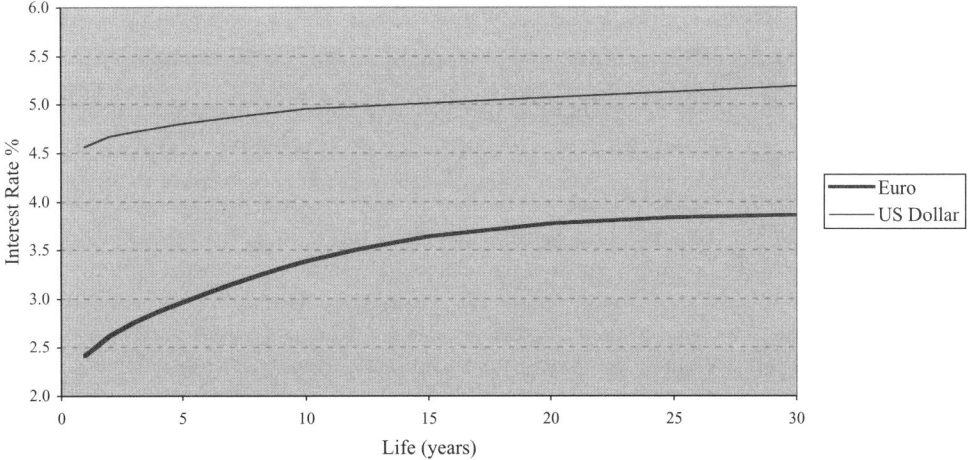

Figure 9.5 US dollar and euro swap curves.
Source: International Swaps and Derivatives Association Inc., (ISDA®). ISDAFIX® is a registered trademark of ISDA.

Table 9.3 ISDAFIX daily interest swap rates

Currency	Maturities (years)
CHF	1–10
EUR – EURIBOR	1–10, 12, 15, 20, 25 and 30
EUR – LIBOR	1–10, 12, 15, 20, 25 and 30
GBP	1–10
HKD	1–5, 7 and 10
JPY	1–10, 12, 15, 20, 25 and 30
USD	1–10 and 30
USD spreads	1–10 and 30

In order to establish a recognized benchmark for swap rates the International Swaps and Derivatives Association (ISDA) in cooperation with Reuters and Garban-ICAP established ISDAFIX in 1998, which provides on a daily basis a benchmark for fixed rates, against LIBOR or EURIBOR, on interest rate swaps for six currencies and selected maturities. ISDAFIX rates are based on mid-day, and in some markets end-of-day, polling of mid-market rates. These rates are referred to in the 2000 ISDA definitions and can be used in connection with swap terminations, marking a portfolio to market, and for various exchange products, such as on LIFFE. ISDAFIX provides daily data on the currencies and maturities as given in Table 9.3.

If we now look at the structure of a plain vanilla interest rate swap, you will see that it consists of the following components:

- One side of the swap offers a fixed rate of interest for the period of the swap.
- The other side pays a floating rate of interest which is set equal to a major floating-rate interest rate (such as LIBOR, EURIBOR or the US Prime Rate, in the appropriate currency and for the appropriate period). Each payment is determined in advance just before the start of the coupon payment.
- The payment frequency of the two interest streams is the same. They will usually be quarterly, semi-annually or annually.
- The period of the swap may be for up 30 years.
- The amount of the principal on which the swap is based does not change during the swap's life.

Needless to say, as this is a derivatives market, any of the characteristics can change to meet the clients need. Some of the variations are discussed below.

Sometimes for presentation or accounting reasons the parties to a swap do not want to record an interest rate swap as one where the exchange was a fixed rate r against LIBOR or EURIBOR. Instead they want to record it with the rates for both sides increased by a margin, e.g. as a swap for a fixed rate $(r + m)$ against a floating rate of LIBOR $+ m$. Such an interest rate swap is called a 'margin swap'.

It is possible for the floating-rate interest payment frequency to be different to that of the fixed leg. For example, in the euro interest rate swap market nearly all the fixed-rate bonds pay annual coupons, but for all maturities over one year the rates are compared against a six month EURIBOR/LIBOR.

Sometimes the floating-rate payments for a period are determined in arrears as opposed to in advance, as is normal.

A 'zero-coupon' interest rate swap may replace the fixed coupon payments which replaces the flow of coupon payments by a single payment at either the beginning or the end of the swap agreement.

It is possible for the principal amount of the swap to change over its life. The amount of principal could even decrease to zero, as occurs with an annuity.

Let us now consider how it may be possible for two companies to reduce their borrowing costs by swapping their cash flows.

Example 9.2

Consider two companies, A and B, whose borrowing costs for a £100 million loan for 10 years are:

Company A   Fixed rate 6% or floating rate LIBOR + 100 basis points; would prefer to pay floating rate

Company B   Fixed rate 6.75% or floating rate LIBOR + 150 basis points; would prefer to pay fixed

If there is no swap, Company A will pay LIBOR + 100 basis points and Company B 6.75%. The two companies directly, or more generally through an intermediary, agree to raise the monies as fixed for Company A and floating for Company B and swap the following income streams: A pays B LIBOR and receives from B 5.10% on the full amount of the loans (see Figure 9.6).

As a result of the swap the cost of raising the monies for A becomes:

$$6.00 + \text{LIBOR} - 5.10 = \text{LIBOR} + 0.90 - \text{a saving of 10 basis points}$$

For company B the cost becomes:

$$\text{LIBOR} + 1.50 + 5.10 - \text{LIBOR} = 6.60\% - \text{a saving of 15 basis points}$$

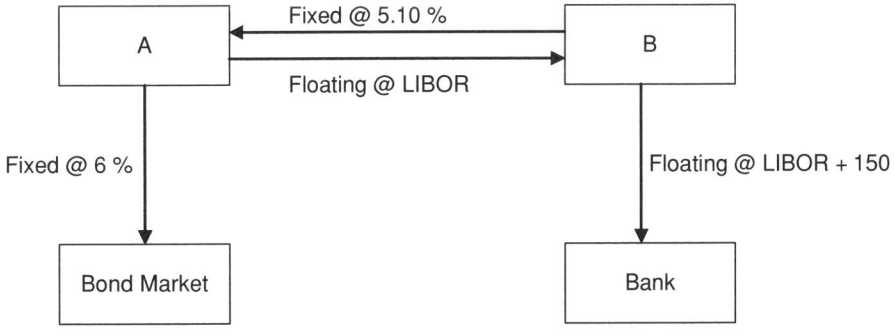

Figure 9.6 Company income stream swap.

130   An Introduction to the Bond Markets

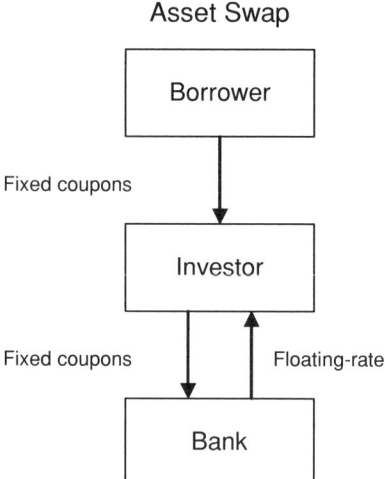

Figure 9.7 Asset swap.

9.1.2 Asset swap

An investor holds an investment that pays a fixed rate of interest. The investor would like to swap this interest stream to a floating-rate one as the expenditure varies according to short-term interest rates. This can be achieved by going to an investment bank who will swap the fixed-rate interest stream for a floating-rate one. Such an arrangement is called an 'asset swap' (Figure 9.7).

Example 9.3

An investor holds €50 million of a fixed-rate three year bond which pays annual coupons of 4 %. The investor is happy to hold the bond until maturity, but would prefer to have floating-rate coupons. As a result, the investor approaches a bank that is prepared to swap the coupon payments received for floating-rate payments equal to 12 month EURIBOR + 100 basis points payable annually on the coupon payment date. The EURIBOR rate, which is used in the calculations, will be the closing rate two business days before the start of the coupon period.

If the EURIBOR rate for the first year is 2.9 %, then after one year the investor will give the bank $50\,000\,000 \times 4/100 = €2\,000\,000$ and will receive $50\,000\,000 \times (2.9 + 1)/100 = €1\,950\,000$ from the bank. This process will be repeated for the following two years.

9.1.3 Cross-currency swap

A 'cross-currency swap' is similar to an interest rate swap, except that now the swapped streams of payments are in different currencies. The two streams may now be fixed rate and floating rate, as is normal with an interest rate swap, or both fixed rate or both floating rate. At the beginning of the swap, the counterparties normally swap the nominal amount of the two currencies at the current exchange rate. At the end, they swap back the nominal amounts at the original exchange rate. Hence at the end of the swap there is no exchange rate profit or loss. However, during the life of the swap there may be considerable credit risk due to a change in the exchange rates. As a result, in the agreement the parties may agree to post collateral with each other to compensate for any imbalance.

The cash flows involved in a cross-currency swap are illustrated in the following example.

Example 9.4

Company A has just issued $160 million of a fixed-rate bond at par. The bond pays an annual coupon rate of 6% paid semi-annually, and will be redeemed in five years' time. The company wants to invest the proceeds of this issue in a project in the UK and pay interest at a floating rate.

The company goes to a bank to arrange a five year cross-currency swap as follows (see Figure 9.8):

- The bank swaps the principal from the sale of the bonds ($160 million) into £100 million, based on a current exchange rate of $1.60 = £1.
- The bank agrees to swap a stream of sterling payments based on a nominal of £100 million and at interest rate of six month sterling LIBOR plus 100 basis points for a stream of fixed-rate coupons based on a nominal of $160 million with an annual coupon of 6% paid

Start – Exchange of Capital

Periodic coupon swaps

End – Exchange of Capital

Figure 9.8 Cross-currency swap.

semi-annually. In this way the income stream received from the bank is just sufficient to service the coupon payments on the bond.
- After five years the swap contract and the bond issue mature. The payments stop and the principals are exchanged back at the original exchange rate. The company now has sufficient dollar funds to redeem the bond issue.

9.1.4 Basis swap

A 'basis' swap is very similar to an interest rate swap, except that now both parties to the agreement exchange floating-rate cash flows. There are innumerable varieties of cash flows that can be exchanged. Some examples are:

- The parties agree to swap interest on a nominal of €100 million. Party A agrees to swap interest calculated on the basis of the one year euro swap rate plus 20 basis points, in exchange for interest on the ten year euro swap rate. This swap is in effect a derivative based on the shape of the euro swap yield curve during the life of the contract.
- The parties agree to swap interest based on the US prime rate with that of the dollar LIBOR in London.
- The parties agree to swap interest based on $100 million nominal at a rate of 6 month US dollar LIBOR with an equivalent cash flow stream based on 6 month euro EURIBOR plus 200 basis points. Normally at the beginning of the agreement, the two parties also exchange the principal amounts of the two currencies. At the end of the swap agreement, the currencies are swapped back at the original exchange rate.

9.1.5 Forward rate agreement

A 'forward rate agreement' (FRA) is essentially a special type of interest rate swap. With an FRA there is a swap of a single fixed-rate payment against a floating-rate payment. The agreement refers to a single period that starts at a date in the future. The floating-rate interest payment is normally determined two working days before the start of the period. At this time the profit or loss on the transaction can be calculated. This difference is now payable at the beginning instead of at the end of the forward rate agreement period, but to compensate for this the amount due is discounted by the floating-rate interest rate.

Example 9.5

Consider the following forward rate agreement. In 2005, party A agrees to exchange with party B the income earned on $10 million nominal at a rate of 5% per annum with that earned on a six month US dollar LIBOR, for the six month period between 15 January 2009 and 15 July 2009.

On 13 January 2009, two days before the start of the forward rate agreement, the quoted rate for the six month US dollar LIBOR is 4%. As a result of this FRA,

$$\begin{array}{ll} \text{Party A owes party B} & 0.05 \times 10\,000\,000/2 = \$250\,000 \\ \text{Party B owes party A} & 0.04 \times 10\,000\,000/2 = \$200\,000 \end{array}$$

Net position:

$$\text{Party A owes party B} = \$50\,000$$

The net amount is discounted back to 15 January 2009 at a discount rate of 4%. Thus, on 15 January 2009, party A owes party B:

$$50\,000/(1 + 0.04/2) = \$49\,019.61$$

Program 9.2 FRA

This program allows users to enter the terms of a forward rate agreement (FRA). It calculates the associated profit/loss for the parties.

9.2 CREDIT RISK IN SWAPS

If a bank makes an unsecured loan of, say, $100 million to a company for three years, then the bank is at risk that the company may go bankrupt during this time and as a result it could lose a substantial part of this loan. The credit risk is much less with interest swaps, as it is only the income streams that have been swapped, but it still exists.

If you consider a 30 year interest rate swap, during its life interest rates can vary considerably, with the result that the amounts payable and receivable on the swap can get very much out of line. For example, if a swap is taken out when interest rates are 3% and they rise to 9%, then the floating-rate payer will have to pay three times as much as when the contract started. If the floating-rate payer defaults with, say, 10 years of the contract still to run, then the fixed-rate payer would lose out on a very profitable contract. To compensate for this, the swap agreement might include a clause to evaluate the credit risk (mark-to-market) on a regular basis and for the losing party to post an appropriate amount of collateral with the winning party.

9.3 SWAPTIONS

A 'swaption' is just an option on a swap. The buyer of a swaption has the option but not the obligation to purchase an interest rate swap agreement during the life of the option. The terms of the agreement will specify whether the buyer is a fixed-rate payer or a floating-rate payer. The counterparty to the swaption (the seller or writer) becomes the counterparty to the interest rate swap if the buyer exercises the option.

Swaptions are valued in the same way as other options. Similarly, the profit and loss profiles for the buyers and the writers are very similar. A buyer of a swaption cannot lose more than the initial cost, unless of course the buyer exercises the option.

9.4 FUTURES

A future contract is an agreement between two parties that commits them to exchange some goods at a specified rate at a specified future date. Futures trading, especially in commodities, has been around for a very long time. Today most of the trading in financial derivative futures products is conducted on an exchange as opposed to being on the over-the-counter market. This inevitably means that the contracts have become a lot more standardized.

In the US both the Chicago Board of Trade (CBOT) and the Chicago Mercantile Exchange (CME) trade a number of interest rate futures and options products, such as those listed below.

CBOT
30 year US Treasury bond
10 year US Treasury note
5 year US Treasury note
2 year US Treasury note
10 year interest rate swap
5 year interest rate swap
30 day Federal funds
10 year municipal note index

CME
10 year swap rate
5 year swap rate
2 year swap rate
13 week US T-Bill
Eurodollar
Eurodollar – forward rate agreement
Euroyen
Euroyen – LIBOR
LIBOR

In Europe, much of the bond derivatives trading is conducted on Euronext.Liffe or EUREX. Together they offer a range of futures and options on futures products. The following lists some of the available futures contracts.

Euronext.Liffe and EUREX futures products
One-month EONIA indexed futures
One-month EURIBOR futures
Three-month EURIBOR interest rate futures
Three-month LIBOR interest rate futures
Three-month sterling interest rate futures
Three-month EuroSwiss interest rate futures
Three-month Euroyen interest rate futures
Short-term German Government futures (Schatz)
Medium-term German Government futures (BOBL)
Long-term German Government futures (BUND)
Very long-term German Government futures (BUXL)
Long-term gilt futures
Long-term Swiss Government futures
Long-term Japanese Government bond futures

In addition, it is possible to trade options on some of these products. For example, there are exchange tradeable options on the CME eurodollar, LIBOR and euroyen products, and in

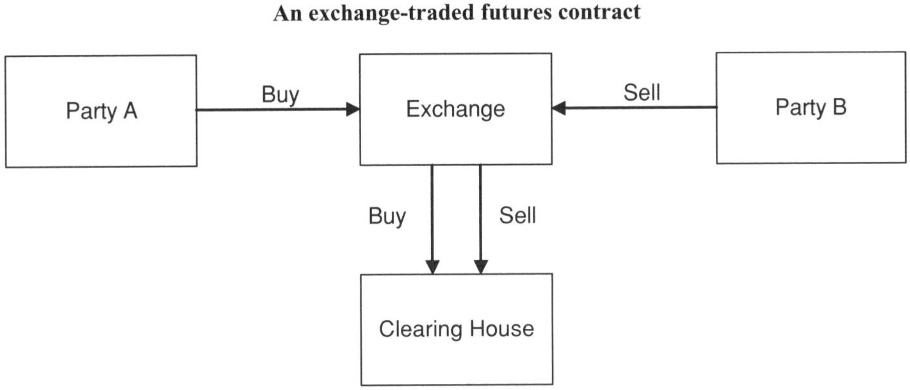

An exchange-traded futures contract

Figure 9.9 Exchange-traded futures transaction.

Europe on the German Government short-, medium- and long-term futures contracts and on the long-term gilt future.

When a party A buys an exchange-traded futures contract from another party B, the exchange arranges for a 'clearing house' to intervene and become the counterparty of both A and B (see Figure 9.9). In this way, neither A nor B are subject to any credit risk. For taking over this responsibility, the clearing house will charge both parties an 'initial margin' and will calculate on a daily basis how much 'variation margin' is needed to cover any trading losses of any open positions. The position of the clearing house also enables the parties to close out their positions, by selling the same contract if they previously bought, or vice versa, as the clearing house is the counterparty to all trades.

A purchaser of a futures contract can either let the contract run to maturity or can close it out at any time between the trade date and the maturity date. When the purchaser closes out the position in a contract, usually at a different price, an immediate profit or loss is established.

Most of the exchange contracts work in a similar way. Two of the most liquid contracts, the CBOT 10 year US Treasury note futures contract (Table 9.4) and the long-term gilts futures contract as traded on Euronext.Liffe (Table 9.5) are examined and compared.

If the Treasury note contract is not closed out prior to delivery, the seller of the contract has to deliver the chosen bond and the purchaser has to pay a price that is dependent on the bond that is being delivered. In order to make all the deliverable bonds have approximately the same value, the exchange calculates a 'conversion factor' for each deliverable bond. The conversion factor is the price that the delivered note would have if it were to yield 6%, compounded semi-annually, divided by 100. Thus the conversion factor is greater than one if the bond has a coupon greater than 6% and less than one if its coupon is less than 6%. The buyer of the contract has to pay:

$$\text{Futures price} \times \text{conversion factor} + \text{accrued interest}$$

where the accrued interest is that of the delivered bond.

Table 9.5 shows that at any one time there are three different long-term gilt contracts that can be traded. If you are in January, then you can trade the contracts for delivery in March, June and September, but not December. Every day the exchange calculates the 'exchange delivery settlement price' (EDSP). The final EDSP is normally the average traded price during the last trading day for the contract.

Table 9.4 CBOT 10 year US Treasury note futures contract

Contract size	US Treasury note having a notional value of $100 000 and a coupon of 6 %
Delivery months	March, June, September and December
Quotation	Per point ($1000)
Minimum price movement (tick size and value)	In multiples of one-half of 1/32 point per 100 points ($15.625 rounded up to the nearest cent per contract), except for intermonth spread, where the minimum price fluctuation shall be one-quarter of 1/32 point per 100 points ($7.8125 per contract)
Last trading day	Seventh business day preceding the last business day of the month
Last delivery day	Last business day of the delivery month
Trading hours	Open auction: 7:20 am–2:00 pm US Central time, Monday–Friday Electronic: 6:00 pm–4:00 pm US Central time, Sunday–Friday
Contract standard	The seller of a contract, which has not been closed out prior to the maturity date, has to deliver US Treasury notes maturing at least $6\frac{1}{2}$ years, but not more than 10 years, from the first day of the delivery month

If you buy one long-term gilt futures contract, you have committed yourself to purchasing £100 000 nominal of a theoretical 10 year 6 % gilt-edged stock on the delivery date. Since this bond does not exist, the exchange allows the seller of the option to deliver instead a fixed amount of selected gilt-edged stocks, which have a life to maturity of between $8\frac{3}{4}$ years and 13 years. (This is a longer maturity profile than the CBOT 10 year Treasury note futures contract.) Similarly, the deliverable stocks will have different values in the cash market. As a result, a few days before the delivery date, the exchange will calculate the theoretical value P for each of the deliverable bonds. This price is the price the bond would have if it were to yield 6 %, compounded semi-annually. A ratio (the 'price factor') $P/100$ is then calculated for each bond.

Table 9.5 Long-term Euronext.Liffe gilts futures contract

Contract size	£100 000 nominal amount of a 6 % bond
Delivery months	March, June, September and December, such that the nearest three delivery months are available for trading
Quotation	Per £100 nominal
Minimum price movement (tick size and value)	0.01 (£10)
Last trading day	11:00, two business days prior to the last business day in the delivery month
Delivery day	Any business day in the delivery month
Trading hours	08:00–18:00
Contract standard	The seller of a contract, which has not been closed out prior to the maturity date, has to deliver gilts, which are on the exchange's delivery list. In general terms, this means that any standard gilt with a remaining life of between $8\frac{3}{4}$ years and 13 years on the first day of the relevant delivery month, and has an outstanding amount in issue in excess of £1.5 billion

If the buyer of a contract has not closed out the position the buyer has to pay an amount for each contract equal to:

$$1000 \times \text{EDSP} \times \text{price factor} + \text{accrued interest}$$

where:

EDSP   exchange delivery settlement price for the notice day
Accrued interest   interest calculated to the settlement day

The seller of a contract, who has not closed out the position prior to the delivery date, has to deliver £100 000 of nominal of his or her chosen deliverable bond.

It can be seen that the terms of the two contracts are very similar. The method of calculating the conversion or price factor in the above contracts means that some bonds are cheaper to deliver than others. The market players always calculate which bond is likely to be the 'cheapest to deliver' in the few days before the contract matures. This, in turn, can increase the price of this bond relative to its peer group.

In addition, in the US market, it is possible by buying and selling the 2 year, 5 year, 10 year and 30 year Treasury note and bond futures to protect oneself from a major change in the shape of the US Treasury yield curve, as any change is likely to change the spread between the prices of at least two of the futures contracts.

9.5 CREDIT DEFAULT SWAPS

A 'credit default swap' (CDS) is basically an insurance policy against a specified credit risk. A credit default swap most frequently consists of a corporate bond investor buying protection against a default by the issuer of the bond. However, these investments can also be used to protect the investor from other types of corporate credit risk. For example, credit default swaps can be created to protect the buyer from:

- a corporate bankruptcy;
- failure of the issuer to pay interest or a repayment of the principal;
- debt restructuring in a way that is unfavourable to the debt holders;
- debt obligations becoming due before the original scheduled redemption date;
- the bond being downgraded to an unacceptable rating.

A CDS contract can allow the owner of a bond to remove the relevant credit risk from its portfolio by transferring the specified risk to another party without transferring the title to the underlying bond. Prior to the emergence of credit default swaps there was no readily available vehicle that enabled this to be done. This has proved enormously popular and credit default swaps now represent a very significant proportion of the global credit derivatives market.

In a credit default swap (see Figure 9.10), one party 'sells' risk and the other counterparty 'buys' that risk. The 'seller', usually the holder of the bond or other instrument, of the credit risk pays a periodic fee to the risk 'buyer'. In return, the risk buyer agrees to pay the seller if there is a default.

The settlement terms of the CDS are determined when the contract is written. If the default event occurs, then this often involves exchanging the bonds at their par value, although alternatively there may be a cash settlement, where the buyer of the risk pays the seller an amount equal to the difference between the current market price and par.

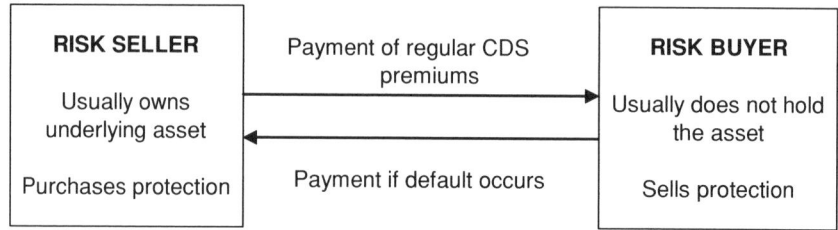

Figure 9.10 Credit default swap.

Example 9.6

A five year CDS has been agreed between an investor A and a bank B, whereby if there is a default during the period of the agreement in bond X, then bank B will pay A an amount equal to the difference between par and the current market price of bond X. The agreement is for a nominal amount of CHF 10 million.

A relevant default does occur in bond X, and after the event the bond is priced in the market at 40. As a result bank B has to pay A an amount equal to:

$$10\,000\,000 \times \left(\frac{100 - 40}{100}\right) = \text{CHF } 6\,000\,000$$

Credit default swaps range in maturity from one year to 10 years although the five year CDS is the most frequently traded. They can refer to a single bond or other asset, or they may be based on a portfolio of credits or even a CDS index.

Investors are not obliged to own the underlying bond or other assets and can trade the credit default swap, which can be tailored to their specific needs, separately, with the result that the liquidity in the CDS market can be much greater than in the market of the underlying instrument. In particular, credit default swaps allow parties to:

- access maturity periods, which are not available in the cash markets;
- access credit risk in the bond market, where there is only a very limited supply of the underlying bonds;
- remove the currency risk from foreign currency credits.

Prices on credit default swaps are quoted in basis points, which represents the annual cost of protection against default of a principal of 100.

Example 9.7

Suppose that an investor has been quoted 50 basis points for a five year CDS on a Ford issue. If the investor wants to protect an investment of $10 million nominal, then the annual cost will be:

$$10\,000\,000 \times 0.50/100 = \$50\,000$$

As you can imagine, the cost of a CDS can change extremely rapidly. The cost of CDS contracts can also vary considerably within an overall group structure. In the case of General Motors, for most of 2005 the cost of CDS protection for its bond issues was somewhat more than that for the bonds of its profitable financing arm subsidiary GMAC. The gap increased considerably following its announcement in October 2005 of its intention to sell a significant stake in GMAC, thus decoupling the CDS ratings.

10
Portfolio and Other Considerations

10.1 HOLDING PERIOD RETURNS

A portfolio manager, or for that matter any investor, may want to liquidate a portfolio of bonds at a specified date, the horizon date, in the future. Needless to say, the portfolio manager would like to have a certain amount of confidence in the amount of money that would be received at this date. In achieving this objective, the portfolio manager is presented with several challenges:

- Would any coupons received before the horizon date be able to be reinvested at a satisfactory rate?
- Would the proceeds of any redemption amounts received before the horizon date be able to be reinvested at a satisfactory rate?
- What will be the value of the bond portfolio at the horizon date?
- Would it be possible to redeem any outstanding bonds at a 'fair' value? This can sometimes be a problem as the market makers may widen the spreads considerably for all but the most liquid bonds.

The portfolio manager can solve this problem if he or she can find and invest in either zero-coupon bonds or bond strips of suitable quality that yield an appropriate amount and mature on the horizon date. This is because there are no coupons or redemption proceeds to reinvest and, irrespective of movements in interest rates, the value of the portfolio at the horizon date will equal its redemption amounts. Unfortunately, such a satisfactory solution very rarely exists.

Let us now consider the performance of a single bond from now until a horizon date in five years' time. The bond, which has been trading at a price of around 100, pays an annual coupon of 5 % and will be redeemed in 20 years' time at par (100).

Such a bond has a yield of 5 %. If in five years' time the bond is still yielding 5 %, it will still be priced at 100. However, if the yield on the bond at the horizon date has increased to 6 %, its capital value will have decreased. Conversely, if it is then yielding 4 %, its capital value will have increased. The possible price movements for such a bond against changes in yields are illustrated in Figure 10.1. However, as has already been demonstrated, if the life of the bond is decreased, the volatility of its price (modified duration) also decreases.

The total return on this bond from now to the horizon date in five years' time comprises a capital gain or loss plus a return from the coupons received, which will have been reinvested. The capital return per annum over the five years to the horizon date is shown for this bond for a range of yield assumptions in Figure 10.2.

So far we have not considered the effect of reinvesting the coupons. The standard redemption yield calculation assumes that all coupons are reinvested in the original bond as soon as they are received at the original redemption yield without any cost to the holder. In practice this is usually an impossible goal. There is obviously no possible guaranteed reinvestment rate for the coupons, so calculations have been performed assuming they have been reinvested using the original yield and the horizon yield in Figure 10.3. Frequently the average reinvestment rate should be between these two values. It can be seen that the assumption made about the

142   An Introduction to the Bond Markets

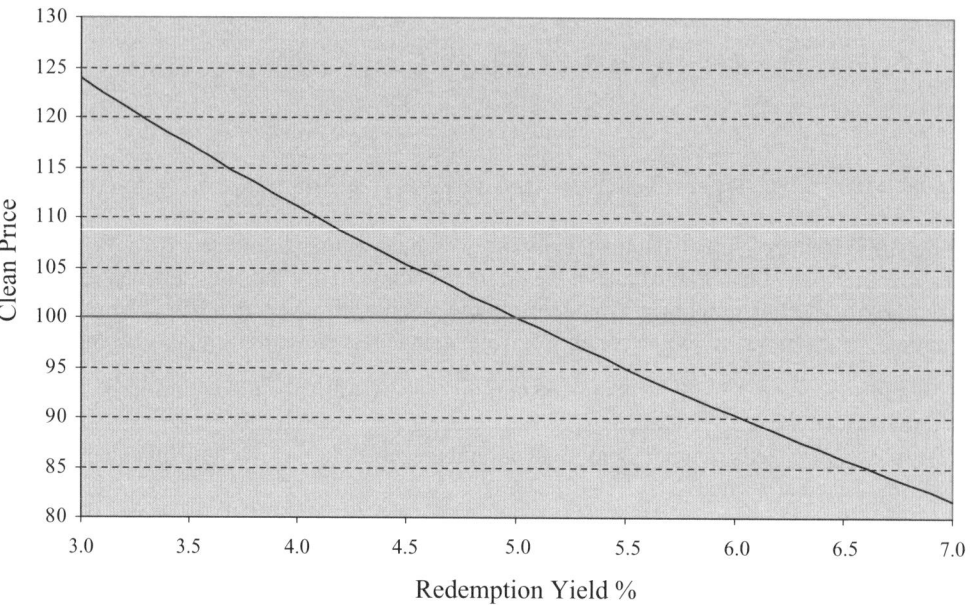

Figure 10.1 Price versus yield of a 5 % bond with a life of 15 years.

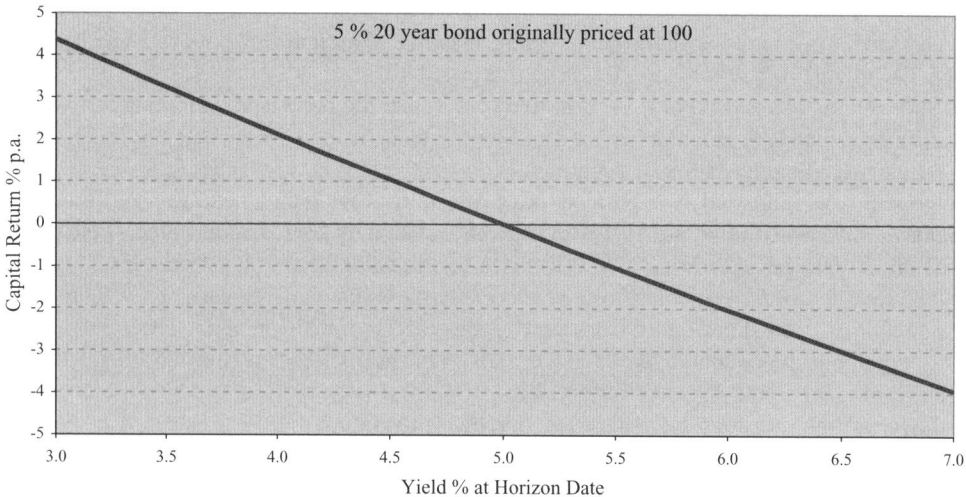

Figure 10.2 Capital gain/loss versus yield at the horizon date.

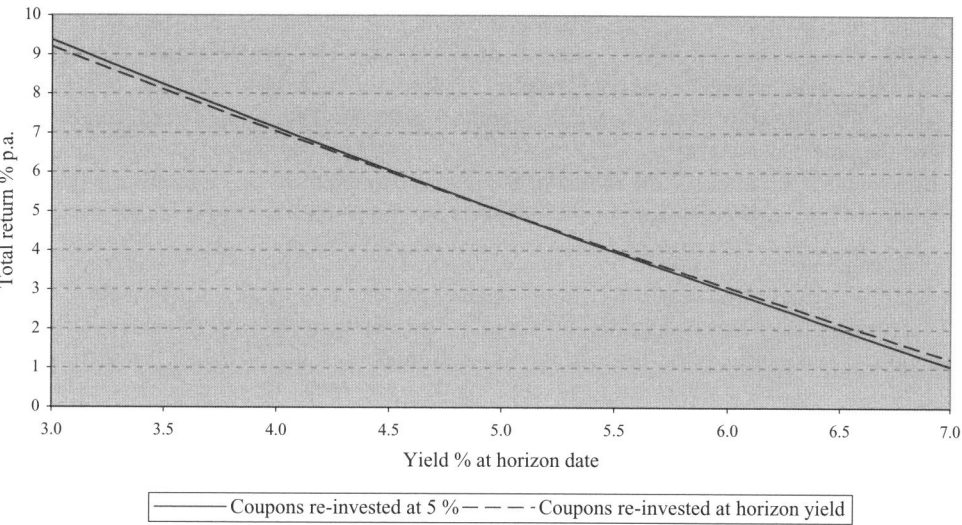

Figure 10.3 Total return versus horizon yield.

reinvestment rate of the bond's coupons does not significantly affect the rate of return on the bond to the horizon date.

Program 10.1 Horizon

This program enables the user to enter the details of a bond and specify a horizon date. It then calculates the return on the bond for a range of interest rate scenarios at the horizon date. The results are displayed in both a tabular and a graphical format.

10.2 IMMUNIZATION

A pension fund or insurance company bond investment manager often has an obligation to make specified payments at a range of future dates. We have also seen that a fixed interest bond portfolio rises in value when interest rates fall, and falls in value when interest rates rise. 'Immunization' is the process of attempting to minimize, or even occasionally eliminate, the effect of interest rate changes on the value of the investments at the horizon date or dates.

A number of software programs have been produced to assist in the management of this process. However, in constructing a portfolio to service future obligations, the following should be considered:

- The only way that you can be certain that you can meet the future obligation, assuming that you do not have surplus funds, is to invest in a zero-coupon bond or strip that is redeemed on the obligation due date. Unfortunately, suitable instruments rarely exist, and even in the rare cases where they do, they may provide an unattractive return.

- Investing in floating-rate notes enables the fund manager to preserve the capital of the fund, since the floating-rate coupon rate is reset at the beginning of each coupon period. Unfortunately, it gives no guarantee about the income that can be used for reinvestment. Future interest rate movements with a floating-rate note can significantly affect its return over the period, as there is no compensating capital profit or loss.
- The capital values of fixed-rate bonds become less sensitive to interest rate changes as the bond approaches maturity.
- Bonds with a duration similar to that of the required time horizon tend to offset any capital losses against any interest rate gains and vice versa for a small change in yield.

The techniques used in immunization programmes try to minimize the possible variations in portfolio values at the horizon date by keeping the duration of the portfolio close to that of the horizon date. This is achieved by periodically reviewing the portfolio and adjusting its duration, if necessary, by selling investments with a shorter duration than the horizon date and buying investments with a longer duration, or vice versa, depending on whether it is desirable to increase or decrease the portfolio's duration. Similarly, when sufficient monies, from dividends, capital repayments, new money, etc., have been accumulated to make a new investment, they are invested in a bond or bonds that will reduce the difference between the portfolio's duration and the horizon date.

It should be pointed out that immunization is not in any way a protection for credit risk, and the credit rating of the bonds in the portfolio ought to be maintained when making substitutions. Similarly, it is necessary for some investors to take into account the effect of tax on coupon payments.

10.3 PORTFOLIO MEASURES

The correct way to calculate the overall yield or duration of a bond portfolio is to calculate all the expected future cash flows of all the bonds in the portfolio, and then calculate the internal rate of return, based on the discounted values of all the cash flows, that gives a total value equal to the current value of the portfolio. Given this internal rate of return, it is then possible to calculate the portfolio's duration, modified duration and convexity. This is a significant effort even with computers. Luckily it is relatively easy to produce acceptable approximations from the holdings, prices, yields, durations, etc., of the individual bonds.

A reasonable estimate for the duration of a portfolio consisting of two or more bonds is simply the weighted average of the duration of the bonds.

Example 10.1

Consider a portfolio that consists of just two bonds, A and B. The portfolio holds $10 million worth of bond A, which has a duration of 2 years, and $20 million worth of bond B, which has a duration of 5 years. The estimated portfolio duration (PD) is given by:

$$PD = \frac{10 \times 2 + 20 \times 5}{10 + 20} = 4 \text{ years}$$

The formula for the portfolio duration calculation is given in Appendix B. In a similar way, a good approximation for the modified duration of a portfolio is the average of the modified durations of all the bonds in the portfolio weighted by their current values.

Unfortunately, this approach does not work satisfactorily for calculating the average redemption yield of a portfolio. This is illustrated in the following example.

Example 10.2

Consider a portfolio that consists of two bonds, A and B. Bond A has a market value of £10 million, a redemption yield of 3 %, a life to maturity of 1 month and a modified duration of 1 month (0.0833 years). Bond B has a market value of £10 million, a redemption yield of 6 %, a life to maturity of 5 years and a modified duration of 4.2 years.

The weighted average portfolio redemption yield (PRY) if calculated in the same way as that for duration, is:

$$PRY = \frac{10 \times 3 + 10 \times 6}{10 + 10} = 4.5\%$$

However, the yield on bond A is only for one month, when the proceeds of the redemption become available for reinvestment. If the market does not move significantly during the month, these funds could be reinvested at a higher rate, even possibly in bond B.

The situation could have been reversed in the above example if bond A had yielded more than bond B, potentially making it impossible for the portfolio to obtain the projected return. The solution, which gives a good approximation, is to weight the holding values by both the redemption yields and their modified durations (i.e. a discounted measure of the average time of holding the bonds).

Example 10.2 (*Continued*)

The estimated portfolio redemption yield (PRY) is now given by:

$$PRY = \frac{10 \times 3 \times 0.0833 + 10 \times 6 \times 4.2}{10 \times 0.0833 + 10 \times 4.2} = 5.94\%$$

A value of 5.94 % for the portfolio's redemption yield is clearly a better approximation to the true portfolio yield than 4.5 %. The portfolio redemption yield formula is given in Appendix B.

Program 10.2   Portfolio

This program allows the user to enter details of the bonds in a small portfolio. It then calculates for the portfolio its projected cash flow (which is shown in a graphical format), its average yield, and Macaulay and modified durations.

10.4   ALLOWING FOR TAX

The returns on bonds in the hands of an investor are often subject to income and possibly capital gains tax. The tax on the income is sometimes deducted before the coupon is received by the investor. On the other hand, especially with over-the-counter products, any income is received gross and it is up to the holder to declare it to the relevant tax authorities. Although in these two cases there is a considerable difference in the timing of the tax payments, when calculating returns net of tax the timing differences are often ignored, and the tax is assumed to have been paid at the same time as the coupons are received.

To calculate a yield and the related calculations, such as duration and convexity, for a bond investment that is subject to an income tax deduction, the bond's coupon is just netted down by the tax rate.

Example 10.3

An investment in a 5 % bond, where the coupon payments are subject to income tax of 30 % is treated as an identical bond with a 3.5 % coupon which is not subject to tax, as $5 \times (1 - 30/100) = 3.5\,\%$.

If the holder of the bond has to pay capital gains tax on at least part of the difference between the buying and selling price, then it usually suffices to reduce the selling price by the tax liability in calculating any returns.

Example 10.4

A holder purchased a bond some time ago for 90 and is now selling it for 100. As a result of this sale, the holder is subject to a tax liability of 1% on the capital gain. The return on the investment should now be calculated as if the holder were now selling it for 99 without any capital gains tax liability.

11
Indices

So far we have discussed how individual bonds work together with various options and derivatives on specific bonds. The problem we have not discussed is how to measure the performance of a portfolio of bonds against the average market performance of a similar group of bonds. In order to aid us in this comparison, a number of companies calculate a variety of bond indices. If you just consider the domestic and international bond markets for straight bonds there are innumerable numbers of indices. The list below gives you a flavour of the available types of indices:

- Domestic government bond indices (government indices are calculated for nearly all the OECD countries).
- Composite government bond indices, e.g. composite indices are calculated for all the eurozone countries.
- Indices for supranational agencies, such as the World Bank or European Investment Bank. Indices are calculated for the whole category and individual issuers, and are subdivided according to the currency of issue.
- Indices containing issues by government agencies, regional governments, municipal councils, etc.
- Asset-backed security indices. These are often called Pfandbriefe.
- Corporate indices. These are often categorized by country of issuer, currency and even industry sector. They may also be categorized by the rating of the issue.

11.1 BOND INDEX CLASSIFICATIONS

Bond indices are often classified according to:

- the currency of the issues;
- the type of issuer, e.g. government, supranational, public sector, corporate, financial and asset-backed issuers;
- the maturity band of the issues;
- the rating of the bonds.

Unlike equity indices, the industrial sector of a corporate issuer is of secondary importance. Any difference between the prospects of individual industries is often reflected in the rating of the bonds.

Most bond calculators split their index calculations into eligible bonds that fall into a number of maturity subdivisions. The standard maturity subdivisions are:

Bonds with a life to maturity of	1–3 years
	3–5 years
	5–7 years
	7–10 years
	10–15 years
	Over 15 years
	All eligible bonds with an outstanding life of at least one year

These maturity bands are often combined together to form, for example, a '1–5 year' or an 'over 10 year' index. As you can see, the number of different available bond indices is multiplying rapidly.

Bonds are frequently removed from the indices[1] when they reach one year to maturity. This is partly because they are now regarded as money market instruments and it is often harder to trade in them.

Producing valid and consistent bond indices is not a simple task. In fact, in some ways it is more difficult than calculating equity indices. With equity indices, their constituent members tend to change less often than with bonds, as each equity share normally has an indefinite life. The constituents can potentially continue to remain indefinitely in the index, and the reasons for its removal are unpredictable, e.g. the company is taken over, it changes its nature with the result that it is no longer eligible for index or it ceases to exist. Nearly all bonds have a finite life, although possibly quite a long one.[2] Even with bonds that are originally issued with a very long maturity date, during their life, using the standard maturity subdivision classification above, they will fall into six different maturity subgroups. This is not something that usually happens to equity shares.

11.2 CHOOSING INDICES

The process of choosing appropriate equity indices against which to measure one's portfolio performance is slightly different to that of choosing appropriate bond market indices.

In the case of equity indices, the primary selection criterion is frequently the market where the equities are traded and the secondary criterion is the size of the companies in the portfolio. The equity market in turn usually specifies the currency of the indices. For example, even if companies that do not have a US domicile produce their accounts in US dollars, there is often a sterling quotation if they are quoted in London, e.g. Standard Chartered Bank. Similarly, some portfolios tend to specialize in smaller or mid-sized companies as opposed to large companies or not to restrict the company size. In the UK, indices such as the FTSE All-share, FTSE 100, FTSE 250 and FTSE 350 cater for these requirements. In addition, indices are also calculated for many industry classifications and for one of the more general indices less the companies in a specific sector, e.g. all UK shares excluding tobacco companies and companies involved in the arms trade.

Bond indices, on the other hand, tend to be classified by issuer type and currency. The most common indices reflect the performance of bonds issued by governments in their domestic currency. This is mainly because governments have in the past been the largest issuers, with the result that their bonds tend to remain liquid over time. This is in contrast to corporate issuers, where bonds frequently start their lives being very liquid, but the liquidity rapidly dries up as the bonds are placed in permanent homes with pension funds or insurance companies. However, even when corporate bonds are first issued the bid-offer price spread tends to be greater than that of equivalent government securities. It is also unusual to combine bonds denominated in different currencies in the same bond index, even if they are all issued by the same issuer. This is, at least partly, because the currency variations may, and often do, account for larger changes than the returns on the underlying bonds in their denominated currency.

---

[1] The FTSE Actuaries fixed-rate UK gilt-edged indices do not normally remove the bonds before redemption, provided they have not been put on to the Debt Management Office's rump stock list.

[2] In 2005 several issuers, including the French and UK Governments and Telecom Italia, have started to issue bonds with a 50 year maturity to satisfy the demands of pension fund managers.

Pension fund and insurance companies often have long-term liabilities; hence it is sometimes not appropriate to compare their performance with a general bond index in the appropriate market, since it may be dominated by bonds with a short life to maturity, which by their nature are unlikely to be as volatile as longer-dated bonds.

Similarly, care should be taken to ensure that if, for example, a proxy index of a government bond index is used for comparison instead of a corporate bond index because a suitable one does not exist, full allowance is made for the change in corporate credit spreads relative to the government issues. These credit spreads can change relatively quickly and make any comparison almost meaningless. Credit spreads can also vary considerably across different rating bands.

11.3 INDEX DATA CALCULATIONS

With equity indices, providers tend to produce only a price index and possibly a dividend yield. However, with bond indices, much more data is produced. This is due to the nature of bonds, where a clean price index on its own does not indicate whether a fund manager has done well or badly. The following values are frequently calculated:

Clean price index
Dirty price index
Total return index
Interest paid this year
Average coupon
Average life
Average duration
Average convexity
Average redemption yield
Average current yield

In addition, occasionally the average dispersion of the constituents may also be calculated. Of the above calculations, the one that most closely resembles the equity price index is the total return index, although it should be noted that there are significant differences in its calculation.[3]

The great majority of equity and bond indices use a chain-linking mechanism, whereby today's value is calculated to be equal to the previous value multiplied by the change in value of the current constituents since the previous calculation.

Example 11.1

Consider an index that is calculated daily and consists of three constituents (A, B and C) that all have the same amount in issue, or number of shares if an equity index. After the calculation is performed on day 2 security C is removed. If the value of the index on day 1 is 120 and the prices of the three components:

	Day 1	Day 2	Day 3
A	80	81	80
B	90	91	90
C	100	98	—

---

[3] The EFFAS Standardized Rules on constructing bond indices are described fully by Patrick Brown (2002).

the index calculation for day 2 is:

$$\text{Index}_{\text{Day2}} = 120 \times \frac{81 + 91 + 98}{80 + 90 + 100} = 120$$

Similarly, the index calculation for day 3 is:

$$\text{Index}_{\text{Day3}} = 120 \times \frac{80 + 90}{81 + 91} = 118.605$$

This shows how as the overall value of the three constituents did not change between days 1 and 2 the index remained unchanged at 120. However, the index for day 3 which is based only on two securities drops as the prices for the remaining securities drops. However, note that their prices are the same as they were on day 1.

Equity indices just compare the prices of the shares, suitably weighted, at the end of the period with those at the beginning. The total return index, on the other hand, takes the clean prices today of the bonds, adds the current accrued interest and any coupon received today, and compares this with the clean prices and accrued interest for the previous calculation. In effect, from one date to the next, if all the bond prices are unchanged, the total return index will increase by the average increase in accrued interest after taking into account the payment of any coupons.

11.4 INDEX CONTINUITY

One of the most important things when creating a 'useful' index is to ensure that there is continuity over time of the index calculations. Problems about continuity can, and do, arise quite frequently with bond indices. The following sections list some of the problems that may arise.

11.4.1 Large changes in the constituents of the index

With many bond index providers, the constituents of the index are reviewed every month. This means that, especially with subindices based on maturity bands, from one month to the next you might be looking at greatly differing securities.

Example 11.2

Consider a bond index that includes bonds that mature on 5 January 2011, 15 January 2011, 10 January 2013, 20 January 2013 and 1 June 2013. All the other bonds mature before the end of 2010.

In December 2005, the 5–7 year maturity band index will contain bonds maturing on 5 January 2011 and 15 January 2011, whereas the other three bonds will be in the 7–10 year maturity band index.

In January 2006, they will still be in the same maturity bands but in February 2006, the 5 January 2011 and 15 January 2011 will have moved to the 3–5 year maturity band index and will have been replaced by the 10 January 2013 and 20 January 2013 bonds in the 5–7 year maturity band. The 7–10 year maturity band will now only consist of one bond, the one maturing on 1 June 2013.

If all the bonds in the above example have similar characteristics and the same, or an interchangeable, issuer, then there may be no problem with continuity. However, even if all the bonds are issued by the same issuer, if the 2011 bonds have high coupons and the 2013 ones low coupons, then the nature of the subindices may change. This can often cause problems if the market is subject to a significant rate of tax on income, but not on capital gains.

11.4.2 Gaps in subindex calculations

Another problem that can happen when a number of maturity band subindices are calculated is that over time it is possible for a specific maturity band to have valid constituents, then to lose them and then to acquire new constituents.

Example 11.3

Consider an index where, on 1 January 2006, there are four bonds with lives to maturity of between 5 and 10 years. They have lives of 5.1 years, 5.9 years, 9.1 years and 9.6 years.

Thus on 1 January 2006 there are two bonds in the 5–7 year maturity band and two bonds in the 7–10 maturity band. By 1 January 2007, both the bonds in the 5–7 year maturity band have moved into the under five year band, but the other two bonds are still in the 7–10 year band. In early 2008 one of these bonds moves into the 5–7 year category.

The problem now is 'what should be the policy on calculating an index for the 5–7 year sector?' If the closing 5–7 year index value prior to losing the first two bonds was 150, then obviously it could not be calculated during the period it contained no securities, but at what value should the index recommence when a security moves into the maturity band? There are three obvious contenders:

- Start the index again at 100.
- Start the index at the last closing value prior to losing its constituents.
- Based on the performance of the other maturity band indices, estimate how you would have expected the index to perform during the interregnum, and restart at a value that adjusts the last closing value for this change.

The first option of restarting the index at 100 is obviously the safest option and in many ways the only one that can be justified. Unfortunately, it does not allow one to compare the performance of two indices over periods that include a gap. However, arguably this is not something that should be done.

The second option of continuing at the last calculated value of the index does not have much to recommend it as it does not reflect the market changes when it could not be calculated.

The third option, although superficially it gives a sense of continuity, is by its nature very subjective and sometimes cannot be done in a satisfactory way. It also encourages users to believe that the maturity band has performed in a specific way over a period when it was impossible to invest in it.

11.4.3 Bonds dropped due to lack of prices

As has been discussed, there are very many more extant bond issues than there are equity issues. This in turn means that many bond issues are not regularly traded and as a result there is a lack of price information on them. As a consequence, index providers ignore them, but these bonds still exist in many portfolios. Hence, this can mean that the bonds do not properly represent the relevant bond sector from an investor's point of view, with the associated knock-on effect on the relevance of the index calculations.

However, there is more of a problem when some bonds have been included in the index and then the market makers cease to provide prices for them. Although this occurs mainly in the corporate sector, it can also occur in the government bond markets. For example, in the UK gilt-edged market GEMMs have an obligation to make continuous two-way prices in all the main outstanding UK Government bonds, but from time to time the UK Debt Management Office transfers some of these bonds to their 'rump' stock list, whereupon the market maker's obligation ceases.

If the quotations cease during a month and the index constituents are only revised at the month end, this produces a problem. There are several ways to get round this problem, although some index providers always remove such issues immediately. They are:

- exceptionally to remove the bond;
- to leave the bond in at its last price and remove it at the first review date; or
- to calculate a matrix price for the bond based on the yields of similar bonds in the index, assuming that the yield relationship will continue to be the same until the next review date, when it will be removed.

Unfortunately the last option, which may produce the best result, is not always possible. This is especially true in the corporate bond market where there may not be any equivalent bonds.

In practice, in any one area, the bonds with continuous quotations will tend to be those that are the most traded, although not necessarily the largest ones.

11.4.4 Ratings downgrade

Especially when calculating corporate indices, many index providers restrict the securities to those with a specific rating. In particular, the indices may be restricted to investment grade[4] issues. Interesting effects can occur when a significant proportion of the issues are removed for this reason.

A very well signposted example of this occurred in May 2005 when Standard & Poors downgraded the Ford and General Motors issues to junk bond status. These two companies had $161.3 billion and $291.8 billion of debt outstanding.[5] Ford was downgraded from BBB− to BB+ and General Motors, which only four years ago had an A− rating, from BBB− to BB.

The effect on some indices was spectacular. For example, FTSE calculate a motor manufacturing sector investment grade corporate index in both sterling and euros. The yields on the longer-dated sterling General Motors issues were already over 12 % prior to the former announcement, at a time when the yields on Toyota Motor Credit issues, another major issuer in the sector, were less than 5 %. The increase in yields and the associated reduction in price pushed down the indices. However, because of the chain nature of index calculations, the removal of Ford and General Motors bonds at the end of May 2005 did not, *per se*, move the indices, but they had a dramatic effect on the motor manufacturing index yield, which dropped considerably.

---

[4] Rated at least BBB−.
[5] The previous largest downgrade of bonds to 'junk' status was in May 2002 when $30.0 billion of WorldCom debt was downgraded.

Appendix A
Using the Companion Website
www.wiley.com/go/introductiontothebondmarkets

Although it is not essential to use the companion website to appreciate the scope of the book, using it will enable the user to get a better feel of how bonds and derivatives react to changes in market conditions in an interactive way. It is hoped that its use will enable the user to get a better understanding of why traders and portfolio managers enact different trading and investing strategies.

In order to use the contents on the website, the user will need to have installed Microsoft Windows 98, Windows NT, Windows 2000 or Windows XP and Microsoft Excel 2002. (The routines were developed on Windows XP.) To use just select the required program and this will cause an Excel spreadsheet or user form to appear with certain data already filled in.

The following programs have been supplied on the website:

- *Annuity.*
  This program allows the user to enter the life, payment frequency and required interest rate for an annuity. It then calculates the annuity payments and the breakdown between interest and capital repayments. These may be displayed in tabular and graphical form.
- *Yield1.*
  This program allows users to enter the basic terms of a fixed-rate bond issue together with either its price or yield. It then calculates the accrued interest, the clean and dirty prices, redemption yields compounded both annually and semi-annually, and various associated calculations, such as Macaulay and modified durations and convexity.
- *Yield2.*
  This program is similar to Yield1, except that now it is possible to specify and modify the expected cash flow stream, before performing the calculations.
- *PriceProgression.*
  This program allows the user to specify the terms of a bond and to plot its price progression to maturity with various interest rate scenarios.
- *FRN.*
  This program allows the user to set up a floating-rate note and specify a price. It then calculates a simple margin, a discounted margin and a redemption yield for the note.
- *Discount.*
  This program allows the user to enter the price or discount, accrual basis and life of a money market instrument, and calculates its discount/price, money market yield and equivalent redemption yields compounded both annually and semi-annually.
- *YieldCurve1.*
  This program allows the user to either modify the shape of a normal yield curve or enter one's own yield curve and, based on the assumption that all the bonds forming the yield curve have the same coupon, which can be specified, automatically create a zero-coupon yield curve.

It will be noticed that sharp changes in yield over time can make dramatic changes to the zero-coupon curve.

- *YieldCurve2.*

  This program allows the user to specify the annual spot rates, and calculate the resulting par and one, two and three year forward yield curves. The results are shown in both tabular and graphical form.

- *YieldCurve3.*

  This program allows the user to enter the current yield curve in the market, make assumptions about its change in shape, or enter a projected yield curve at a specified date in the future. It then displays the two yield curves and, for a specified coupon rate and payment frequency, the expected change in prices.

- *Swap.*

  This program enables the user to enter the details of an interest rate swap, together with details of the projected yield curve of the floating-rate indicator rate. It then calculates and displays the projected cash flows, and calculates the returns for both parties.

- *FRA.*

  This program allows users to enter the terms of a forward rate agreement (FRA). It calculates the associated profit/loss for the parties.

- *Horizon.*

  This program enables the user to enter the details of a bond and specify a horizon date. It then calculates the return on the bond for a range of interest rate scenarios at the horizon date. The results are displayed in both a tabular and a graphical format.

- *Portfolio.*

  This program allows the user to enter details of the bonds in a small portfolio. It then calculates for the portfolio its projected cash flow (which is shown in a graphical format), its average yield, and Macaulay and modified durations.

Appendix B
Mathematical Formulae

In order to make the formulae easier to understand, the following notation has been used throughout this section:

- P dirty price of a bond
- AI accrued interest to the settlement date
- g annual coupon rate (%)
- ND number of days accrued
- CP clean price; hence $P = CP + AI$
- C redemption value
- n number of future cash flows until the assumed redemption date
- CF_i ith cash flow
- L_i time in years to the ith cash flow, allowing for the market conventions used in calculating any fraction of a year
- v discounting factor, i.e. $v = 1/(1 + y)$
- y redemption yield compounded annually ($y = 0.06$ for a yield of 6%)

B.1 ACCRUED INTEREST

The accrued interest on a security varies according to the type of security and the market on which it is traded. The accrued interest (AI) is, although there are exceptions, generally defined as:

$$AI = g \times \frac{ND}{\text{days in year}}$$

where:

- AI accrued interest to the settlement date
- g annual coupon rate (%)
- ND number of days accrued from either the issue date or the last coupon date to the settlement date

It should be noted that there are several ways of calculating the number of days accrued up to the settlement date, and a further several ways of calculating the number of days in a year.

The accrued interest on a bond is almost always calculated from the issue date or, if there has been a subsequent coupon payment, the last coupon date up to the settlement date of the transaction and not the trade date. However, it should be pointed out that sometimes, especially with new tranches of existing securities, bonds may be issued with a certain amount of accrued interest included in the issue price.

A further complication arises when bonds are being traded ex-coupon. In this case, the last coupon date is the date a few days ahead of the settlement date, with the result that the amount of accrued interest becomes negative.

Example B.1

If a bond is being traded ex a coupon payment on 15 May for settlement on 13 May, then it is being traded with minus two days' accrued interest.

There are three main methods of calculating the number of days accrued. They are:

- actual number of calendar days;
- European method of calculating number of days based on a year of twelve 30 day months; or
- US method of calculating number of days based on a year of twelve 30 day months.

Variations on the above methods include the Japanese markets, where they do not recognize the existence of leap days (i.e. 29 February). Such actual days are interest free.

The differences between the European and US 30 day month methods concern the treatment of periods between month end dates. Under the European 30 day month method (30E), if interest accrues from the date $D_1/M_1/Y_1$ to a value date of $D_2/M_2/Y_2$, the number of days accrued (ND) is given by:

If $D_1 = 31$, set it to 30

If $D_2 = 31$, set it to 30

$$ND = (D_2 - D_1) + 30 \times (M_2 - M_1) + 360 \times (Y_2 - Y_1)$$

For the US 30 day month method (30), the number of days accrued (ND) is given by:

If $D_1 = 31$, set it to 30

If $D_2 = 31$ and D_1 is 30 or 31 set D_2 to 30, otherwise leave as 31

$$ND = (D_2 - D_1) + 30 \times (M_2 - M_1) + 360 \times (Y_2 - Y_1)$$

Example B.2

The number of day's accrued interest between 15 July and 31 August according to the main methods is:

$$\text{Actual calendar days} = 16 + 31 = 47 \text{ days}$$
$$\text{European 30 day month} = 15 + 30 = 45 \text{ days}$$
$$\text{US 30 day month} = 15 + 31 = 46 \text{ days}$$

Similarly, there are several ways of calculating the number of days in a year. The main ones are:

- calendar days in period × number of periods in year, where a period is defined to be the fraction of a year between the normal coupon payments for the instrument;
- 365;
- 365 days in a non-leap year and 366 days in a leap year; or
- 360.

However, there are again a number of variants. For example, in the swap markets with some contracts an interest period that spans parts of a leap and a non-leap year is split into two with a day being regarded as 1/365 of a year in one part and 1/366 of a year in the other.

With the above conventions, it can be seen that the number of days in a year can vary from 360 to 368. If a bond only pays once a year, then the number of calendar days between interest payments is either 365 or 366. However, if a bond pays twice a year, the number of calendar days between payment days can vary between 181 and 184.

Example B.3

If a bond that accrues interest on an actual day method pays interest twice a year on 1 January and 1 July then:

- there are 181 days from 1 January to 1 July in a non-leap year and 182 days in a leap year and
- there are always 184 days from 1 July to 1 January.

A further complication arises if a bond that accrues interest on an actual/actual basis is issued with either a short or a long first coupon. In order to be consistent with existing bonds, it is assumed that the bond has been issued for the full period for the calculation of the number of days in the period in the case of a short first coupon, and a long coupon period is divided into two separate periods with different numbers of days.

Example B.4   Short first coupon period

A 6 % bond issued on 1 May will pay regular coupons on 1 September and 1 March each year. The bond accrues interest on an actual/actual basis and the first coupon payment is on 1 September following the issue in May.

The accrued interest calculation requires a number of calendar days from the issue date in the numerator and the number of days in the period in the denominator. The period for the denominator is assumed to start on 1 March (a pseudo interest payment date) prior to the issue on 1 May. The accrued interest calculation for 10 May, nine days after issue is thus:

$$Accrued\ interest = 3 \times \frac{9}{184} = 0.1467\,\%$$

as there are 184 days from 1 March to 1 September.

Example B.5   Long first coupon period

A 6 % bond issued on 1 May will pay regular coupons on 1 September and 1 March each year. The bond accrues interest on an actual/actual basis and the first coupon payment is not until 1 March the following year, which is not a leap year.

The 10 month first coupon period is now divided into two separate six month periods. The first one goes from 1 March to 1 September, which includes the 1 May issue date. The second one goes from 1 September to 1 March the following year. The bond accrues interest at different rates during these two pseudo periods. The first pseudo period is deemed to have 184 days, as in the short coupon period example above. The second has 181 days (the number of calendar days from 1 September to 1 March in a non-leap year). The accrued interest for this bond for 10 May, nine days after issue is as above:

$$\text{Accrued interest} = 3 \times \frac{9}{184} = 0.1467\,\%$$

whereas the accrued interest calculation for 10 September in the same year is:

$$\text{Accrued interest} = 3 \times \frac{123}{184} + 3 \times \frac{9}{181} = 2.1546\,\%$$

B.2 CURRENT YIELD

The current yield (CY) of a bond is given by:

$$CY = \frac{g \times 100}{CP}$$

where:

g annual coupon rate (%)
CP clean price

Example B.6

A 4% bond is priced at 90. It has a current yield (CY) of:

$$CY = \frac{4 \times 100}{90} = 4.444\,\%$$

B.3 SIMPLE YIELD TO MATURITY

The simple yield to maturity (SY) of a bond is given by:

$$SY = \frac{g + (C - CP)/L}{CP} \times 100$$

where:

g annual coupon rate (%)
CP clean price
C redemption value
L time in years to maturity

Example B.7

A 5% bond, which will be redeemed at par (100) in four years' time, is priced at 90. Its simple yield to maturity (SY) is given by:

$$SY = \frac{5 + (100 - 90)/4}{90} \times 100 = 8.333\%$$

B.4 REDEMPTION YIELD

The redemption yield (y) of a dated security, compounded annually, can be calculated from solving the following formula:

$$P = \sum_{i=1}^{n} CF_i \times v^{L_i}$$

where:

- P dirty price
- n number of future cash flows
- CF_i ith (future) cash flow
- L_i period in years to the ith cash flow, allowing for the market conventions for any fractional part of a year
- v discounting factor, i.e. $v = 1/(1+y)$
- y redemption yield compounded annually ($y = 0.06$ for a yield of 6%)

Except in a few special cases, if it is desired to calculate the redemption yield, the above equation has to be solved by an iterative process. The equation always produces a yield compounded annually. This redemption yield can be converted to one being compounded semi-annually (see below), or alternatively in markets where most bonds pay interest twice a year (e.g. the UK and US) the formula may be modified slightly, by counting time in periods of six months instead of years, to produce directly a semi-annually compounded redemption yield (y_s):

$$P = \sum_{i=1}^{n} CF_i \times v^{L_i}$$

where:

- P dirty price
- n number of future cash flows
- CF_i ith (future) cash flow
- L_i time in periods (i.e. six months) to the ith cash flow, allowing for the market conventions for any fractional part of a period
- v discounting factor, i.e. $v = 1/(1 + y_s/2)$
- y_s redemption yield compounded semi-annually ($y_s = 0.06$ for a yield of 6%)

The above formula for calculating a yield compounded semi-annually differs from the previous annually compounded one solely in the definitions of L_i and v.

In the case of a fixed-rate bond with identical coupon payments paid h times a year, which is redeemed on a coupon payment date, the above formula with compounding h times a year can be rewritten as:

$$P = \sum_{i=1}^{n} \frac{g}{h} \times \left(1 + v + v^2 + \cdots + v^{n-1}\right) \times v^f + C \times v^{n-1+f}$$

where:

- P dirty price
- C redemption amount
- n number of future coupon payments
- g annual coupon (%)
- h number of coupon payments per year
- f fraction of period (i.e. $12/h$ months) to the next coupon payment
- v discounting factor, i.e. $v = 1/(1 + y/h)$
- y redemption yield compounded h times a year ($y = 0.06$ for a yield of 6%)

The above formula reduces to:

$$P = \frac{g}{h} \times \frac{1 - v^n}{1 - v} \times v^f + C \times v^{n-1+f}$$

It should be noted that the above generalized formulae can be applied equally well to index-linked bonds and floating-rate notes, albeit with various assumptions being made about future coupon payments and the final maturity value. However, in the case of index-linked bonds a more useful measure is the real redemption yield, i.e. the net return after inflation is taken out (see Section B 12). In the case of index-linked bonds, using the indexation techniques first used in the Canadian Real Return Bond market, e.g. UK index-linked gilts with a three month indexation lag, the above formula may be used to calculate a real clean price from a yield and vice versa. However, in this case the dirty price has to be adjusted by the relevant index ratio to derive the settlement amount.

With floating-rate notes, when calculating a redemption yield, one often assumes that all future coupon payments, after the next which is usually known, are equal to the coupon rate that would be set if today were a coupon-fixing date. In other words, the standard redemption yield formula for floating-rate notes becomes:

$$P = v^f \times \left(k + \sum_{i=1}^{n-1} \frac{I2 + QM}{h}\right) \times v^i + C \times v^{n-1}$$

where:

- P dirty price
- C redemption value
- n number of future coupon payments
- k first/next coupon payment

Appendix B: Mathematical Formulae   161

$I2$	assumed market indicator rate for subsequent coupon payments (%)
QM	quoted margin (%)
h	number of coupon payments per year
f	fraction of period (i.e. $12/h$ months) to the next coupon payment
v	discounting factor, i.e. $v = 1/(1 + y/h)$
y	redemption yield compounded h times a year ($y = 0.06$ for a yield of 6 %)

In the final period before redemption, some people prefer to discount the future payments using simple as opposed to compound interest. The reason for this is that the return on the bonds can then be directly compared with that on money market instruments.

The redemption yield formula compounded annually in the last period reduces to:

$$P = CF_1 \times v^{L_1}$$

$$P = \frac{C + g/h}{(1 + y)^f}$$

where:

P	dirty price
g	annual coupon rate (%)
h	number of coupon payments per year
CF_1	final cash flow, i.e. redemption value + coupon payment
L_1	period in years to the final cash flow, allowing for the market conventions for any fractional part of a year; in this case it is just the fraction of a year f to redemption
v	discounting factor, i.e. $v = 1/(1 + y)$
y	redemption yield compounded annually ($y = 0.06$ for a yield of 6 %)

Restating this formula discounting with simple interest you get:

$$P = \frac{C + g/h}{1 + f \times y}$$

which is just the money market yield.

In the special case of an undated bond, it is assumed that the price is the present value of an infinite stream of coupons, with the result that the redemption amount is valueless. The above equation for an undated bond with an annual coupon (g) paying twice a year thus becomes:

$$P = \sum_{i=1}^{\infty} \frac{g}{2} \times v^{i+f-1}$$

$$p = \frac{g}{2 \times (1 - v)} \times v^f$$

where:

P	dirty price
g	annual coupon rate (%)
$i + f - 1$	time in periods (i.e. six months) to the ith cash flow, allowing for the market conventions for any fractional part (f) of a period
v	discounting factor, i.e. $v = 1/(1 + y_s/2)$
y_s	redemption yield compounded semi-annually ($y_s = 0.06$ for a yield of 6 %)

By convention the fractional part (f) of a period is defined using the same convention with regard to the day count as that used for calculating the accrued interest for the bond.

It should be noted that this differs slightly from the current yield of a bond as it allows for the accrued interest in the price of the bond and the fraction of a period to the first coupon payment. However, on a coupon payment date there is no accrued interest and so the clean price (CP) is the same as the dirty price (P), and the fraction of a period (f) to the next interest payment is 1. The redemption yield equation now reduces to:

$$CP = \frac{g \times v}{2 \times (1 - v)}$$

$$CP = \frac{g}{2 \times (1 + y_s/2 - 1)}$$

$$CP = \frac{g}{y_s}$$

This is the current yield.

B.5 DURATION

The (Macaulay) duration of a bond is the average period in years of all the future cash flows of the bond discounted at the redemption rate. In other words it is given by:

$$D = \frac{\sum_{i=1}^{n} CF_i \times L_i \times v^{L_i}}{\sum_{i=1}^{n} CF_i \times v^{L_i}}$$

where:

D Macaulay duration
n number of future cash flows
CF_i ith (future) cash flow
L_i period in years to the ith cash flow, allowing for the market conventions for any fractional part of a year
v discounting factor, i.e. $v = 1/(1 + y)$
y redemption yield compounded annually ($y = 0.06$ for a yield of 6%)

This formula can be rewritten as:

$$D = \frac{1}{P} \times \sum_{i=1}^{n} CF_i \times L_i \times v^{L_i}$$

where:

P dirty price

Appendix B: Mathematical Formulae 163

In the special case of an undated bond with a constant annual coupon, the above duration formula reduces to:

$$D = \frac{\sum_{i=1}^{\infty} g \times (f+i-1) \times v^{f+i-1}}{\sum_{i=1}^{\infty} g \times v^{f+i-1}}$$

$$D = f + \frac{v + 2v^2 + 3v^3 + \cdots}{1 + v + v^2 + \cdots}$$

$$D = f + \frac{v}{(1-v)^2} \times (1-v)$$

$$D = f + \frac{1}{y}$$

where:

- D Macaulay duration
- g annual coupon rate (%)
- f fraction of a year to the next coupon payment
- v annual discounting factor, i.e. $v = 1/(1+y)$
- y redemption yield compounded annually ($y = 0.06$ for a yield of 6%)

This shows that for undated bonds the duration calculation is independent of the coupon and is related to the inverse of the yield.

B.6 MODIFIED DURATION

The modified duration (MD) of a bond measures the percentage change in price for a unit change in yield. It is given by:

$$MD = -\frac{dP}{dy} \times \frac{1}{P}$$

where:

- MD modified duration
- P dirty price
- dP small change in price
- dy corresponding small change in yield

Using the redemption yield formula for a conventional bond above, this equation can be modified as below:

$$MD = -\frac{dP}{dv} \times \frac{dv}{dy} \times \frac{1}{P}$$

$$MD = -\left(\sum_{i=1}^{n} CF_i \times L_i \times v^{L_i-1}\right) \times \left[\frac{-1}{(1+y)^2}\right] \times \frac{1}{P}$$

$$MD = D \times v$$

where:

- D Macaulay duration
- n number of future cash flows
- CF_i ith (future) cash flow
- L_i period in years to the ith cash flow, allowing for the market conventions for any fractional part of a year
- v discounting factor, i.e. $v = 1/(1+y)$
- dv small change in v, corresponding to the small change in y
- y redemption yield compounded annually ($y = 0.06$ for a yield of 6 %)

The modified duration or volatility for a fixed-rate bond is simply the Macaulay duration multiplied by the annual discounting factor.

On the other hand, for a floating-rate note, since the interest payments are adjusted for each coupon period, price movements, other than those caused by a rerating of the issue, are only sensitive to the next known interest payment being out of line with the current interest rates. As a result the modified duration of a floating-rate note is very small and always less than the period between two coupon payments.

B.7 CONVEXITY

Convexity measures the curvature of the price/yield relationship. Using the notation above, convexity is given by:

$$CX = \frac{1}{P} \times \frac{d^2 P}{dy^2} = \frac{1}{P} \times \frac{d}{dy}\left(\frac{dP}{dy}\right)$$

$$CX = \frac{1}{P} \times \sum_{i=1}^{n} CF_i \times L_i \times (L_i + 1) \times v^{L_i+2}$$

or

$$CX = \frac{\sum_{i=1}^{n} CF_i \times L_i \times (L_i + 1) \times v^{L_i+2}}{\sum_{i=1}^{n} CF_i \times v^{L_i}}$$

where:

- CX convexity
- P dirty price
- n number of future cash flows
- CF_i ith (future) cash flow
- L_i period in years to the ith cash flow, allowing for the market conventions for any fractional part of a year
- v discounting factor, i.e. $v = 1/(1+y)$
- y redemption yield compounded annually ($y = 0.06$ for a yield of 6 %)
- dP small change in price
- dy corresponding small change in yield
- dv small change in v, corresponding to the small change in y

In the case of a zero-coupon bond, where there is only one payment C at redemption in L years' time, the convexity formula above reduces to:

$$CX = \frac{L \times (L+1)}{(1+y)^2}$$

as

$$P = C \times v^{L_i}$$

In this case it is easy to see that the convexity increases with life to maturity and decreases with increasing yield.

The above formula gives convexity compounded annually. The method of adjusting the calculations so that they are compounded with a different frequency is described later in Section B.18.

B.8 DISPERSION

The dispersion of a bond DS measures the variance in the timing of a bond's cash flows around its duration. The cash flows are weighted by their discounted amounts. Using the same terminology as before, dispersion is given by:

$$DS^2 = \sum_{i=1}^{n} \frac{CF_i}{P} \times v^{L_i} \times (L_i - D)^2$$

$$DS^2 = \sum_{i=1}^{n} \frac{CF_i}{P} \times v^{L_i} \times (L_i^2 - 2L_i \times D + D^2)$$

$$DS^2 = \sum_{i=1}^{n} \frac{CF_i}{P} \times v^{L_i} \times L_i^2 - D^2$$

$$DS^2 = \frac{CX}{v^2} - D - D^2$$

where:

- DS dispersion
- D duration
- CX convexity
- P dirty price
- n number of future cash flows
- CF_i ith (future) cash flow
- L_i period in years to the ith cash flow, allowing for the market conventions for any fractional part of a year
- v discounting factor, i.e. $v = 1/(1+y)$
- y redemption yield compounded annually ($y = 0.06$ for a yield of 6%)

The last formula may be rearranged to define convexity in terms of dispersion, duration and yield:

$$CX = \frac{DS^2 + D + D^2}{(1+y)^2}$$

It should be noted that for a zero-coupon bond of life (L), the duration is L, the convexity is L^2 and the dispersion is 0.

B.9 ANNUITIES

An annuity is just a bond where the regular payments, which consist of both interest and capital repayments, are designed to repay all the capital during its life. There is no separate final redemption payment, as nearly all the capital has already been repaid. For each successive payment, the amount of interest decreases and the amount of capital repaid increases. The yield on an annuity paying an annual amount a, h times a year, is given by solving:

$$P = \sum_{i=1}^{n} \frac{a}{h} \times (1 + v + v^2 + \cdots + v^{n-1}) \times v^f$$

where:

- P dirty price
- n number of future annuity payments
- a annual annuity amount (%)
- h number of annuity payments per year
- f fraction of period (i.e. $12/h$ months) to the next annuity payment
- v discounting factor, i.e. $v = 1/(1 + y/h)$
- y redemption yield compounded h times a year ($y = 0.06$ for a yield of 6%)

The above formula reduces to:

$$P = \frac{a}{h} \times \frac{1 - v^n}{1 - v} \times v^f$$

If an annuity (of 100) pays interest h times a year at an annual rate of g% per annum, then the first interest payment I_1 and the first capital repayment C_1 are respectively:

$$I_1 = \frac{g}{h} \quad \text{and} \quad C_1 = \frac{a}{h} - I_1$$

Similarly, the second payments are respectively:

$$I_2 = \frac{g}{h} \times \frac{100 - C_1}{100} \quad \text{and} \quad C_2 = \frac{a}{h} - I_2$$

or more generally for the tth period:

$$I_t = \frac{g/h \times [(1 + g/100h)^n - (1 + g/100h)^{t-1}]}{(1 + g/100h)^n - 1}$$

$$C_t = \frac{g/h \times (1 + g/100h)^{t-1}}{(1 + g/100h)^n - 1}$$

where:

- a annual annuity payment amount (%)
- g annual interest rate on the annuity (%)
- h number of annuity payments per year
- n number of annuity payments
- I_t interest proportion of the tth annuity payment
- C_t capital repayment proportion of the tth annuity payment

The above formulae for I_t and C_t can be easily proved as initially the annuity is priced at par with a yield of g %. Thus the price formula above reduces to:

$$100 = \frac{a}{h} \times \frac{1 - v^n}{1 - v} \times v$$

where $v = 1/(1 + g/100h)$. Similarly:

$$I_t + C_t = \frac{g/h \times (1 + g/100h)^n}{(1 + g/100h)^n - 1} \quad \text{reduces to} \quad \frac{a}{h}$$

B.10 SIMPLE MARGIN

The simple margin formula measures the return that can be obtained on an FRN relative to its indicator rate. It is given by:

$$SM = \frac{C - [P + (I + QM) \times f - k]}{L} + QM$$

where:

- SM simple margin (%)
- C redemption value
- P dirty price
- I current market indicator rate to the next coupon date (%)
- QM quoted margin (%)
- f fraction of a year from value date to the first/next coupon date
- k first/next coupon payment
- L life in years (actual days/assumed number of days in a year)

B.11 DISCOUNTED MARGIN

The discounted margin for an FRN redeemed on a normal coupon date is given by:

$$P \times \left(1 + \frac{I + DM}{100} \times f\right) = k + \sum_{i=1}^{n-1} \frac{(I2 + QM)}{h} \times v^i + C \times v^{n-1}$$

where:

- DM discounted margin (%)
- C redemption value
- P dirty price
- I current market indicator rate to the next coupon date (%)
- $I2$ assumed market indicator rate for subsequent coupon payments (%)
- QM quoted margin (%)
- n number of future cash flows
- f fraction of a year from value date to the first/next coupon date
- k first/next coupon payment
- L life in years (actual days/assumed number of days in a year)
- h number of coupon payments per year adjusted, if not eurosterling, for the assumed number of days in the year
- v discounting factor; i.e. $v = 1/[1 + (I2 + DM)/100h]$

B.12 REAL REDEMPTION YIELD

Real redemption yields for index-linked bonds are calculated in a similar way to those for fixed-rate bonds, although there are two differences:

- In solving the standard redemption yield equation, future cash flows, unless they are already known, are grossed up by the assumed inflation rate.
- The resulting calculated discount factor has to be netted down by the assumed rate of inflation.

The real redemption yield, compounded on a semi-annual basis, is calculated by solving:

$$P = \sum_{i=1}^{n} CF_i \times v^{L_i}$$

where:

- P dirty price; if appropriate, this may be the (real clean price + real accrued interest) × index ratio
- n number of future cash flows, i.e. future coupon payments and the final capital repayment
- CF_i ith (future) cash flow, i.e. interest and capital payments grossed up by the assumed future inflation rate
- L_i time in semi-annual periods to the ith cash flow, allowing for the market conventions for any fractional part of a period
- v discounting factor; i.e. $v = 1/[(1 + ry/2) \times i^{0.5}]$
- ry required real redemption yield compounded twice a year
- i assumed annual inflation rate (%); e.g. $i = 0.05$ for 5% inflation

In the UK, all index-linked bonds first issued prior to September 2005 used as their indexation measure the UK Retail Price Index (RPI) with an 8 month lag. This meant that as the bonds paid coupons every six months, the next coupon payment was known before the bond started to accrue interest for that period. This indexation lag method, which was at least in part responsible for the real yields differing considerably according to the inflation assumption, was not widely accepted outside the UK.

In the meantime, the Canadians in their Real Return Bond market proposed a system that only involves a three month lag. This method has been adopted by a number of countries for their index-linked bonds, and will be used in the UK for index-linked bonds from September 2005 for new issues.

However, a three month indexation lag does mean that now dividend and redemption payments are not known until a few weeks before the actual payments. The reference RPI for a bond being redeemed on the first of a month is that for the calendar month falling three months earlier. For example, if a bond is being redeemed on 1 July, the final redemption amount will be based on the RPI for April, which is published in mid May. If the bond is redeemed on any other day in July the final redemption amount will be based using linear interpolation on the RPI values for the previous April and May.

Example B.8   When final redemption amounts are known for three month lag UK index-linked bonds

Bond is redeemed on 1 July
The redemption value is based on the previous April RPI, which is known in mid May.

Bond is redeemed on 2 July
The redemption value is based on the previous April and May RPIs, which are not known until mid June; i.e. the final redemption amount is not known until just over two weeks before redemption.

Bond is redeemed on 31 July
The redemption value is based on the previous April and May RPIs, which are not known until mid June; i.e. the final redemption amount is now known just over six weeks before redemption.

The UK Debt Management Office has published a booklet (2005) that goes into the calculation details.

B.13   CONVERTIBLE CALCULATIONS

A convertible is a bond with a holder's option to convert the bonds into usually, but not always, an equity at specified dates and rates. In a liquid market the price investors will pay for a convertible is thus the current value of the underlying assets plus an amount for the option. The convertible premium (or occasionally discount) is a measure of the percentage extra amount that the market is prepared to pay for this option. The convertible premium/discount is derived by first calculating the exercise cost of the asset via the purchase of the convertible. This is given by:

$$EC = \frac{P}{100} \times PC$$

where:

- EC exercise cost
- P dirty price of the convertible
- PC conversion price

Sometimes the asset into which the convertible bond is converted is in a different currency to that of the bond. In this case, the currency exchange rate is normally specified and the conversion price has to be adjusted appropriately.

The conversion premium/discount is then:

$$PM = \frac{(EC - AP)}{AP} \times 100\%$$

where:

- PM convertible premium/discount (%)
- EC exercise cost
- AP price of purchasing the underlying asset directly in the market

When a bond is convertible into an equity share, the conversion is often exercisable on specific dates over a number of years. Normally the convertible will yield more than the equity, as a result it is often interesting to calculate the breakeven period over which one must hold the convertible for the extra income, assuming the equity dividends do not change, to compensate for the conversion premium. The breakeven period is given by:

$$BE = \frac{EC - SP}{g \times PC/100 - d}$$

where:

- BE breakeven period in years
- EC exercise cost of purchasing one share via the convertible
- SP price of one share in the market
- PC conversion price
- g annual convertible coupon rate (%)
- d gross annual equity dividend payment

B.14 DISCOUNT

Money market instruments such as Treasury bills, commercial paper, bankers acceptances etc., are frequently traded on the basis of a discount to par or redemption value. Discounts are quoted at an annual percentage rate, based normally on a 360 or 365 day year. The percentage price paid for a money market instrument quoted at a discount rate is given by:

$$P = \left(1 - \frac{R \times f}{100}\right) \times 100$$

where:

- P percentage price of the instrument
- R annual percentage discount rate
- f fraction of a year from settlement to redemption based on actual calendar days usually divided by 360 or in the case of sterling 365

B.15 MONEY MARKET YIELD

The discount on a money market instrument can be converted into a yield so that it can be compared with other securities. The formula for a money market yield is:

$$MMY = \frac{R}{P} \times 100$$

$$MMY = \frac{R}{1 - R \times f/100}$$

where:

- MMY money market yield (%)
- P percentage price of the instrument
- R annual percentage discount rate
- f fraction of a year from settlement to redemption based on actual calendar days usually divided by 360 or in the case of sterling 365

It should be noted that the money market yield discounts the payment on a linear and a not compounded basis. Hence the yield is not directly comparable with a redemption yield that has been compounded semi-annually or annually.

B.16 CERTIFICATE OF DEPOSIT YIELD

Most certificates of deposit (CDs) pay a single coupon at redemption. This coupon is based on the percentage annual coupon rate and the fraction of a year to which it applies. CDs with only a single payment at redemption are quoted on a yield basis, and their price is given by:

$$P = \frac{C + g \times f}{1 + y \times f}$$

where:

- y quoted yield (%)
- P percentage price of the instrument
- C percentage redemption value – with CDs this is usually 100
- g quoted annual interest rate (%)
- f fraction of a year from settlement to redemption based on actual calendar days usually divided by 360 or in the case of sterling 365

The yield y in the formula above is comparable to the money market yield.

B.17 WARRANT CALCULATIONS

Bonds are sometimes issued with warrants attached to allow the holder to purchase further bonds or equity shares at a predefined price, the exercise price. After a while the warrants are usually traded on their own. The exercise cost of purchasing the designated security via the warrant is given by:

$$EC = \frac{WP}{n} + EP$$

where:

- *EC* exercise cost
- *WP* warrant price
- *n* adjustment factor to allow for the number of bonds or shares that can be purchased with each warrant
- *EP* exercise price

Since a warrant is an option, the exercise cost of purchasing the asset via the warrant is often more expensive than directly in the market. As a result a warrant premium/discount is often calculated. Its formula is:

$$PM = \frac{EC - AP}{AP} \times 100$$

where:

- *PM* warrant premium/discount (%)
- *EC* exercise cost
- *AP* price of purchasing the underlying asset directly in the market

If the exercise price of a warrant is less than the price of the security in the market, the warrant is said to have an intrinsic value, which is given by the following formula:

$$IV = (AP - EP) \times n \quad \text{if} \quad AP > EP$$

where:

- *IV* intrinsic value
- *EP* exercise price
- *AP* price of purchasing the underlying asset directly in the market
- *n* adjustment factor to allow for the number of bonds or shares that can be purchased with each warrant

As the price of a warrant is usually less than that of the underlying asset, its price tends to be more volatile. As a result a warrant gearing or leverage ratio is often calculated. The formula for this is:

$$WG = \frac{AP \times n}{WP}$$

where:

- *WG* warrant gearing or leverage
- *AP* price of purchasing the underlying asset directly in the market
- *n* adjustment factor to allow for the number of bonds or shares that can be purchased with each warrant

B.18 COMPOUNDING FREQUENCY ADJUSTMENTS

Since interest is paid on a bond at the end of a period, if you compare two otherwise identical bonds, where one pays interest once a year and the other pays interest twice a year, the one paying twice a year pays half the annual interest to an investor six months before the other one. Hence, it is valued more highly than the bond that pays just once a year.

Appendix B: Mathematical Formulae

It is very easy to convert yields that are compounded once a year to twice, four times or 12 times a year and vice versa. The yields are related as follows:

$$(1 + y_a) = \left(1 + \frac{y_s}{2}\right)^2 = \left(1 + \frac{y_q}{4}\right)^4 = \left(1 + \frac{y_m}{12}\right)^{12} = \exp(y_c)$$

where:

- y_a yield compounded annually ($y_a = 0.06$ for a yield of 6 %)
- y_s yield compounded semi-annually
- y_q yield compounded quarterly
- y_m yield compounded monthly
- y_c yield compounded continuously

More generally we have:

$$y_r = r \times \left[\left(1 + \frac{y_h}{h}\right)^{h/r} - 1\right]$$

where:

- y_r yield compounded r times a year
- y_h yield compounded h times a year
- r required compounding frequency per year
- h original compounding frequency per year

Table B.1 compares equivalent yields compounded at different frequencies. Similarly, it is possible to convert and compare modified duration and convexity calculations based on different compounding frequencies.

When calculating a Macaulay duration it does not matter whether you calculate it using yields compounded annually in years or semi-annually in half years. The result in both cases is a period of years. In other words we have:

$$D_a = \frac{D_h}{h}$$

Table B.1 Equivalent yields compounded at different frequencies

	Compounding frequency			
Annual	Semi-annual	Quarterly	Monthly	Continuously
0.0000	0.0000	0.0000	0.0000	0.0000
1.0000	0.9975	0.9963	0.9954	0.9950
2.0000	1.9901	1.9852	1.9819	1.9803
3.0000	2.9778	2.9668	2.9595	2.9559
4.0000	3.9608	3.9414	3.9285	3.9221
5.0000	4.9390	4.9089	4.8889	4.8790
6.0000	5.9126	5.8695	5.8411	5.8269
7.0000	6.8816	6.8234	6.7850	6.7659
8.0000	7.8461	7.7706	7.7208	7.6961
9.0000	8.8061	8.7113	8.6488	8.6178
10.0000	9.7618	9.6455	9.5690	9.5310

where:

D_a Macaulay duration calculated in years using yields compounded annually
D_h Macaulay duration calculated in periods, there being h periods in a year, using yields compounded h times a year
h number of compounding periods a year

Since modified duration is equal to the Macaulay duration multiplied by the discounting factor using annual or semi-annual compounding, it varies according to the compounding frequency:

$$MD_h = \frac{D}{1 + y/h}$$

where:

MD_h modified duration calculated with compounding h times a year
D Macaulay duration in years
y redemption yield of the bond compounded h times a year
h number of compounding periods a year

As the Macaulay duration is usually quoted in years, the modified duration is also usually quoted in years.

In order to convert the convexity of a bond from being compounded annually to periodically, you have to multiply the annual figure by the square of the number of periods per year:

$$CX_a = \frac{CX_h}{h^2}$$

where:

CX_a convexity calculated with annual compounding
CX_h convexity calculated with compounding h times a year
h number of compounding periods a year

B.19 PORTFOLIO YIELD

A reasonable estimate for the overall yield of a bond portfolio is given by the following formula, which weights the contribution of the yield of each holding by the size of the holding and by their modified duration, which is a proxy for the average time that they could be held:

$$PY = \frac{\sum_{i=1}^{n} N_i \times P_i \times MD_i \times RY_i}{\sum_{i=1}^{n} N_i \times P_i \times MD_i}$$

where:

PY estimated portfolio yield
n number of bonds in the portfolio
N_i nominal value of the nth bond
P_i dirty (or gross) price of the nth bond
MD_i modified duration of the nth bond
RY_i redemption yield of the nth bond

and where the summation is performed on all the bonds in the portfolio.

B.20 PORTFOLIO MACAULAY DURATION

A reasonable estimate of the Macaulay duration of a bond portfolio is given by the weighted average of the durations of the bonds weighted by their current values:

$$PD = \frac{\sum_{i=1}^{n} N_i \times P_i \times D_i}{\sum_{i=1}^{n} N_i \times P_i}$$

where:

- *PD*   estimated Macaulay duration of the portfolio
- *n*   number of bonds in the portfolio
- N_i nominal value of the nth bond
- P_i dirty (or gross) price of the nth bond
- D_i Macaulay duration of the nth bond

and where the summation is performed on all the bonds in the portfolio.

B.21 PORTFOLIO MODIFIED DURATION

A reasonable estimate of the modified duration of a bond portfolio is given by the weighted average of the modified durations of the bonds weighted by their current values:

$$PMD = \frac{\sum_{i=1}^{n} N_i \times P_i \times MD_i}{\sum_{i=1}^{n} N_i \times P_i}$$

where:

- *PMD* estimated modified duration of the portfolio
- *n*   number of bonds in the portfolio
- N_i nominal value of the nth bond
- P_i dirty (or gross) price of the nth bond
- MD_i modified duration of the nth bond

and where the summation is performed on all the bonds in the portfolio.

Appendix C
Bond Market Glossary

30/360

Method of calculating interest, including accrued interest, on an instrument based on a calendar of twelve 30 day months. With this method interest does not accrue on the 31st of a month and there is always assumed to be three days between 28 February and 1 March. This method originally arose in the pre-computer era. There are slight differences to the calculations in North America and Europe.

AAA or Aaa

The highest security risk rating awarded to a bond or issuer by a rating agency. Standard & Poor and Fitch rate such securities AAA, whereas Moody rates them Aaa.

ABS

See 'Asset-backed security'.

Accrued interest

Bonds normally pay predefined interest amounts on predefined days. Accrued interest is the interest earned on the bond since the last interest date or, in the case of a new issue from the issue date, up to the value date. When buying or selling a bond, the accrued interest is usually added to, or in a few markets immediately before a coupon payment, when the seller keeps it, deducted from the price of the bond.

Actual/actual

Method of calculating accrued interest on a daily basis based on the number of actual calendar days since the last coupon date or for a new issue from the issue date, divided by the actual calendar days in the period.

ADR

See 'American Depository Receipt'.

AER

See 'Annual equivalent rate'.

All-in price

The dirty or gross price of a security.

American Depository Receipt

The shares of a non-US company that have been repackaged to make them more attractive to US investors.

American option

An American option gives the holder the right to exercise the option at any time up to the expiry date of the option. This is in contrast to a European option which is only exercisable on a specified date.

Annual equivalent rate

This is a UK term which means the compounded interest rate or yield on the security or other instrument. The interest is compounded annually.

Annuity

An annuity is an instrument that pays regular amounts of money like a normal bond, but the payments represent a mixture of interest and return of capital. If the payments are of a fixed amount, over time the interest proportion will reduce and conversely the capital repayment proportion will increase.

Insurance companies issue 'life annuities', which pay out regular amounts until the death of the beneficiary. When this occurs, there is often no residual value.

APR

Annual percentage rate. This term is sometimes used instead of the 'annual equivalent rate' (see above).

Arbitrage

The process of buying instruments in one market, currency or country, and selling identical instruments in another to take advantage of price differences.

Asset-backed security

An asset-backed security is a security where the payment of coupons and the return of the principal are guaranteed by a claim on the underlying assets. The underlying collateral is often a pool of mortgages, but it could be credit card receivables, car loan backed securities or similar other types of loans.

Frequently these securities have been created by taking loans off a bank's balance sheet and putting them into a special-purpose vehicle by a process called 'securitization'. Initially the bonds often have a credit rating of AAA or AA, but this can change over time as the underlying assets are redeemed, which results in a partial prepayment of the bond.

Ask price

The price at which a market maker will sell the security to an investor. It is also known as the 'offer price'.

At-the-money

For a warrant this means a security where the cost of exercising the option is the same as the current price of the exercisable security.

Auction

A process whereby securities are issued to the market. Investors submit bids for the securities on a price or yield basis. If there are more bids than securities, the securities are issued to those people with the highest bids. The auction rules vary considerably from market to market.

Average life

If a bond is redeemed in more than one tranche, its average life is the period to the weighted average of the redemption dates.

> **Example C.1**
>
> If 40 % of a bond is redeemed on 1 July 2010 and the remaining 60 % is redeemed on 1 July 2015, then its weighted average redemption date is 1 July 2013. The bond's average life is the period from now up to the weighted average redemption date.

Backwardation

Backwardation means it is possible to buy a security for less than it is possible to simultaneously sell the same security, thus making a profit. Such occurrences for obvious reasons do not usually last for long.

> **Example C.2**
>
> Consider a security where two market makers make quotations. The first market maker quotes 90–91 and the second 92–93 for the security. If this occurs it is theoretically possible to buy the security from the first market maker for 91 and simultaneously sell the same security to the second market maker for 92.

Bankers' acceptance

A banker's acceptance starts as an order by a bank's customer to a bank to pay an amount of money in the future, usually within six months. Effectively it starts as a postdated cheque. When accepted the bank assumes responsibility for the payment. They are used in foreign trade where the credit worthiness of one trader is unknown to the trading partner. Acceptances are traded in the secondary market at a discount to their face value.

Barbell

An investment strategy involves investing in two securities, one with a short maturity/duration and the other with a long maturity/duration, instead of a single security with a medium-term maturity/duration.

Example C.3

Consider the following three bonds from the same issuer which pay coupons once a year:

Bond	Coupon rate	Life to maturity (years)	Price	Yield (%)	Duration
A	5.0	5.0	100	5.0	4.53
B	5.5	10.0	100	5.5	8.06
C	6.0	20.0	100	6.0	12.62

An investment of 1 000 000 in bond B would have a duration of 8.06 and yield 5.5 %.

On the other hand, an investment of 564 000 in bond A and 436 000 in bond C will have the same duration of 8.06, but will produce a different yield. Such a strategy is called a barbell or butterfly strategy.

Basis point

A yield or price change of 0.01 %. For example, if the price on a security changes from 98.00 to 98.25, then the price is said to have changed by 25 basis points.

Basis risk

Basis risk occurs when one kind of market risk is hedged with an instrument that performs in a similar but not necessary identical way.

Bearer bond

A bond where the physical possession of the certificate implies ownership, e.g. as is the case with ordinary bank notes. Most international bonds are in fact bearer bonds, but the certificates are frequently all held centrally by Euroclear or Cedel, with the result that many of the advantages of registered bonds are achieved.

Benchmark security

A liquid security, relative to which some securities are compared or sometimes quoted and traded.

Beta

Although usually associated with equities and equity-related products, based on historic information it measures the sensitivity of an instrument to its market.

If a security has a beta of 1 then, based on historic performance, it is expected to increase or decrease in value by the same amount as the appropriate market. If it has a value of 2 then historically it will move by twice the amount of the market. If a security moves countercyclically then its beta will be negative.

Bid-offer spread

The difference between the price that a market maker will sell a security to an investor (offer or ask price) and the price that the market maker is prepared to buy the same security from an investor (bid price).

Bid price

The price at which a market maker will buy a security.

Bill

Bills are short-term money market instruments. They are usually issued for a period of not more than 12 months.

BOBL

Bundesobligationen. German Government bonds issued with a life to maturity of up to five years.

Bond Market Association

A trade organization of over 200 securities firms, banks and other market participants that underwrite, trade and sell debt securities and other financial products globally. It has offices in New York, Washington and London. It represents the interest of its members in these markets before regulators and legislators, establishes market practices and standardization of procedures and documentation to promote market efficiency and integrity.

BOT

Buoni Ordinari del Tesoro. Italian Government Treasury bills.

bp

See 'Basis point'.

Brady bonds

Brady bonds represent the restructuring of non-performing bank loans of emerging market governments into marketable securities. An agreement for the restructuring of non-performing bank loans was first worked out between the United States and Mexico by the then Secretary of the Treasury Nicholas Brady.

BTAN

Bons du Trésor à Taux Fixe et Interêt Annuel. French Government bonds issued with a life to maturity of less than five years.

BTF

Bons du Trésor à Taux Fixe. French Government bills.

BTP

Buoni del Tesoro Poliennali. Italian Government fixed-rate notes.

Bulldog

A sterling bond issued in the United Kingdom by a non-UK issuer.

Bullet bond

A bond that has been issued without any call or other options, i.e. a bond that should normally be redeemed on its maturity date irrespective of prevailing interest rates. Bullet bonds are also called 'option free bonds'.

Bund

Bundesanleihen. A German Government bond issue, which has been issued with an initial life of more than five years.

Bundesschatzanweisungen

Short-term German Government bond issues. They usually have an initial life of two years.

Butterfly

See 'Barbell'.

Buy/Sell Back

A reverse repo. (see Chapter 6 on repos).

Call

For a bond, the ability of the issuer to redeem (i.e. call) the bond early. The bond's prospectus specifies the circumstances and the notice period required for a bond to be called. Sometimes a bond can only be called at a premium.

CCT

Certificati di Credito del Tesoro. Italian Government floating-rate notes.

CD

See 'Certificate of deposit'.

CDO

See 'Collateralized debt obligation'.

CDS

See 'Credit default swap'.

Cedulas

A Spanish covered bond or *Pfandbrief*.

Central counterparty

In some markets, in order to reduce counterparty risk, a central counterparty has been created, which is guaranteed by the members of the market (exchange). The central counterparty is thus less likely to default than an individual member.

As soon as a transaction has been agreed between two members, it is replaced by two separate transactions with the central counterparty: a sale of the security from the seller to the central counterparty, and a purchase of the same security with the same terms from the central counterparty by the buyer. This process is called 'novation'.

In addition, the existence of the central counterparty potentially allows transactions to be netted out, thus further reducing the counterparty risk.

Example C.4

In the morning member A sells 1 000 000 of a security to member B for 950 000. Later that day member A buys back 1 000 000 of the same security from B for 945 000. If these two transactions are netted out, the only obligation is for member B to pay A 5000.

Central Securities Depositary

An organization that holds securities in either a dematerialized or immobilized form, thus enabling transactions to be processed by book entry transfer.

Certificate of deposit

A certificate of deposit is a money market instrument that has normally been issued with a life to maturity of up to one year, although some have been issued with lives of up to five years. The majority of certificates of deposit pay a single coupon at maturity.

CGO

UK Central Gilts Office.

Classic repo

See Chapter 6, section 6.1.

Clean price

The price of a bond excluding any accumulated accrued interest. This is normally the way that bonds are quoted.

Closing leg

The second and closing half of a repo transaction.

CMO

See 'Collateralized mortgage obligation'.

Collateralized debt obligation

Collateralized debt obligations are securities backed by a portfolio of bonds or loans that can be divided into different slices of risk. This enables the securities to appeal to a range of investors.

Collateralized mortgage obligation

Similar to a collateralized debt obligation, but secured on a pool of mortgage-backed securities.

Commercial paper

Commercial paper is a short-term unsecured promissory note that has been issued by a company in the open market. Normally, commercial paper is issued with a zero coupon.

Common stock

A term used, especially in the US, for 'ordinary shares'.

Compounding period

Redemption and holding yield calculations usually assume that any interest and other payments are reinvested periodically, i.e. compounded. If the reinvestment period is one year, then the yield is said to be compounded annually. Similarly, if it is reinvested every six months, then it is said to be compounded semi-annually.

Conversion premium/discount (%)

For a convertible the percentage premium or discount that has to be paid for buying the underlying security (into which the convertible can be converted) via the convertible as opposed to buying the security directly.

Convertible

A convertible is a bond that gives the holder the option on specific dates or during a specific period to convert the bond into another security. Although the other security is normally an ordinary share, convertibles have been issued with the option to convert into other bonds.

Convexity

The relationship between yield (to maturity) and price for a bond is not linear and varies from bond to bond. This measures the degree of curvature.

Counterparty

The other party in the purchase or sale of a security: i.e. the counterparty of a purchaser of a security is the seller and vice versa. For most investors the counterparty is usually the market maker.

Coupon

The annual rate of interest of the bond, which may be paid in one or more instalments. Nearly all interest-paying bonds pay interest annually, semi-annually, quarterly or monthly.

With a bearer bond, the physical coupons are attached to the bearer certificate. For the holder to get a payment the coupons have to be detached by the paying agent.

Coupon frequency

The number of coupon payments for a bond in a year. Bonds usually pay interest one, two, four or twelve times a year. In the UK and USA for fixed-rate bonds, this is usually two, whereas in most of Continental Europe it is usually one.

Coupon payment

An actual interest payment: not to be confused with the annual coupon rate.

Coupon payment date

The date on which an interest or coupon payment is due. With fixed-rate bonds, but not normally with floating rate notes, the payment date may be a non-business day (e.g. at a weekend or on a bank holiday). When this occurs the payment will be delayed until the following business day.

Covered bonds

Covered bonds are bonds issued by banks and are secured on a pool of mortgages or public loans on the bank's balance sheet. The bonds are considered to be very secure since they are covered by the issuer and have preferential claim over the cover pool in the event of insolvency. In Germany, the covered bond market, where they are known as *Pfandbrief*, has been in existence for over a century. The covered bond market is growing fast in a number of European countries. They are called *Obligation Foncières* in France, *Lettres de Gage* in Luxembourg and *Cedulas Hipotecarias* in Spain.

Credit default swap

Credit default swaps (CDS) allow investors to insure the credit risk of their bond and loan holdings. They also allow them to take on risks where they think that the terms are attractive.

An investor who holds a normal bond can buy a credit default swap for the bond. The investor makes regular payments to the market maker, who in turn guarantees payment of the whole amount of the underlying bond regardless of whether the issuer defaults during the life of the CDS.

CTO

Certificati del Tesoro con Opzione. Italian Government putable fixed-rate notes.

CTZ

Certificati del Tesoro – Zero Coupon. Italian Government two-year zero-coupon bonds.

Cum-dividend

The trading status of a bond where the purchaser is entitled to receive the next interest payment. In some markets it is possible for bonds to have the alternative status of ex-dividend, where the seller has the right to receive the next interest payment.

Cumulative preference shares

A preference share issued by a company where the entitlement to dividends continues to accumulate even if the company cannot afford to pay any dividends.

Example C.5

Consider a company whose share capital consists of 5 % cumulative preference shares and ordinary shares. For some years the company makes reasonable profits and as a result it pays out 5 % on the preference shares and a dividend on the ordinary shares. The company then has two very lean years and as a result it cannot afford to pay either the preference or the ordinary dividend. In the third year the company starts making profits again. However, before it can pay an ordinary dividend it has to pay the cumulative preference shares a dividend of 15 % (5 % for each of the missed years and 5 % for the current year).

Current yield

A yield that does not allow for any potential gain or loss, e.g. at redemption. For a bond this is just the annual coupon divided by the clean price. This is similar to the dividend yield on an equity share. It is also known as a flat, interest or running yield.

> **Example C.6**
>
> For a bond with a 6% coupon priced at 90% this is:
> $$6 \times 100/90 = 6.67\%$$

Day count method

Method of calculating accrued interest for a bond. Although there are many variants, there are five main methods. They are:

Actual days/actual days
Actual days/365
Actual days/360
30/360 (European method)
30/360 (US method)

These methods are described in more detail under 'Accrued interest' in Appendix B.

Day trading

Buying and selling the same security during the same day.

DBV

See 'Delivery by value'.

Debenture

A bond frequently issued by a company, which is often secured on a specific asset or a group of assets, e.g. on a property.

Debt Management Office

The UK Debt Management Office, which was established on 1 April 1998, carries out the function of debt management for the UK Government. It is an executive agency within HM Treasury.

Default risk

The credit risk associated with the issuer of a bond failing to pay all the coupons and to repay the principal in a timely way is called the default risk of a bond. Even if a bond goes into default, the holder normally recovers a percentage of the investment. This percentage is called the 'recovery rate'.

Delivery by value

A process that enables a UK CGO member to borrow from or lend money to another CGO member against overnight gilt-edged collateral.

Delivery versus payment

A mechanism that enables the simultaneous exchange of securities and cash. As a result neither the purchaser nor the seller of the securities is at risk of default by the other party.

Dematerialized securities

Securities held in a book transfer system with no certificates.

Denomination

The denomination of a bond is usually the smallest amount of the bond that it is possible to hold. This could be on a central register or on the certificate with bearer bonds.

Example C.7

In the UK gilt-edged market, where the holdings are held on a central register, it is possible to hold £0.01 of a bond – hence the bonds have a denomination of just 1 p. However, in the eurodollar market the bond denominations are usually at least $1000 and in some cases as much as $100 000 or even $1 million.

A few bearer bonds have been issued with multiple denominations, e.g. $10 000, $25 000 and $100 000.

Derivative

A generic term for an option and/or a future to buy or sell a security or a combination of instruments. The terms may be very complicated.

Dirty price

The price of a bond including any accrued interest. If you purchase a bond, this is the price you will have to pay. The 'dirty' or 'gross' price of a bond is its clean price plus or minus any accrued interest.

Discount rate

A measure, expressed as an annual rate per cent, of how much the price of a security is less than its redemption value. This is usually applied to money market instruments that do not have a coupon.

> **Example C.8**
>
> If an instrument that will be redeemed at 100 in 3 months' time is priced at 98, it has a discount of $(100 - 98) \times 4/100 = 8\,\%$.

Discounted margin

The discounted margin for a floating-rate note measures the yield premium or discount of the note relative to its indicator rate. It allows for both the current yield effect on the margin and allows for any capital gain.

Dispersion

A measure of the variance of a bond's cash flows around the date of its Macaulay duration.

Dividend

Although dividend usually refers to an interest payment for a preferred or ordinary share, it is sometimes used to denote a coupon payment on a bond.

Dividend yield

For an equity share this is the estimated current annual dividend divided by the price. Dividend yields are sometimes grossed up to allow for tax that has been paid on the dividends. This is similar to the current yield on a bond.

DMO

See 'Debt Management Office'.

Domestic bond

A bond issued in a country in the currency of that country by a domestic issuer.

> **Example C.9**
>
> A bond issued in sterling by the UK Government (i.e. a gilt-edged security). A bond issued in the US in US dollars by Ford.

Dragon bond

A bond issued in Asia but denominated in US dollars.

Dual currency bonds

Bonds that pay interest in one currency but repay the capital in another are referred to as dual currency bonds. There is a variety of different models of dual currency bonds. Some fix the exchange rate between the currencies at the issue date, whereas others use the exchange rate at the time of the cash flow payment, and others even offer the investor the choice of the payment currency.

Duration

The average life of all the anticipated future cash flows of a bond discounted at the redemption yield rate. This is the average time your investment in the bond will be outstanding assuming you hold the bond until maturity allowing for the cost of money.

DV01

Dollar value of an oh one. It measures the sensitivity of the price to a change in yield of 0.01 (i.e. one basis point). DV01 is similar to 'modified duration', but instead of measuring the percentage change in price as modified duration does, it measures the actual change.

Example C.10

Consider a bond with a modified duration of 5.0.

If the bond has a dirty price of 120, then its DV01 will be $1.2 \times 5 = 6$.
If the bond has a dirty price of 100, then its DV01 will be $1.0 \times 5 = 5$.
If the bond has a dirty price of 80, then its DV01 will be $0.8 \times 5 = 4$.

DVP

See 'Delivery versus payment'.

ECP

See 'Euro commercial paper'.

EONIA

'Euro OverNight Index Average'. It is the effective overnight rate calculated as a weighted average of overnight unsecured lending transactions in the interbank market, initiated within the euro area by the panel banks.

Equity shares

See 'Ordinary shares'.

EURIBOR

Euro interbank offer rate. The rate of interest at which prime quality banks can borrow euros. EURIBOR rates are quoted for periods of 1 week up to 12 months.

Eurobond

An international bond issued in Europe. They are often listed on the Luxembourg or London Stock Exchanges. It may be issued in many different currencies, not just euros.

Euro commercial paper

A money market loan created on demand as part of a euro commercial paper (ECP) issue program. The paper is usually issued for a period of less than a year at a discount and does not pay a coupon.

Eurodollar bond

An international bond issued in Europe and denominated in US dollars.

European option

A European option is an option to purchase securities or currency for a defined price at a specified future date. The option, unlike American options, cannot be exercised prior to the date.

Exchangeable bond or note

The name sometimes given to a convertible bond where the conversion terms specify that it is convertible into a security that is not the ordinary share of the bond issuer.

Example C.11   Swiss Life Finance Ltd 1 % Exchangeable Bonds 2005

Although these bonds are guaranteed by Swiss Life Insurance and Pension Fund Company, they are exchangeable for UBS AG registered shares from 20 May 1998 at CHF 3450 each.

Ex-coupon date

The date on which the buyer of a bond or share does not get the next coupon payment. The seller keeps it, although this is after the seller has sold the shares. International bonds do not go ex-coupon until the coupon date. In the UK gilt-edged market securities (other than $3\frac{1}{2}$ % War

Loan) go ex-coupon seven business days before the coupon date. War Loan goes ex-coupon 10 business days before the coupon date.

Ex-dividend

A security is said to be traded ex-dividend or ex-coupon if the seller of the security keeps the next coupon payment instead of the purchaser.

Ex-dividend date

See 'Ex-coupon date'.

Exercise cost

The cost of purchasing the underlying security via the convertible or warrant. For a warrant, the exercise cost is the exercise price plus the cost of purchasing the warrant after adjusting for currency and the number of securities associated with the warrant.

Exercise price

For a warrant, this is the cost of exercising the option to purchase the security. It is also called the strike price.

Expiration date

The date at which an option or a futures contract expires.

Face value

See 'Nominal amount/value'.

Fannie Mae

Federal National Mortgage Association. Set up in the 1930s by the US Congress with the responsibility of creating a liquid secondary market in mortgages.

Flat price

The price of a bond where accrued interest is not added. It is usually applied to bonds where the issuer has defaulted and/or the payments are uncertain.

Flat yield

See 'Current yield'.

Floating-rate note

A debt instrument where the coupon payments are not fixed, but vary according to some external rate such as a three month LIBOR or a six month EURIBOR.

Example C.12

A floating-rate note might commit to pay quarterly coupons equivalent to one-eighth plus the three month dollar LIBOR rate two days prior to the beginning of the coupon period.

Foreign bond

A bond issued in a country in the currency of that country by a foreign issuer.

Forward contract

An agreement between two parties to conduct a transaction at a future date on terms that have been agreed.

Forward rate

An interest rate that will commence at some time in the future.

Example C.13

If an interest rate of 4.5 % is agreed for a period of, say, one year on a deposit that will be made in one year's time, 4.5 % is said to be a forward rate.

Freddie Mac

Federal Home Loan Mortgage Corporation.

FRN

See 'Floating-rate note'.

Future

An agreement to transact a deal at a future date at a specified price, e.g. an agreement to buy 1000 BT shares at 200 p each on 1 January 2008.

GDR

See 'Global depository receipt'.

GEMM

A UK gilt-edged market maker.

General collateral

Securities that can be used as collateral against cash borrowing in a repo contract.

Gilt-edged securities

Securities issued and guaranteed by the UK Government.

Gilts

See 'Gilt-edged securities'.

Ginnie Mae

Government National Mortgage Association. Formed in 1968 out of Fannie Mae to support the market in US Government insured mortgages.

Global bond

A global bond is one that was issued and is traded in both the eurobond market and the US Yankee bond market. The first global bond was issued by the World Bank in 1989.

Global certificate

Some bonds are issued with a single global certificate for the entire issue. Trading in such bonds is effected by changes in the record of ownership and not by the physical transfer of the securities.

Global depository receipt

The shares of a company that have been packaged to make them more attractive to international investors. For example, Asian company shares repackaged in US dollars.

GMRA

Global Master Repurchase Agreement. The GMRA is a standard master agreement for repo transactions. The first version of the TBMA/ISMA GMRA was published in 1992. The most recent version, taking account of market developments, was published in 2005.

Grey market

Trading a security on the 'grey market' refers to trading a security after it has been announced, but prior to it being formally issued. Such trades are transacted on a 'when issued' basis. This means that if the security is pulled for any reason, the transaction is deemed to be null and void.

Gross price

See 'Dirty price'.

Haircut

A term, originating in the USA, referring to the margin on a repo transaction.

Hedge fund

An investment partnership whose prospectus allows for the fund to take both long and short positions and use leverage and derivatives.

Hedging

Balancing an investment by buying or selling another instrument that moves in a similar way to the original investment, with the result that changes in interest rates etc. have very little impact on the value of the portfolio.

High-yield bond

A bond rated BB+, Ba1 or less by the rating agencies. They are also called 'junk bonds'.

ICMA

See 'International Capital Market Association'.

Immunization

Immunization is the process by which a bond portfolio is created to have an assured return for a specific time horizon, irrespective of changes in interest rates. If interest rates increase, then the return from reinvesting the coupons will increase, but the value of the underlying bonds will decrease, and vice versa. Immunization is the process of equalizing these effects.

Index-linked bonds

Bonds issued by a variety of issuers (e.g. the UK and US Governments) which promise to increase the coupon payments and the redemption amounts in line with some index. In the case of UK index-linked gilts, these will rise in line with the Retail Price Index, albeit lagged by three or eight months according to the issue.

Initial margin

The amount of additional collateral that has to be put up in a repo or other transaction to give protection to the lender of the money.

Instrument

Used to indicate any type of security, e.g. a bond, an equity or a derivative.

Interest

See 'Coupon'.

Interest payment date

See 'Coupon payment date'.

Interest yield

See 'Current yield'.

International bond

A bond that does not fall into the domestic or foreign bond categories. It frequently has an international issuing syndicate.

International Capital Market Association

The International Primary Market Association and the International Secondary Market Association merged in July 2005 to form the International Capital Market Association (ICMA). In addition, the ICMA includes the European activities of the Bond Market Association, which has sponsored the establishment of the European Securitization Forum (ESF) and the European Primary Dealers Association (EPDA) and provided advocacy on various issues in the global capital markets.

International Primary Market Association

The International Primary Market Association is the trade association that represents the interests of the international banks and securities firms that underwrite and distribute equity and debt securities in the primary market.

International Securities Market Association

The International Securities Market Association is the self-regulatory organization and trade association for the international securities market. The international nature of the market means that it is not subject to the same controls as the domestic primary and secondary markets. Since conception it has, *inter alia*, played the role of providing a global framework of industry-driven rules and recommendations that guide and regulate trading and settlement in the international securities market.

International security

A security governed by ISMA's Rule 2.2, i.e. international bonds and MTNs in most currencies, global bonds, GDRs and international warrants.

International Swaps and Derivatives Association

The International Swaps and Derivatives Association is the global trade association representing participants in the privately negotiated derivatives industry, a business covering swaps and options across all asset classes (including interest rates, currency, commodity and energy, credit and equity).

In-the-money

For a warrant this means a security where the cost of exercising the option is less than the current price of the exercisable security.

> **Example C.14**
>
> A warrant gives the holder the right to buy security A at 100, and security A has a current value of 120. The warrant is said to be in-the-money with an intrinsic value of $(120 - 100) = 20$.

Intrinsic value

The intrinsic value of an option is the difference between the strike price and the current underlying asset price. In other words, it is the value of the option if it were to be exercised immediately, assuming that this is possible.

Investment grade bond

A bond that has been rated BBB− or better by the rating agencies.

IPMA

See 'International Primary Market Association'.

Irredeemable bond

Although strictly incorrect, this term is often used to refer to an 'undated bond'.

ISDA

See 'International Swaps and Derivatives Association'.

ISIN

International security identification number. ISINs have been issued for securities quoted on most stock exchanges (China is an exception). The ISIN code is 12 characters long: the first two characters identify the ISIN code issuer (usually a country code or XS in the case of international issues), followed by a nine character issuer code and a check digit. Its definition conforms with ISO 6166.

Islamic bond

A bond that has been constructed in such a way that it does not conflict with Shariah principles. In particular, it does not pay a fixed rate of interest.

> **Example C.15**
>
> In January 2005, the Pakistan International Sukuk Company issued a five year floating-rate note based on these principles, which was designed to yield 220 basis points over a six month dollar LIBOR. Instead of interest, investors will receive regular payments on profits from subsequent approved investments.

ISMA

See 'International Securities Market Association'.

ISMA Rules

Rules governing how international securities should be traded. These are specified in the ISMA Statutes, By-laws, Rules and Recommendations.

ISO

International Standards Organization.

ISO 4217

The ISO standard that specifies three character currency codes for all the currencies in the world, e.g. 'USD' for US dollars and 'JPY' for Japanese yen.

Japanese yield

Usually refers to the 'simple yield to maturity' calculation.

JGB

A Japanese Government bond.

Junk bond

A bond that has been rated BB+, Ba1 or lower by the rating agencies. They are sometimes called 'high-yield bonds'.

Keepwell agreement

A contract between a parent company and one of its subsidiaries to maintain solvency and financial backing throughout the term of the agreement.

LBO

Leveraged buyout. In a leveraged buyout, a company is taken over by another company (the leveraged buyout) in such a way that the debt burden is increased with the aim of maximizing the return to the equity shareholders.

LIBID

London interbank bid rate. This is the rate at which a top quality bank will expect to have to borrow money.

LIBOR

London interbank offer rate. This is the rate at which banks will lend money to other top quality banks.

LIBOR fixing

The various LIBOR rates are agreed ('fixed') by the British Bankers Association at 11:00 am on each business day. LIBOR rates are fixed for a variety of currencies (e.g. sterling, US dollars and euros) and for a variety of periods up to one year (e.g. one month, three months or six months).

Life

The life of a bond from the calculation date to its expected maturity date.

LIMEAN

London interbank mean rate. This is the average of the London interbank bid rate (LIBID) and the offer rate (LIBOR).

Liquidity

A term describing the ease with which one can undertake transactions in a particular security or market. A market where there are always buyers and sellers at competitive prices is regarded as liquid.

Margin

The amount of excess collateral that has to be put up in a repo or other transaction to give protection to the lender of the money.

Market maker

A market maker is someone who makes a market in certain securities. With some securities the market maker has an obligation to continuously make two-way prices. The higher 'offer' price is the price at which the market maker is prepared to sell the security, and the lower 'bid' price is that at which the market maker is prepared to buy it.

Mark-to-market

Portfolio managers have a regular requirement to value the assets that they hold. Valuing their assets against the current market price is called 'marking to market'. Especially with some less liquid bonds, it is possible to obtain a mark-to-market price, even when it is not possible to get a dealing price.

Matched book

In the repo market, if a trader has transacted repos and reverse repos in the same securities in such a way that the net position is flat, then the trader is said to have a matched book.

Matilda bond

A bond issued in Australia in Australian dollars by a non-Australian issuer.

Maturity date

The final date when an instrument will be redeemed.

MBO

Management buy out.

MBS

See 'Mortgage-backed security'.

Medium-term note

A loan issued as a tranche of a pre-announced program. As a result it can be issued at less expense than a public bond issue. It is often distributed directly to a small group of investors. Medium-term notes trade in the same way as bonds.

Mezzanine debt

Mezzanine debt or finance is subordinated debt that sits between the senior debt of a company and its equity capital. It is used by companies as a means of raising capital when they are unable to raise more senior debt and do not want to dilute the equity base more than necessary. In order to make the mezzanine debt more attractive, it may have attached equity warrants.

Modified duration

A measure of the price volatility of a bond. It is defined as the percentage change in price for a unit change in yield.

Example C.16

A bond has a price of 90, a yield of 6%, and a modified duration of 4. If the yield changes to 5%, then the price will change to approximately:

$$90 + (6 - 5) \times 4 = 94$$

Money market

The money market usually refers to financial instruments (such as Treasury bills) that are issued with an initial period to maturity of between one day and one year.

Money market yield

A yield that measures the increase in value of the security at maturity but does not allow for the compound effect of time.

Example C.17

If a security that will be redeemed at 100 including any accrued interest in six months' time is priced at 98, the money market yield is:

$$(100 - 98)/98 \times 12/6 = 4/98 = 4.08\%$$

Mortgage debenture

A loan that is secured on property.

Mortgage-backed security

A type of asset-backed security, which is secured on a basket of mortgages on property.

MTN

See 'Medium-term note'.

Negative pledge

A commitment not to issue other debt instruments with a higher priority to receive interest and capital in the case of a default.

Nominal amount/value

The face value or amount of a bond, i.e. the amount of capital a holder receives when the bond is redeemed at par.

Nominal amount/value (uplifted)

The face value or amount of an index-linked bond that has been increased (uplifted) by the relevant index since the issue of the bond.

Note

A term that is often interchangeable with bond, e.g. a floating-rate note. Fixed-rate notes frequently have an original maturity of less than five years; e.g. US Treasury notes are issued with an original life of not more than five years, whereas Treasury bonds have a life of more than five years at issue.

OAT

Obligations Assimilables du Trésor. French Government bonds that have been issued with an initial life to maturity of more than five years.

Odd lots

An amount of securities that is not a multiple of some minimum amount; i.e. it is not a round lot.

Offer price

The price at which a market maker will sell a security to an investor. It is also known as an 'ask price'.

OLO

Obligations Linéaires – Lineaire Obligaties. OLOs are medium- or long-term dematerialized linear bonds issued by the Belgium Government.

On-the-run

The most liquid securities in a market; e.g. in the US Treasury market this refers to the latest, and usually most liquid, 1, 2, 3, 5, 10 and 30 year bonds. The opposite of 'on-the-run' is 'off-the-run'.

Opening leg

The first half of a repo transaction.

Option

The right to buy securities at a predetermined price at a date in the future.

Option free bond

See 'Bullet bond'.

Ordinary shares

The ordinary shareholders of a corporation own the assets of the company after all debts and prior commitments have been met. Ordinary shares are also called 'equity shares' or 'common stock'.

OTC

See 'Over-the-counter'.

Out-of-the-money

For a warrant, this means a security where the cost of exercising the option is more than the current price of the exercisable security. In other words, the option has no intrinsic value.

Over-the-counter

A trade that is not conducted on a stock exchange; e.g. most international securities are traded under ISMA Rules over the telephone and so are traded 'over-the-counter'.

Par value

The nominal value of a bond or loan. The majority of bonds are redeemed at par (normally 100). However, there is often a premium if they are called by the issuer at an earlier date

Permanent interest bearing shares

A type of preference share, issued in sterling by UK building societies. Their advantage is that the interest payments are tax deductible for the building society.

Perpetual bond

See 'Undated bond'.

Pfandbrief

A type of bond originally issued by German mortgage banks that is collateralized by long-term assets. These types of bonds represent the largest segment of the German private debt market and are considered to be very safe debt instruments. Instruments that are often referred to as 'covered bonds' and behave very similarly to *Pfandbrief* have now been issued by companies in a number of European countries.

The term Jumbo *Pfandbrief* is used to refer to the larger, more liquid segment of the *Pfandbrief* market. Such bonds need to have a nominal value of at least €500 million, and at launch at least three market makers who are committed to providing two-way prices throughout normal market hours.

PIBS

See 'Permanent interest bearing shares'.

Pik loan notes or bonds

Pik (payment-in-kind) loan notes or bonds pay interest in the form of more loans or obligations, instead of actual interest. They tend to be deeply subordinated debt and as a result in the event of a default lead to large losses. The deals generally have the option for the issuer to redeem the debt early with typically a reduced rate of interest. Michael Glazer's takeover of Manchester United is believed to have involved the use of Pik loans.

Preference shares

Shares, issued by companies, that receive dividends and any return of capital after tax, but before the ordinary shares.

Preferred shares

Usually the same as 'preference shares'.

Price spread

The difference between the bid and offered prices for the security.

Primary market

The primary market refers to the issuance and placing of new securities or new tranches of existing securities. It does not refer to the trading of securities after issuance.

Principal

The nominal amount or value of a bond.

Purchase fund

An issuer of a bond with a purchase fund may use it to repurchase some of the bonds early in the market place. There is usually a restriction on the price that can be paid to repurchase the bonds. A purchase fund may in certain circumstances enable the issuer to stabilize the price of the bonds in the market.

Put

The ability of the holder of a bond to ask for early redemption on specific dates.

Rating

A measure of the ability of the issuer to pay the coupons and repay the capital. A number of companies rate bond issues, of which Moody, Standard & Poor and Fitch are the largest international players. The highest rating that a bond can get is AAA or Aaa. This is awarded to bonds issued by issuers such as the French Treasury or the World Bank. The rating agencies also rate issuers for short-term money market instruments.

Real yield

The yield on an instrument after allowing for inflation.

> **Example C.18**
>
> If a security has a yield of 5.00 % when inflation is 3.00 % per annum, then it is said to have a real yield of 2.00 %.

Redemption date

The final date at which a bond will be redeemed. If a bond is redeemed in several tranches, this refers to the last date. Note that a bond may often be redeemed prior to the redemption date, e.g. if it has a call option.

Redemption value

The amount the issuer will repay when a bond is redeemed. Although in most non-indexed issues this is normally par (the nominal value), bonds are often redeemed at a premium if they are redeemed early.

Redemption yield

A measure of the return that an investor will get if the security is held to maturity from the coupons received and any capital gain/loss at redemption.

Registered security

A security where ownership is determined by whose name is on the central register, and not by who holds the certificate. See 'Bearer bonds'.

Registrar

An organization that keeps and maintains a record of all the holders of the security. By definition, bearer securities do not have a registrar.

Repo

An agreement to sell a security and buy it back at a later date. It is effectively a secured loan.

Retail price index

A UK measure of retail price inflation. UK index-linked gilt-edged securities use this index to adjust the interest and redemption payments.

Reverse repo

An agreement to buy a security and sell it back later, usually at a profit. It is the opposite of a repo.

Risk-free investment

There is no such thing as a totally risk-free investment. However, the term often refers to domestic government issues, denominated in the currency of the country, where the government has the possibility of just printing more, albeit possibly devalued, bonds.

Round lots

A quantity of securities that is a multiple of some minimum amount. In the US equity market, this is considered to be a multiple of 100 shares, whereas in the eurodollar bond market it is considered to be a nominal value of $100 000.

RPI

See 'Retail price index'.

Running yield

See 'Current yield'.

Samurai bond

A Japanese yen bond issued in Japan by a non-Japanese issuer (e.g. in February 2005 Ford sold JPY 160 billion ($1.5 billion) of three year Samurai bonds to Japanese investors).

Secondary market

The market for trading an instrument after the initial offering. The initial offering is called the 'primary market'.

Secured bond

A bond where the interest and capital repayments are secured on a portfolio of assets or a specific asset. If the issuer of the bond defaults in any way, the bond holders can take possession of the assets.

Sell/buy-back

An agreement to sell a security and buy it back at a later date. It is similar to a repo, but uses different legal documentation and involves the ownership of the securities being transferred to the other party.

Settlement date

The date on which the monies and the securities change hands. It is usually one or more business days after the transaction date.

Shares

See 'Ordinary shares'.

Simple margin

With a floating-rate note, the simple margin measures the return that can be obtained on the floating-rate note taking into account both the quoted margin and the capital gain or loss over the life of the note.

Sinking fund

A sinking fund is an amount of money used by the issuer of a bond to redeem part of the issue before the final redemption date. The bonds to be redeemed may be chosen by lot or a proportion of each holding is redeemed each time. Sometimes the issuer may buy back bonds in the market if it is cheaper than redeeming them.

Example C.19

A 6 % bond which is being redeemed in 10 years' time has a sinking fund that commits the issuer to redeem 10 % after eight years and a further 10 % after nine years. The selection is performed equally for all holders by reducing the principal of the bond held by 10 % after eight years, and then by a further 10 % of the original principal one year later. The bond pays coupons annually and is redeemed at par.

Thus a holder of 1 000 000 of the bond would receive:

After 1 year, interest of 60 000

....

After 7 years, interest of 60 000

> After 8 years, interest of 60 000 and a capital repayment of 100 000
> After 9 years, interest of 54 000 and a capital repayment of 100 000
> After 10 years, interest of 48 000 and a capital repayment of 800 000

Special collateral

In the repo markets, the cost of borrowing collateral of a certain type is frequently the same. However, if it is required to borrow a specific security that is in demand, the cost may have a lower repo rate. Such a bond is said to be 'tight' or 'special'.

Spens clause

A clause used in many sterling corporate bond issues, which defines the terms under which the issuer may redeem the issue early. The term allows the borrower to redeem (call) its bonds at a price that gives the same redemption yield as its reference UK gilt-edged issue.

In practice, the Spens-call clause is rarely exercised as it is prohibitively expensive for borrowers, especially for long-dated issues, as the corporate bond would usually trade at a yield premium to the relevant gilt.

Spot rate

An interest rate for an investment from today until the agreed maturity, without any intervening payments.

Spread

See 'Price spread' and 'Yield spread'.

Spread quotation

When a security is quoted as a spread over the yield of a benchmark security, the yield spread is usually quoted in basis points. For example, if a security is quoted with a spread of 55 basis points and the benchmark has a yield of 4.1 %, it will be priced to yield 4.65 %.

Stock

The term 'stock', especially in the US, usually refers to the ordinary shares of a company. However, the Bank of England has used 'stock' to refer to UK gilt-edged securities, e.g. $3\frac{1}{2}$ % War Stock.

Stock borrowing

Institutional borrowers such as insurance companies and pension funds sometimes prefer to lend out their holdings for a fee instead of becoming involved in a repo agreement. Such arrangements are called 'stock borrowing' or 'stock lending'.

Strike price

The price at which at an option may be exercised.

Strips

Investors would sometimes like to have a zero-coupon bond maturing on a specified date, which has been issued and guaranteed by a certain issuer. Unfortunately, government and other issuers do not tend to issue a range of zero-coupon bonds. To remedy this situation, in some markets, such as the UK gilt-edged market, arrangements have been made to disaggregate all the future coupon payments and the final redemption amount of some conventional fixed-rate bonds into separate securities. These are called 'strips'.

Sukuk

An Islamic bond.

$T + n$

Refers to a transaction being settled n business days after the transaction date (T).

> **Example C.20**
>
> For example, if a trade is agreed on Wednesday 10 January 2005 for settlement on $T + 1$, then the settlement date will be Thursday 11 January 2005. On the other hand, if the trade is agreed on Wednesday 12 January 2005 for settlement on $T + 3$, then the settlement date will be Monday 17 January 2005.

Some of the major government bond markets (e.g. US Treasury market and the UK gilt-edged market) usually trade on $T + 1$, whereas the Eurobond market usually trades on $T + 3$. It is normally possible to agree to a different settlement, although there may be a price penalty.

T-Bill

See 'Treasury bill'.

Tap issue

Another name for a new tranche of an existing security.

TARGET

'Trans-European Automated Real-time Gross settlement Express Transfer system'.
    TARGET is the real-time gross payment system for the eurozone. It consists of the national payment systems and the European Central Bank.

TBMA

See the 'Bond Market Association'.

Trade date

The date on which a transaction is agreed. This is usually one or more business days before the settlement date, when the transaction is concluded.

Tranche

An issuer may issue bonds with the same security and coupon and maturity terms on two or more dates. The bonds issued on a specific date are referred to as a 'tranche'. Sometimes new tranches are immediately fungible (i.e. interchangeable) with previous tranches. However, sometimes a new tranche will have a different first interest payment, and as a result it will not become fungible until after this payment.

Treasury bill

A short term money market instrument. Treasury bills have been issued by a number of governments (e.g. United States, Canada, United Kingdom and even Kenya). They are usually issued for periods of one month, three months, six months or one year.

It is conventional for bills not to pay a coupon, but be issued at a discount to their redemption value.

Treasury bond

In the US market a government debt security, which was originally issued with a life to maturity of at least 10 years. Other governments also issue 'Treasury Bonds', where the original life to maturity may be different.

Treasury gilt

In the UK market, a UK Government gilt-edged security originally issued on or after 1 April 2005. This means that all 8-month lag index-linked bonds are called 'Treasury Stock' and all 3-month lag index-linked bonds are called 'Treasury Gilt'.

The first Treasury gilt to be issued was $4\frac{1}{4}$ % Treasury Gilt 7/12/2055 on 26 May 2005.

Treasury note

In the US market, a US Government debt security that was originally issued with a life to maturity of less than 10 years.

Treasury stock

In the UK market, all UK Government gilt-edged bonds originally issued before 1 April 2005.

Undated bond

A bond without a specified final redemption date. Such bonds usually contain call and/or put options, which can be exercised in certain circumstances.

> **Example C.21**
>
> The UK Government has had the right to redeem its $3\frac{1}{2}$% War Loan Stock at par at any time since 1952. However, during this period there have been very few times when it would have made sense for the government to exercise this option, as the bond has normally been priced in the market at a significant discount to par. Hence, if the government had redeemed it, it would have cost it more money to refinance the debt.

Undated bonds are also referred to as 'irredeemable' or 'perpetual bonds'.

Unsecured loan stock

A bond that is not secured on any specific asset. In the event of a default it is treated as a normal creditor.

Value date

The date to which the details of a transaction refer. This is usually the same as the settlement date.

Vanilla straight bond

A 'bullet' or 'option-free' bond.

Variation margin

During the life of a repo transaction, if the value of the collateral changes significantly, either up or down, then the agreement may specify that the amount of collateral should be changed to equate with the cash part of the transaction. This is called 'variation margin'.

Volatility

For a bond this is the same as 'modified duration'. However, it is not as well defined for an equity issue, where it is just an indication of how variable its price movement has been.

Warrant

A right, but not an obligation, to buy or sell an instrument at a predetermined price during a specified time period.

When-issued trading

See 'Grey market'.

Withholding tax

A tax on coupon payments, which is deducted at source.

Writer

A party who receives the option premium in exchange for the risk of the option being exercised against him.

XD

See 'Ex-dividend'.

Yankee bond

A US dollar bond issued in the United States by a non-American issuer.

Yield

A measure of the return an investor will get on a security. The markets use a variety of calculations. These include: current yield, dividend yield, money market yield and redemption yield. For a bond, if the type of yield has not been specified, it normally means the redemption yield.

Yield compounding frequency

The redemption yield of a bond differs according to its compounding frequency. In the UK Government and US markets the compounding frequency is every 6 months, as the majority of bonds pay coupons every 6 months. Similarly, in the euro market it is paid annually as bonds tend to pay just one coupon a year.

It is very easy to convert a yield that has been calculated on an annual basis to a semi-annual basis and vice versa.

Yield Gap

The difference between the redemption yield on government fixed interest securities and that on equities. In the sterling market, the average yield on long-term gilt-edged securities is used. Although government securities are regarded as safer investments than equities, the yield gap is usually positive as the market expects the dividends on equity shares to grow.

Yield spread

Sometimes the price of a security is quoted as the spread over the yield of a specified benchmark security. The spread is usually quoted in basis points. For example, if a security is quoted with a spread 55 bps and the benchmark has a yield of 4.1 %, it will be priced to yield 4.65 %.

Yield to call

The redemption yield of a bond to its call date. Some bonds are callable on a variety of dates, often with different call values. Hence, there can be more than one yield to call. If not specified, this is usually the yield to the earliest call date.

Yield to maturity

This is the redemption yield of a bond if it is held to maturity (the redemption date). However, it should be noted that the assumption about the expected redemption date can change over time.

Yield to put

The redemption yield of a bond to the, normally first, putable date, i.e. the first date at which the holder can demand that the bond is redeemed.

Yield to worst

The redemption yield of a bond, from the holder's point of view, to the worst of the call and maturity dates, i.e. the yield that is the lesser of the yields to call and maturity. In some circumstances this calculation is useful as it is assumed that the issuer will behave in a way that minimizes costs.

YTM

See 'Yield to maturity'.

Zero-coupon bond

A bond that only pays out at maturity; i.e. it does not pay any dividends or coupons. In order to give an investor a return, such bonds are issued at a discount to their redemption value. Sometimes this discount can be very large, especially if the bond is not going to be redeemed for 20 or more years.

References

Braudel, Fernand (1982), *Civilization and Capitalism 15th–18th Century, The Wheels of Commerce*, William Collins Sons and Company Ltd; translated from French edition, *Les Jeux de 'Echange*, Libraire Armand Colin, Paris, 1979.

Brown, Patrick (1998), *Bond Markets: Structures and Yield Calculations*, GDP in association with International Securities Market Association.

Brown, Patrick (2002), *Constructing and Calculating Bond Indices*, 2nd edition, GDP.

United Kingdom Debt Management Office (2005), *Formulae for Calculating Gilt Prices from Yields*, 3rd edition, 16 March 2005.

Index

3G mobile phones 75
30/360 day-count convention 32–4, 156–7, 177, 187
30E/360 day-count convention 32–4, 156–7, 187

ABSs *see* asset-backed securities
accrued interest
    concepts 20–1, 32–65, 135–7, 155–8, 177
    mathematical formulae 155–8
actual prices 35
actual/360 convention 33–4
actual/365 convention 33–4
actual/actual convention 33–4
AER *see* annual equivalent rate
agencies, credit ratings 5–6, 29–30, 65, 75, 115–21, 152
agreements, repos 97–8, 100–3
Allied Domecq 116–17
alpha evaluations 52–3
American options 107–13, 178
annual equivalent rate (AER) 46–8
annual percentage rate (APR) 46–8, 178
annuities
    website 153–4
    concepts 15–16, 166–7, 178
    mathematical formulae 166–7
appendices 153–213
APR *see* annual percentage rate
arbitrage 178
asset swaps 123, 130
asset-backed securities (ABSs)
    see also securitization
    concepts 74, 147, 178–9
    indices 147
at-the-money options 111–12, 179
auctions 179
Australia 6, 9–10, 35
average life 149–50, 179

backwardation 179
balance sheets 7
Bank of England 1, 97, 100–1
Bank for International Settlements (BIS) 123
bank loans 1
Bank of Scotland 6–7
bankers' acceptances 64–5, 170–1, 180
    see also money markets
banks, repos 95–105, 182, 184
barbell 180
basis points 138–9, 180
basis risk 180
basis swaps 123, 132
bearer bonds 180
benchmarks 120–1, 147–52
beta evaluations 52–4, 181
bid-offer spreads 36–9, 181
BIS *see* Bank for International Settlements
BMA *see* Bond Market Association
BOBL 181
Bond Market Association (BMA) 95–6, 100
bonds
    see also coupon; *individual types*
    complex structures 120
    concepts 1–8, 9–26, 27–65, 120–1
    conditional coupon changes 75–6
    convertible bonds 4–5, 65, 69–73, 169–70, 185
    convexity 45, 56–65, 68, 144–6, 149, 164–5, 185
    currency of issue 2, 24–5, 31, 73, 120–1, 147–52, 193
    definition 1
    derivatives 1–2, 3–6, 30, 48–50, 65–78, 107–14, 123–39, 178, 188, 191, 203
    description 1–7, 147–52
    embedded options 1–2, 4–6, 9, 27, 30, 42, 48–50, 65–78
    equity contrasts 1, 7–8, 148–9

218 Index

bonds (*Continued*)
  guarantees 5–6
  indices 63–4, 147–52
  issuers 1–8, 29–30, 120–1, 147–52
  Macaulay duration 30, 45, 50–65, 144–5, 149, 162–3, 173–5, 190
  maturity dates 1–8, 16, 147–8, 200
  modified duration 45, 53–65, 144–5, 149, 163–4, 174–5, 201
  parties 1–8, 120–1
  performance measures 144–52
  portfolios 31, 52–3, 141–6, 174–5
  price unavailability 151–2
  prices 6–7, 29–40, 42–52, 101, 155–8, 188
  pricing 36–65, 68–9, 115
  profile examples 6–7
  quotes 6–7, 29–30, 32–6
  redemption yield 39–65, 68, 81–94, 117, 141–4, 149–50, 159–62, 168–9, 174–5, 205
  sinking funds 13–14, 65, 207
  tax 4, 26, 70, 145–6
  types 1, 2, 9–26, 30
  valuations 27–65, 115
  warrants 5, 78, 171–2, 211
  yield types 29, 39–65, 212
Brady bonds 181–2
break-even prices 70–3
bubble (humped) yield curves 79–82, 87–8
bullet (straight-coupon) bonds 9–10, 41–2, 49–50, 109–10, 182
Bunds 182
butterfly *see* barbell
buy/sell backs 182, 207
buying
  call options 107–8
  put options 108–9

call options 3–4, 16–17, 30, 42, 48, 65–9, 107–13, 182
  see also options
  buying 107–8
  concepts 107–13
  long call positions 107–8
  short call positions 108–9
  writing 108–9
call spread options 112–13
callable bonds, concepts 5, 65–9
Canada 7, 9–10, 20, 79
capital depreciation 90
capital gains 40–1, 145–6
caps, FRNs 18–19
car loan debt 74–5
cash flows
  dispersion 58–65, 165–6
  future cash flows 27–65, 144–5
CBOT *see* Chicago Board of Trade

website 153–4
CDOs *see* collateralized debt obligations
CDs *see* certificates of deposit
CDSs *see* credit default swaps
Cedel 95
certificates of deposit (CDs)
  concepts 22–3, 171–4, 184
  yields 22–3, 171
Chicago Board of Trade (CBOT) 134–7
Chicago Mercantile Exchange (CME) 134
Citigroup 97
classic moves, yield curves 93–4
classic repos 95–6, 100–5
  see also repos
classifications, indices 147–8
clean prices 32–4, 35–40, 43–4, 155–8
clearing houses, futures 135–7
Clearstream 95, 97
CME *see* Chicago Mercantile Exchange
collateral, repos 99–100, 101–4
collateralized debt obligations (CDOs) 74–5, 184
collateralized mortgage obligations 65, 184
combinations, options 112–13
commercial paper 23–4, 64–5, 170–1, 184
  see also money markets
commodities, futures 133–4
common stock
  see also equities
  concepts 1
complex structures, bonds 120
compound interest
  concepts 27–9, 85–6, 159–62, 172–4, 184–5
  frequency adjustments 28, 30, 172–4, 212
  mathematical formulae 159–62, 172–4
continuity needs, indices 150–2
conversion factors, futures 135–7
convertible bonds
  concepts 4–5, 65, 69–73, 169–70, 185
  mathematical formulae 169–70
  premiums 4–5, 70–3, 169–70, 185
convexity
  see also Macaulay duration
  concepts 45, 56–65, 68, 144–6, 149, 164–5, 185
  mathematical formulae 164–5
  pricing effects 56–7, 68
corporate bonds
  see also bonds
  concepts 2–8, 29–31, 79, 147–52
  equity contrasts 7–8, 148–9
  indices 147
'corridor' issues 18–19
counterparty risk 183, 185
  see also credit risk
coupons
  see also bonds
  accrued interest 32–65, 155–8

Index   219

concepts 1–8, 9–65, 75–6, 149–52, 155–8, 185
conditional coupon changes 75–6
frequency 2–3, 9–10, 28, 30, 42
indices 149–52
modified duration 55–6
step-up bonds 14–15
types 30
covenants, concepts 116–17
covered bonds 186
credit card debt 74–5
credit default swaps (CDSs) 123, 137–9, 186
concepts 137–9
definition 137
parties 137–8
pricing 138–9
credit derivatives 123, 137–9, 186
credit ratings 5–6, 29–30, 65, 75–6, 115–21, 147–8, 152, 178–9, 205
agencies 5–6, 29–30, 65, 75, 115–21, 152
concepts 115–21, 147–8, 152
downgrades 152
indices 152
credit risk 52–3, 100–1, 115–21, 133, 137–9, 183, 185, 187–8
concepts 115–21, 133
covenants 116–17
swaps 133
cross-currency swaps 123, 130–2
cum-dividend 186
cumulative preference shares 25–6, 186
currency of issue 2, 24–5, 31, 73, 120–1, 147–52, 193
current yield
concepts 39–43, 158, 187
mathematical formulae 158

day-count conventions 32–4, 156–7, 177, 187
debentures 4, 187
Debt Management Office 22, 152
default risk 100–1, 137–9, 187–8
see also credit risk
delivery 188
delivery versus payment (DVP) 95
demand and supply factors, yield curves 92–3
dematerialisation 188
Denmark 116
denomination 35, 148–9
derivatives 1–2, 3–6, 30, 48–50, 65–78, 107–13, 123–9, 178, 188, 191, 203
see also futures; options; swaps
concepts 123–9
types 123
uses 123
description, bonds 1–7, 147–52
dirty prices 32–4, 35–9, 42–52, 101, 155–8, 188

discounted margin
concepts 59–63, 167–9, 189
mathematical formulae 167–9
discounts
website 153–4
concepts 22–3, 27, 29–65, 170–1, 189
mathematical formulae 170–1
money markets 64–5
dispersion
cash flows 58–65, 165–6
concepts 58–65, 165–6, 189
mathematical formulae 165–6
dividends 7–8, 25–6, 189
yields 189
dropped bonds, index problems 151–2
dual currency bonds 73, 190
duration *see* Macaulay duration
DVP *see* delivery versus payment

EDSP *see* exchange delivery settlement price
electronic settlement 95–9
embedded options 1–2, 4–6, 9, 27, 30, 42, 48–50, 65–78
EONIA 97
equities 1, 148, 169–70, 185, 203
bond contrasts 1, 7–8, 148–9
convertible bonds 4–5, 65, 69–3, 169–70, 185
indices 148–9
EUREX 134–7
EURIBOR *see* Euro Interbank Offer Rate
Euro Interbank Offer Rate (EURIBOR) 16–17, 127–9, 191, 192
Eurobonds 31–2, 65–6, 191
Euroclear 95, 97
Euronext.Liffe 134–5
European Currency Unit 2
European Investment Bank 6, 29, 76–7, 79, 147
European markets 97–100, 117, 134–6, 156–7
European options 107–14, 191
European repos 97–100
euros 125–39
ex-coupon bonds (XD) 32–4, 37–9, 155–6, 191–2
ex-dividends 192, 212
exchange delivery settlement price (EDSP) 135–6
exchange-traded transactions 29–30, 134–7
exchangeable notes/bonds 72–3
see also convertible bonds
exercise, options 107–8, 111–13
exercise prices 70–3, 78, 107–13, 192
expected life 48–65, 149–50
expiry date, options 107–13

falling yield curves 79–82
Fannie Mae 192
Fitch 115–21

fixed-rate bonds
    see also bonds
    concepts 2–3, 9–16, 30, 33–4, 45, 54–65, 123–4
    types 9–16, 22
fixed/floating bonds 22
flat yield see current yield
flat yield curves 79–82, 87–8
floating-rate notes (FRNs)
    caps 18–19
    website 153–4
    concepts 1–3, 6–7, 10, 16–19, 30, 34, 59–62, 76–7, 123–4, 144, 160–2, 167–8, 192–3
    examples 17–19
    floors 18–19
    margin 59–62, 167
    payment dates 10, 16–19
    redemption yield 59–62, 160–2
    restrictions 18
    reverse floaters 76–7
floors, FRNs 18–19
Ford 152
foreign bonds 2, 193
forward-forward (forward) yield curves
    concepts 84–9
    zero-coupon yield curves 85–8
forward-rate agreements (FRAs) 123, 132–4, 154
    website 154
    concepts 123, 132–4
forwards 193
France 6–7, 9–10, 12, 20, 35, 55, 79
FRAs see forward-rate agreements
Freddie Mac 193
frequency
    compound interest adjustments 28, 30, 172–4, 212
    coupons 2–3, 9–10, 28, 30, 42
FRNs see floating-rate notes
FTSE 63–4, 148, 152
    100 148
    250 148
    350 148
    All-share 148
    index calculations 152
    UK Gilts Indices 63–4
fund managers 11, 141–6
future cash flows 27–65, 144–5
futures 123, 133–7, 188, 193
    clearing houses 135–7
    concepts 133–7
    definition 133
    parties 134–6

Garban-ICAP 128
GC see general collateral
general collateral (GC), repos 101–2
General Electric Capital 79

General Motors 152
Germany 1, 33–4, 79, 135
gilts 11–13, 29–31, 35–9, 63–4, 79–82, 115, 118–21, 136, 152, 194
    see also government bonds
Ginnie Mae 194
global bonds 194
Global Master Repo Agreement (GMRA) 97, 100–1
glossary 177–213
GMAC 139
GMRA see Global Master Repo Agreement
government bonds 1, 5, 7, 9–22, 29–31, 33–9, 63–4, 67–9, 79–82, 92–4, 99–2, 115–21, 136, 147–52
    see also bonds; gilts
graduated-rate bonds see step-up bonds
Greece 20
grey markets 194
guarantees 5–6

haircut 195
hedging 195
high-yield (junk) bonds 195, 199
holding period returns, portfolios 141–3
horizon dates
    website 154
    concepts 141–3
hybrid bonds, concepts 22

ICMA see International Capital Market Association
immunization programmes, portfolios 143–4
in-the-money options 111–12, 197
index-linked bonds
    concepts 2, 7, 19–22, 30, 34–6, 39, 62–5, 160–2, 168–9, 195
    redemption yield 39, 62–5, 160–2, 168–9
indexation lags 21–2, 35–6, 168–9
indexation techniques 20–2, 160–1, 168–9
indices
    bonds 63–4, 147–52
    classifications 147–8
    concepts 147–52
    constituent changes 150–2
    continuity needs 150–2
    data calculations 149–50
    dropped bonds 151–2
    equities 148–9
    maturity subdivisions 147–8
    problems 150–2
    production difficulties 148
    ratings downgrades 152
    selection 148–9
    subindex calculation gaps 151
    types 147

inflation 19–22, 62–5, 160–1, 168–9
initial margin 100–1, 135–7, 195
institutional investors 31, 35, 92–4, 104–5, 143–4, 149
insurance companies 31, 143–4, 149
interbank interest rates 3, 6, 16–19, 60–1, 76–7, 125–39, 191, 192, 199
interest payments
   see also coupon
   bonds 1–2
interest rate risk
   see also convexity
   concepts 56–65
interest rate swaps, concepts 123–33
interest rates
   concepts 30, 123–33
   expectations 30
   interbank interest rates 3, 6, 16–19, 60–1, 76–7, 125–39, 191, 192, 199
interest yield *see* current yield
internal rate of return 144–5
international bonds 29–30, 196
International Capital Market Association (ICMA) 95, 98–9
International Securities Association (ISMA) 97, 100–1
International Swaps and Derivatives Association (ISDA) 128
intrinsic value 78, 109–12, 197
investment strategies, yield curve changes 89–94
investment vehicles 2, 7
investors, bonds 1–8
irredeemable (undated) bonds 3, 11, 19, 52–4
ISDA *see* International Swaps and Derivatives Association
ISDAFIX 128
ISIN 198
Islamic bonds 198
ISMA *see* International Securities Association
ISO 198
issuers
   bonds 1–8, 29–30, 120–21, 147–52
   types 1, 2, 29–30, 147
Italy 9, 17, 20, 79

Japan 2, 9, 20, 31, 32–3, 40–1, 78, 79, 156, 198
Japanese yield *see* simple yield to maturity
JP Morgan Chase 97
junk bonds 195, 199

LIBID 199
LIBOR *see* London Interbank Offer Rate
life to maturity, concepts 48–65, 79–82, 149–50
LIFFE 128, 134–5
liquidations 8

liquidity 31, 115–21, 199
   concepts 119–21
   determinants 120–1
   market risk 119–21
loans
   books 74–5
   concepts 1–2, 7–8
   seniority 7–8
local authorities 2, 7
London Interbank Offer Rate (LIBOR) 6, 16–19, 60–1, 76–7, 125–39, 192, 199
long call positions 107–8
long put positions 108–9
Luxembourg Stock Exchange 29

Macaulay duration
   see also convexity
   website 154
   concepts 30, 45, 50–65, 144–5, 149, 162–3, 173–5, 190
   mathematical formulae 162–3, 173–5
   portfolios 144–5, 175
margins 59–63, 100–3, 135–7, 167, 200
mark-to-market valuations 100–1, 200
market makers 36–8, 104–5, 120–1, 200
market risk, liquidity 119–20
mathematical formulae 155–73
maturity dates 1–8, 16, 147–8, 200
MBSs *see* mortgage-backed securities
medium-term notes (MTNs) 24–5, 200
   concepts 24–5
mezzanine debt 8, 201
modern portfolio theory 52–3
modified duration
   website 154
   concepts 45, 53–65, 144–5, 149, 163–4, 174–5, 201
   coupon rates 55–6
   mathematical formulae 163–4, 174–5
   portfolios 144–5, 175
money markets
   see also bankers acceptances; commercial paper; Treasury bills
   CDs 22–3, 171–2
   concepts 9, 22–6, 34–6, 64–5, 148, 170–1, 201
   discounts 64–5
   yields 64–5, 171, 201
Moody 75, 115–21
mortgage-backed securities (MBSs)
   see also securitization
   concepts 7, 48, 73–5, 201
mortgages 1, 5, 7, 48, 73–5, 184, 201
MTNs *see* medium-term notes

National Savings 14–15
negative pledge clauses 29–30, 117

Netherlands 65–6
New York Stock Exchange (NYSE) 95
nominal value
see also principle
concepts 2–8, 34–6, 202
redemption amount 3
non-cumulative preference shares 25–6
normal yield curves 79–82
notes
see also floating-rate notes
concepts 1–2, 16–19, 210
NYSE see New York Stock Exchange

OECD 147
offer prices 202
options 1–2, 3–6, 30, 48–50, 65–78, 107–13, 178, 188, 191, 203
see also call . . . ; put . . .
American options 107–13, 178
calculations 107–13
combinations 112–13
concepts 1–6, 9, 27, 30, 42, 65–78, 107–13
definition 107
embedded options 1–2, 4–6, 9, 27, 30, 42, 48–50, 65–78
European options 107–13, 191
exercise 107–8, 111–13
expiry date 107–13
parties 107–13
premiums 107–13
pricing 109–12
straddles 112–13
strike prices 107–13, 209
time value 111–12
types 107–13
valuations 109–12
warrants 5, 78, 171–2, 211
ordinary shares 1, 7–8, 65, 203
see also equities
OTC see over-the-counter transactions
out-of-the-money options 111–12, 203
over-the-counter transactions (OTC) 123–5, 134, 203
concepts 123–5, 134, 145–6, 203
tax 145–6

par value see nominal value
par yield curves
calculation 86–7
concepts 86–9
pension funds 31, 92–4, 104–5, 143–4, 149
performance measures, portfolios 144–52
permanent interest bearing shares (PIBS) 3, 26, 203
concepts 26
tax 26

Pernod Ricard 116
perpetual bonds 6–7, 9–10, 11, 19
see also undated (irredeemable) bonds
Pfandbriefe 147, 204
PIBS see permanent interest bearing shares
portfolio theory 52–3
portfolios
website 154
concepts 31, 52–3, 141–6, 174–5
duration measures 144–5, 175
holding period returns 141–3
immunization programmes 143–4
Macaulay duration 144–7, 175
management considerations 141–6
mathematical formulae 174–5
measures 144–52
modified duration 144–5, 175
performance measures 144–52
redemption yield (PRY) 145
yields 141–6, 174–5
preference shares 7–8, 25–6, 186, 204
see also equities
concepts 25–6
types 25–6
premiums
convertible bonds 4–5, 70–3, 169–70, 185
options 107–13
price progression 46–8
price spreads see bid-offer spreads
price unavailability, index problems 151–2
pricing
bonds 36–65, 68–9, 115
CDSs 138–9
convexity effects 56–7, 68–9
options 109–12
primary markets 204
principle, bonds 2–8
profit and loss accounts 7–8
programs, website 153–4
prospectuses 29–30
protective put options 113
proxy indices 149
put options 4–5, 49, 65–9, 107–13, 205, 213
see also options
buying 108–9
concepts 107–13
long put positions 108–9
writing 109

quarterly coupons 28
quotes, bonds 6–7, 29–30, 32–6

real redemption yield
concepts 39, 62–5, 168–9
mathematical formulae 168–9

redemption amount
    concepts 2–8, 10, 42–52, 90–1
    nominal value 3
redemption date 2, 42–52, 205
redemption yield
    see also yield to maturity
    concepts 39–65, 68, 81–94, 117, 141–4,
        149–50, 159–62, 168–9, 174–5, 205
    index-linked bonds 39, 62–5, 160–2, 168–9
    mathematical formulae 159–62
    portfolios 145
registered securities 1–2, 205–6
registrar 206
reinvestment rates 141–2
repos 95–105, 123, 182, 184
    agreements 97–8, 100–3
    classic repos 95–6, 100–5
    collateral 99–100, 101–4
    concepts 95–105, 123
    definition 95
    historical background 95
    parties 95–7, 101–2
    sell/buy backs 95, 97, 103–4, 182, 207
    statistics 95
    stock borrowing/lending 95–6, 104–5
    types 95
repurchase agreements *see* repos
Retail Price Index (RPI) 3, 20–2, 62–5, 168–9, 206
retained earnings 7–8
returns
    holding period returns 141–3
    internal rate of return 144–5
    performance measures 144–52
    risk 8
Reuters 128
reverse floaters, concepts 76–7
reverse repos 182, 206
rising yield curves 79–82
risk
    credit risk 52–3, 100–1, 115–21, 133, 137–9,
        183, 185, 187–8
    returns 8
risk-free investments 30–1, 111–12, 117–18, 206
RPI *see* Retail Price Index
running yield *see* current yield

Samurai bonds 206
SEC 116
secondary markets 206
secured debt 29–30
securities lending *see* stock borrowing/lending
securitization
    see also asset-backed . . . ; mortgage-backed . . .
    concepts 7, 73–5, 178–9

SegaInterSettle 97
sell/buy backs 95, 97, 103–4, 182, 207
    see also repos
semi-annualized interest rates 3, 9–10, 17–18,
    28–9, 38, 43–4, 159–60, 173–4
seniority, loans 7–8
serial bonds 3
settlement
    conventions 32–4, 155–8, 177, 187
    dates 155–60, 177, 187
    electronic settlement 95–9
short call positions 108–9
simple margin
    concepts 59–63, 167, 207
    mathematical formulae 167
simple yield to maturity
    concepts 39–43, 158–9
    mathematical formulae 158–9
sinking funds 13–14, 65, 207
South Africa 20
'special' bonds 101
Special Drawing Rights 2
special terms 31–2
special-purpose vehicles 2, 7, 29
specific collateral, repos 101
Spens clause 13, 117, 208
spot rates 82–6, 208
spot yield curves *see* zero-coupon yield curves
spread 208, 213
Stagecoach 117
Standard & Poor 75, 115–21, 152
step-up bonds, concepts 14–15
stock
    see also government bonds
    definitions 1–2, 208
stock borrowing/lending 95–6, 104–5
    see also repos
straddles 112–13
straight-coupon (bullet) bonds, concepts 9–10,
    41–2, 49–50, 109–10, 182
strategies, yield curve investment strategies
    89–94
strike prices 107–13, 209
strippable bonds, concept 11–13, 55–6
strips 11–13, 55–6, 141, 209
subindex calculation gaps, index problems 151
subordinated loans 8, 29–30
supply and demand factors, yield curves 92–3
supranational organizations 2, 7, 79, 147
swaps
    asset swaps 123, 130
    basis swaps 123, 132
    website 154
    CDSs 123, 137–9, 186
    concepts 123–33
    credit risk 133

swaps (*Continued*)
 cross-currency swaps 123, 130–2
 FRAs 123, 132–4, 154
 interest rate swaps 123–33
 statistics 123
 types 123
 yield curves 127–8
swaptions 123, 133
Sweden 20
synthetic securities 123

t + n settlement 209
T-bills *see* Treasury bills
TARGET 209
tax 4, 26, 70, 145–6
TBMA 97, 100
time value, options 111–12
Toyota Motor Credit 152
TRAX 98–9
Treasury bills (T-bills) 22–3, 33–4, 64–5, 170–1, 209, 210
 see also money markets
Treasury notes 30–1, 33–4, 95, 210

UK 1–3, 9–22, 29–31, 33–4, 35–9, 55, 62–3, 67–9, 79–82, 92–4, 115–16, 118–21, 148–2, 168–9
UK Debt Management Office 22, 152
undated (irredeemable) bonds 3, 11, 19, 52–4
 see also perpetual bonds
US markets 9–10, 12, 20–2, 30–1, 34, 79, 95, 115, 116–19, 127–39, 156–7

valuations
 bonds 27–65, 115
 mark-to-market valuations 100–1, 200
 options 109–12
vanilla bonds *see* straight-coupon (bullet) bonds
variance 58–65, 165–6
variation margin 100–3, 135–7, 211
volatility 211

warrants
 concepts 5, 78, 171–2, 211
 mathematical formulae 171–2
World Bank 29, 79, 147

writing
 call options 108–9
 put options 109

XD *see* ex-coupon bonds

yield curves
 website 153–4
 changes 89–94
 classic moves 93–4
 concepts 79–94
 forward-forward yield curves 84–6
 investment strategies 89–94
 par yield curves 86–9
 shapes 79–82, 89–94
 supply and demand factors 92–3
 swap yield curve 127–8
 zero-coupon yield curves 82–6
yield gap 212
yield spread 213
yield to call 213
yield to maturity (YTM)
 see also redemption yield
 concepts 39–59, 158–9, 213
 mathematical formulae 158–9
yield to worst 213
yields
 website 153–4
 CDs 22–3, 171
 concepts 29, 39–65, 212
 dividends 189
 Macaulay duration 30, 45, 50–65, 144–5, 149, 154, 162–3, 173–5, 190
 modified duration 45, 53–65, 144–5, 149, 154, 163–4, 174–5, 201
 money markets 64–5, 171, 201
 portfolios 141–6, 174–7
 types 39–59, 158–9, 213
YTM *see* yield to maturity

zero-coupon bonds 3–4, 10–12, 50–65, 82–6, 141, 213
zero-coupon yield curves
 concepts 82–9
 construction 83–4
 forward-forward yield curves 85–8

Index compiled by Terry Halliday